D. C. COLEMAN

The Economy of England
1450–1750

Oxford   New York

OXFORD UNIVERSITY PRESS

Oxford University Press, Walton Street, Oxford OX2 6DP

Oxford New York Toronto
Delhi Bombay Calcutta Madras Karachi
Petaling Jaya Singapore Hong Kong Tokyo
Nairobi Dar es Salaam Cape Town
Melbourne Auckland

and associated companies in
Beirut Berlin Ibadan Nicosia

Oxford is a trade mark of Oxford University Press

ISBN 0–19–289070–0

© Oxford University Press 1977

First published as an Oxford University Press paperback 1977
and simultaneously in a hardback edition
Paperback reprinted 1978, 1982, 1984, 1986

Printed in Great Britain
at the University Printing House, Oxford
by David Stanford
Printer to the University

For F.J.F.

Preface

The title of this book correctly indicates its geographical limitation. It seemed to me impossible, within the word-limit imposed by this series, to do justice to Ireland, Scotland, and Wales; such mention as they receive is therefore incidental to my main concern with England as the dominant economic region of the British islands. Likewise, the book is primarily about economic rather than social or political matters. Nevertheless, it contains some emphasis upon the way in which social and political influences bore upon economic change (or lack of it). This is intentional and reflects a belief that economic history should not be pursued in isolation from other sorts of history.

The text contains numerous arguments, findings, and related examples, derived from other people's books or articles in learned journals. Some are not so derived. Were I to put up signposts to my intellectual indebtedness in the form of the full reference apparatus, the result would be a forest of footnotes. That would neither be appropriate to this sort of book nor conform to the layout of the series in which it appears. Consequently, in order both to meet the potential needs of the reader and to discharge my own sense of indebtedness there are provided:

(1) Note references only to quotations, whether from contemporary or modern works.

(*N.B.* The spelling and punctuation in quotations from contemporary sources have been modernized throughout.)

(2) Source references to all collections of statistics in tables or graphs.

(3) An annotated guide to further reading, which also
     serves to indicate the main sources which have been
     used in compiling the text.

I am grateful to all upon whose labours I have thus drawn,
though they are in no way to blame for the interpretations
which I have put upon their findings. Some of the statistics
used in the tables and graphs have been made available to
me from hitherto unpublished work. This has been made
clear in the relevant source references, but for permission to
use such material I would like here to record my thanks to
Dr. K. N. Chaudhuri, Sir Henry Phelps Brown and Miss
Sheila V. Hopkins, Professor F. J. Fisher, and Dr. E. A.
Wrigley and his colleagues at the Cambridge Group for the
History of Population and Social Structure. A first draft of
the text was read by Dr. Brian Outhwaite and Mr. Keith
Thomas. They each made many helpful comments and
criticisms for which I am extremely grateful.

D.C.C.

Contents

List of Graphs

List of Tables

I

Introduction: the Economy and the Social Order

This book attempts, in a brief compass, to look at three hundred years of the English past from a particular vantage point and with certain assumptions. Specifically, it tries to look through two different pairs of eyes: those of the historian and those of the economist or social scientist. There will be some involuntary squinting. In the cause of comprehension it is important to make clear, at the outset, the nature both of the vantage point and of the assumptions.

The vantage point is the modern industrialized world, a world which, however ominously it may creak and rumble with violence and discontent, knows levels of productivity in its use of economic resources—land, labour, and capital— far higher than those in the period under study. From this vantage point, therefore, that period becomes a part of the wider category of economic and social life which can be called 'pre-industrialized'. An unlovely label, but useful. As a concept it comes from the habits of thought of the economist, rather than from those of historians (to some of whom, indeed, it may be wholly repugnant). Our modern world provides familiarity with such obvious contours of the industrialized society as urbanization, the dominance of industry over agriculture, or the existence of highly mechanized manufacture. The pre-industrialized world is defined not just by the absence of these overt qualities but by the absence of the economic and technical relationships which permitted these qualities to appear; and by the presence of relationships which can be identified, with varying degrees of assurance, as having inhibited their appearance. By thus labelling England between 1450 and 1750 as a specimen of the genus 'pre-industrialized economy', a rough model is set up for analysis and examination, for testing against the infinite diversity of historical reality.

The model and the historical reality stretched outside England. For England, in this sense, was simply an island variation on the continental theme—of pre-industrialized Europe. Within that bigger entity there were of course great extremes, just as there were substantial differences in law, custom, and politics, in standards of life and cultural achievement. Fifteenth-century England looks like a backward rural area against the high culture of urban renaissance Italy; early eighteenth-century England or Holland enjoyed standards of living higher than those of, say, Finland or Sicily. But all territories, irrespective of their national frontiers, shared many common characteristics as they do with some modern countries which we call 'underdeveloped': in the susceptibility of the economy to the play of natural forces; in man's weakness in the face of infectious disease; in his limited, but certainly not primitive, technological achievements. In the course of the three centuries some gaps closed, others widened. One of the central, unanswered questions of European history in this period is why and how England became sufficiently differentiated from the rest of pre-industrialized Europe by 1750 so that its economy could take off into the first industrial revolution. We will return to it later. Meanwhile, whatever the uniquely English developments, the pre-industrialized economy was pervasive; and understanding of its English variant will be aided by seeing its general features as part of a wider European context.

What, then, were the assumed characteristics of early modern England seen in this way? A bare list of some of the more important must suffice. The ratio of population to land was generally much lower than it is today, and the growth and structure of population different from those in the industrialized world—most people lived in small rural communities and were engaged in agriculture; much fixed capital was invested in ways which produced no direct, though perhaps some indirect, gain to the economy; circulating capital, that is, stocks of raw materials or goods, accounted for much of business investment; because of the general absence of the modern sort of investment in fixed capital, embodying certain technical devices, the productivity of all factors of production in all economic activities was low by modern standards; techniques of production were mainly labour-intensive and a reservoir of underemployed labour, varying in size from area to area and from time to time, helped to keep them so; although technology was not static it was sluggish, and cost-reducing innovations were infrequent; the distribution of income in the economy as a whole was very unequal—many people were very poor and had to spend by far the greater part of their small incomes on food, clothing, and shelter; although markets were imperfect, output in general did respond to the stimuli of rising or falling prices. From this undifferentiated catalogue the outlines of a crude and largely static model can perhaps be discerned. Its further implications—for instance, that the harvest was of crucial consequence in most people's lives or that markets were commonly seen as expandable more readily by extension of area than through increase of income—will be considered later in their appropriate contexts.

To seek out the necessary modifications of the economic model, at once to demonstrate its very crudity and to give it the dimensions of particularity which its usefulness demands, is the task of the historian's pair of eyes. They need to search in several directions. It is the historian's empirical techniques which, using whatever the economist can offer him, have to chart the course of change over these three centuries. For there is no agreed theory of economic growth for this sort of pre-industrialized economy which could be tested for fit against the historical experience. Most of the available theories are concerned more with the transition to industrialization than with the long pre-industrialized prelude. Mono-causal explanations, such as those which put all weight upon the relationship of population to resources, are too narrow to be useful. The Marxist interpretation, whilst offering many valuable insights, is too rigid in its insistence upon class-conflict and the revolutionary transition from 'feudal' to 'bourgeois' society to accommodate the variety of English economic and social development.

The theoretical constructs of the modern non-Marxist economist, peopled by wholly economic men engaged upon continuously rational processes of free choice and optimization, seem in a different way remote from the realities of Tudor England. Remoteness apart, however, they, in common with all the economists' theories of change, depend ultimately upon measurement. And it is upon this rock of procedural difficulty that quantitative ships founder, for we have few reliable statistics to steer by in this sea of early modern economic history. National income or wealth, output or employment, costs or profits, the varying size of the population: such crucial indices can rarely be measured. In an economist's ideal world, a fully articulated model fed with a nourishing diet of figures would be capable of so analysing the English economy of 1750 that it would be clear why the first industrial revolution was about to happen here and not elsewhere and how, over the preceding centuries, that state had been reached. Explanation would be complete; prediction would be possible; the model could be taken away and used in the task of helping the economic development of those countries who want it today. Yet this usual absence of the ideal is no reason to throw away the tools of the economist. Nor should it be an excuse to reject the fragmentary statistics which do survive or can be collected. Our knowledge of the English economy in this period has to be built up by the piecemeal mixing of literary evidence and very partial quantitative evidence. The questions to be asked must be economic questions—about the use of scarce resources, about shifts in demand or supply, about the size and distribution of the national wealth—but they must be put with an awareness that the answers can be obtained only with the aid of the tools of the historian.

The true subject of any sort of history is always men and women, their achievements and failures, alone or in groups, in their continuous battle with themselves and with their environment. So the historian has to temper the economist's tools with a regard for sundry diversities, whether imposed by religious faith or political activity, by regional geography or the complex irrationalities of the human spirit. At no time during the period was there a single completely integrated English economy, though it was nearer to being achieved in 1750 than in 1450. Regional evidence and local history are thus vital for our understanding of the economic entity that, for convenience sake, we call England.

(ii)

England as a social entity was seen by contemporaries as a pyramid of status. Yet it was a pyramid conceived in terms not solely of rank but also of wealth and of occupation. This mixture of criteria was as apparent at the beginning as at the end of the period. The categorization of 'rank, degree, or class' set out in an analysis made by Joseph Massie in 1760 differed in detail but not in conception from that to be found in late medieval sumptuary laws, such as those of 1363 and 1463, designed to match apparel to social status. They acknowledged the need for the subdivision by income of the categories, whether categories of rank, such as knights, or of occupation, such as merchants. Yet they equally started with the basic premise of a hierarchy of ranks. It is there in another analysis, made by Thomas Wilson in 1600, and in the well-known one by Gregory King in 1688, *Natural and Political Observations on the State and Condition of England*. His is the most quantitatively expressed analysis of English society and wealth before 1700. It is shown in a modified form in Table 1. At the top of his pyramid were those distinguished solely by rank and status: the nobility, lords temporal and spiritual, baronets, knights, esquires, and gentlemen. Then came the groups distinguished by their occupations: clergy, lawyers, those in the 'sciences and liberal arts', office-holders and officers in the Army and Navy, merchants and tradesmen, farmers, citizens, and handicraftsmen. Finally there was the big group of those whose distinguishing mark was essentially that of inferiority, both in status and occupation:

'labouring people and out-servants, cottagers and paupers, common soldiers, common seamen, vagrants'. A similar pattern was set out by writers concerned with the political nation. In the later sixteenth century four categories were distinguished: the nobility; the gentry; citizens, burgesses,

TABLE 1

Gregory King's estimate of population and wealth, England and Wales, 1688

Number of families	Ranks, Degrees, Titles, and Qualifications	Heads per family	Number of persons	Yearly income per family
160	Temporal Lords	40	6400	2800
26	Spiritual Lords	20	520	1300
800	Baronets	16	12 800	880
600	Knights	13	7800	650
3000	Esquires	10	30 000	450
12 000	Gentlemen	8	96 000	280
5000	Persons in Offices	8	40 000	240
5000	Persons in Offices	6	30 000	120
2000	Merchants and Traders by Sea	8	16 000	400
8000	Merchants and Traders by Sea*	6	48 000	200
10 000	Persons in the Law	7	70 000	140
2000	Clergymen	6	12 000	60
8000	Clergymen	5	40 000	45
40 000	Freeholders	7	280 000	84
140 000	Freeholders	5	700 000	50
150 000	Farmers	5	750 000	44
16 000	Persons in Sciences and Liberal Arts	5	80 000	60
40 000	Shopkeepers and Tradesmen	4½	180 000	45
60 000	Artisans and Handicrafts	4	240 000	40
5000	Naval Officers	4	20 000	80
4000	Military Officers	4	16 000	60
511 586		5¼	2 675 520	67
50 000	Common Seamen	3	150 000	20
364 000	Labouring People and Out Servants	3½	1 275 000	15
400 000	Cottagers and Paupers	3¼	1 300 000	6·5
35 000	Common Soldiers	2	70 000	14
849 000		3¼	2 795 000	10·5
	Vagrants		30 000	
849 000		3¼	2 825 000	10·5
511 586	Increasing the Wealth of the Kingdom	5¼	2 675 520	67
849 000	Decreasing the Wealth of the Kingdom	3¼	2 825 000	10·5
1 360 586			5 500 520	

Source: *Two Tracts by Gregory King*, ed. G. E. Barnett (Baltimore, 1936).

* This second category of maritime merchants is what King wrote; versions in which it appears as 'Merchants and Traders by Land' are subsequent alterations, though it is possible that this is what King intended.

and yeomen; and 'the fourth sort of men who do not rule'. The latter formed no part of the political nation; they were, as an echoing statement of the eighteenth century put it, 'the illiterate rabble, who have neither capacity for judging of matters of government, nor property to be concerned for'.[1]

Concern with rank and status remained powerful throughout the centuries. The vital dividing line was that which separated the gentlemen from the common people. Above that division was an explicit hierarchy of ranks; below it a complex mass of inferiors. Formal recognition of the boundary came in various ways: by the grant of a coat of arms, dependent on genealogical criteria; by the right to wear certain sorts of clothes and to carry a sword; and by the possession of various legal privileges, notably those attaching to the peerage. In practice the dividing line was drawn as much by reference to such informal criteria as behaviour, education, or way of life. Sir Thomas Smith's analysis has often been quoted but deserves quoting again for it serves admirably to catch the flavour of English gentility:

. . . he is a gentleman who is so commonly taken and reputed . . . whosoever studieth in the universities, who professeth the liberal sciences, and to be short, who can live idly and without manual labour and will bear the port, charge, and countenance of a gentleman . . .[2]

The obsession with rank and status became more pronounced during the sixteenth and seventeenth centuries as more yeomen, merchants, and lawyers crossed the vital frontier and set about strengthening from within what they had envied from without. Under the Tudors, the more frequent the sumptuary laws and proclamations, the more they were flouted. But as this method of trying to enforce external social differentiation was abandoned, so did an unwritten code of gentlemanly behaviour, supported by wealth and education, grow stronger. In the church—a focal point of village and parochial life and the symbol of ecclesiastical authority—the congregation had to be seated in a plan which reflected the social order; and along its walls and in its aisles and chapels, the ever more elaborate tombs of dead squires provided further reminders for worshippers. Though lesser beings may have married for love and many marriages were arranged for gain, some of those in gentry families, obsessed by status and lineage, were made for the reasons thus set out by Sir Simonds D'Ewes in the 1630s:

. . . next to religion, my chief aim was to enrich my posterity with good blood, knowing it the greatest honour that can betide a family to be often linked into the female inheritrices of ancient stocks.[3]

Status, lineage, family. The important role of the family in this pre-industrialized society deserves emphasis. King's calculations were cast in terms of families; D'Ewes' was concerned with the honour of his family; marriages were made to sustain or improve family wealth; kinship ties loomed large alike in political allegiance and the provision of credit. Much, probably most, of the country's work was carried on in family units: apprentices became part of a family; the family home—the cottage of the poor weaver, the house-cum-shop of the urban craftsman or retailer, even the country mansion of the landed gentleman—was also the place of work. There were exceptions, such as miners or dockyard workers, but for most people the modern distinction between dwelling-place and work-place was unknown. The family unit in which most people lived was normally a household with an average size of about five persons, comprising parents, children, and some servant or relation. The average concealed great extremes: at one end, the old woman living alone in the village, the typical situation which encouraged suspicions of witchcraft in the seventeenth century; at the other extreme, the great household of the nobleman, still, in the fifteenth century, with retainers drawn from the local gentry, and by the eighteenth, well-supplied with living-in servants tending house and park. But throughout the period 'service' and 'servants' did not bear the connotation which they came to bear later, for many young persons became servants, sometimes for a brief period, in the households of their kin or in those of their parents' friends or neighbours, as did the sisters of those two late seventeenth-century diarists, Samuel Pepys and Ralph Josselin. To become part of a family, as servant, apprentice or craftsman, whether kin or not, provided a certain fixity of abode and thus respectability in the eyes of contemporaries who reserved their disapprobation for 'loose and straggling persons' outside the security of the family and whom the economy could not absorb into employment.

Gregory King's analysis of the distribution of wealth is very rough, and some of his estimates of income are almost certainly wrong. Its importance lies more in its indication of a contemporary view of the structure of wealth and status. He categorized 51 per cent of the population, with 22 per cent of total gross incomes, as 'decreasing the wealth of the kingdom'; yet he also showed a substantial band of middling persons, with family incomes in the range £21 to £69, as accounting for 37 per cent of the population and 44 per cent of total incomes. Right or wrong, his calculations must certainly not be taken as unchanging over time and space. The wealth of England was not only growing and shifting amongst different social groups, but it had a clear pattern of geographical distribution and change. In the late fifteenth and early sixteenth centuries, the richest area of England was heavily concentrated south of a line joining the Severn to the Wash. Within that area, two different regions of relative prosperity existed: London and its group of surrounding counties, i.e. Kent, Surrey, Middlesex, Hertfordshire, Essex, and Suffolk; and the West Country counties of Gloucestershire, Wiltshire, and Somerset. North of the Severn-Wash line not only was there less wealth but less growth in wealth since the fourteenth century. Settlements were fewer and villages sometimes little more than scattered pastoral communities; industry and trade lagged behind their southeastern counterparts; marcher lords and ancient barons ruled and feuded, especially around the border with Scotland, until gradually tamed by Tudor rule or the union of the Crowns in 1603, after which the appeal of more sedate ways of making money or governing men grew stronger. In contrast, the later seventeenth and early eighteenth centuries saw the beginning of a great growth in midland and northern wealth. The textiles of Yorkshire and Lancashire; the North

Sea trade of Hull and the growing Irish and American commerce of Liverpool; iron in the west Midlands and the coal metropolis of Newcastle: all were changing not only the distribution of wealth but patterns of social relationships once founded upon loyalty to such as the Percys and Dacres.

North and south of the line, however, at the end of the period as well as at the beginning, the prestige attached to the ownership of land remained immense. With the ending of its role as a source of men, its role as a source of income, privilege, status, and power became all the more impressive. The landowner's rents allowed him to live the gentlemanly life. Though castles lost their point, conspicuous investment in the building of country houses played a key role in establishing rank. Wealth made in trade, finance, or the law was invested in land, at the most practical level because it provided the safest outlet for profits, and at another level because it conferred social status, provided a base for family advancement, and offered a lever for political power. From about 1700, more towns and new opportunities for investment helped to stimulate the growth of a non-landed or less-landed gentry, identified by money and behaviour but not by acreage. The world of Bath in 1750 was very different from that of Northumberland in 1450. Yet similarities remained, despite such extreme contrasts. This was not a static society, but it was an intensely conservative society. Despite the upheaval of the Interregnum, despite substantial population growth, despite the great disparity in the distribution of wealth, power, and status, despite economic advance which had brought England to the forefront of Europe before the Industrial Revolution, the social conservatism which remained was the concomitant of the persistence of the pre-industrialized economy.

Social structure and attitudes influenced the working of the economy in various ways, and their interaction poses many questions for the historian. For example, in our modern industrialized economy we are used to the concept and the reality of economic change, innovation, and growth. But those who lived in Tudor and early Stuart England were not simply unaccustomed to such notions: they would have been virtually inconceivable to them as social aims desirable in themselves. So, taken in concert with the sluggishness of technical achievement, this meant that those engaged in economic activity only rarely considered cost-reducing innovations based on technical change as methods of solving economic problems. Towards the end of our period, however, this is precisely what did begin to happen more commonly. Why? Or again, did the obsession with land as a source of status lead to a less than optimum allocation of resources for economic growth? Those in power in the State normally desired to preserve the social *status quo*; yet they also sought to encourage industry and the export trade in the interests of national strength. How far did these aspirations conflict? Certainly we should be chary of assuming that contemporary rulers were necessarily swayed or convinced by what we would regard as rational economic considerations. Finally, it is worth considering just how far the social force of the small, local unit—farm and village—reinforced poor transport to ensure a high degree of conformity to local norms of behaviour, thus helping to perpetuate limited economic horizons. As the horizons began to widen so new aspirations began, slowly, to find themselves at variance with the forces of ritual and of customary behaviour which provided so much of the cement of social cohesion.

Population and Prices, mainly to 1650

(i)

Nobody knows how many people lived in England in 1450 or in 1750. Modern research, however, suggests two fairly distinct phases of change: first, a rise in population starting some time between 1470 and 1520 and ending some time around 1640–50; then, about a century in which the long-run trend showed a stable or only slightly rising population, more rapid growth beginning in the later eighteenth century. The mid-seventeenth century turning point in population, and in prices, provides an appropriate division for our period as a whole, not least because of its approximate coincidence in time with other and not directly related happenings of great consequence to English history (see Chapter 6). Some estimates of total population which research has offered for various bench-mark dates are given in Table 2.

TABLE 2

Population estimates, 1430–1750

Approximate date	Approximate total population, England (millions)
1430	2·1
1522–5	2·3
1545	2·8 (+0·25 in Wales)
1603	3·75
1695	5·2 (England and Wales)
1750	6·3 (,, ,, ,,)

Sources: J. Cornwall, 'English Population in the Early Sixteenth Century', *Economic History Review*, 2nd Ser. XXIII (1970); D. V. Glass, 'Gregory King's Estimate of the Population of England and Wales, 1695', *Population Studies* II (1950) reprinted in *Population in History*, ed. D. V. Glass and D. E. C. Eversley (1965); G. T. Griffith, *Population Problems in the Age of Malthus* (Cambridge, 1926).

Allowing for an approximate doubling of the small Welsh population between the mid-sixteenth and mid-eighteenth centuries, it would seem that the population of England and Wales may have increased by nearly 120 per cent between the 1520s and the 1690s but by less than 60 per cent between *circa* 1603 and *circa* 1750. Over the three centuries 1450 to 1750, total numbers roughly trebled, but most of that rise was probably compressed into the period between the mid-sixteenth and mid-seventeenth centuries.

What is the evidence for these estimates, specifically for the period of increase? And what happened between these dates?

(ii)

Just as the actions of individual buyers add up to an aggregate effect in the economy outside the conscious motivation of those individuals, so population change provides a classic example of the effect of large numbers independently of the conscious doings of individual citizens. Do populations, like economies, behave in some regular and predictable fashion? Despite Thomas Malthus' famous *Essay on Population* of 1798, it is only fairly recently that the systematic study of past populations, historical demography, has got under way, and only in the last twenty years or so that its tentative findings have been incorporated into the study of English economic and social history. It is important to bear in mind how tentative they are at this stage, and especially so when they relate to the evidential darkness before the first census of 1801.

Several sorts of sources have been pressed into service to provide the very approximate figures given above. They come from contemporary returns relating to other matters, such as taxation, military service, or ecclesiastical conformity. The muster rolls, or military surveys, of 1522 and the returns to the tax known as the subsidy, in 1524 and 1525, together provide the basis for the 1522–5 estimates; that for 1603 is derived from a return of communicants and recusants; the 1695 figure originated in the contemporary calculations made by Gregory King from the 1688 returns for the hearth tax and the 1694 returns for the tax on births, burials, and marriages. All such estimates have sundry defects: they vary from difficulties in determining the appropriate multipliers by which to convert hearths into persons to those problems which arise from the familiar lack of enthusiasm for paying taxes, serving in armies or revealing unorthodox religious beliefs. Moreover, they tell us nothing about the course and mechanism of change. For this, other sources are needed: literary evidence, local counts, or listings made by contemporaries, and, most important, data on baptisms, burials, and marriages derived primarily from parish registers.

Literary evidence, necessarily subjective and often unreliable, offers little of the precision needed for the systematic quantitative analysis of past populations. But it can give vital clues, suggest confirmation, cast doubt upon findings from other sources, or tell us what some contemporaries believed to have been happening, rightly or wrongly. For example, a number of writers of the late sixteenth and early seventeenth centuries who were busily advocating greater English participation in colonizing ventures in America stressed their value as a safety valve to relieve surplus population at home. In so doing they made such remarks as that of Richard Hakluyt in 1584: 'through our long peace and seldom sickness we are grown more populous than ever heretofore'.[1] Some evidence of this sort can be more specific, like the observations of a contemporary who wrote of 1558 that in that year at harvest time:

. . . the quartan agues continued in like manner or more vehemently than they had done the last year past, where through died many old people and especially priests, so that a great number of parishes were unserved, and no curates to be gotten, and much corn was lost in the field for lack of workmen and labourers.[2]

Putting such literary comment alongside the quantitative evidence of a sharp increase in wills proved in 1557–8 provides a *prima facie* case for a widespread influenza epidemic causing a substantial increase in deaths in those years.[3]

A fair number of contemporary counts of local population

—such as that made by the rector of the Nottinghamshire village of Clayworth in 1676—have survived. When they contain details of age, occupation, and households they are useful both for social analysis and for helping us more directly about numbers of the people. But it is from parish registers—despite their obvious limitations of providing only local coverage and of being impaired by the varying incidence of nonconformity—that we have to derive many of our ideas about population change in this early period. Although the keeping of these registers was required in 1538, few survive from earlier than the 1560s or 70s. In recent years 'aggregative' analyses of the statistics of baptisms, marriages, and burials so recorded have been made for various parishes. Fig. 1 is a graph based upon data drawn from 400 parishes. It is the interim product of work being carried out by the Social Science Research Council Cambridge Group for the History of Population and Social Structure, which will publish revised figures in due course. In their present form the data show clearly the effect of political and religious upheavals, notably during the Civil War and Interregnum, when parochial registration suffered a partial collapse (by no means the only statistics from that period to be defective; see, for example, pages 106, 154). Nevertheless, the gross trends in population history show through strongly and the graph confirms the general picture already painted: that is, of a rise which, having probably started at the end of the fifteenth century, gained momentum after the 1540s and continued its course, despite being punctuated by short-term increases in deaths in the 1550s, 1590s, and 1630s, until around 1640–50 when this whole upward trend ended, to be followed by a century of only slightly rising numbers. This aggregation naturally conceals regional or local variations, but it is an important pointer to the country's general demographic experience. Another way of analysing parish registers, 'family reconstitution', permits insights into the structure of this pre-industrial English population: age at marriage, fertility rates, age-structure, and expectation of life. Although such indices, part of the technical equipment of the demographers, need not concern us in detail here, they are relevant to a

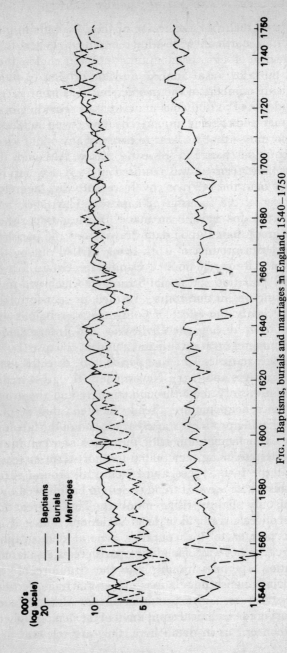

FIG. 1 Baptisms, burials and marriages in England, 1540–1750. Unpublished material reproduced by kind permission of the Director of the Group, Dr. E. A. Wrigley.

Source: The S.S.R.C. Cambridge Group for the History of population and Social Structure.

Baptisms
Burials
Marriages

000's
(log scale)
20
10
5
1

1540 1560 1580 1600 1620 1640 1660 1680 1700 1720 1740 1750

consideration of why the population followed the fluctuating course that it did and with what consequent changes in structure.

Birth- and death-rates are crude tools but they can give some indication of the demographic circumstances of the time. From bits of partial evidence and from what is known about similar populations, it can be inferred that in Tudor and Stuart England the death-rate probably· fluctuated around 30–35 per 1000 (the equivalent 1970 figures for the U.K. were 12·3 for males and 11·2 for females) though sometimes rising very much higher. The corresponding birth-rate would have been about 30–40 (compared with 16·2 for the U.K. in 1970). Infant mortality was often very high, from 100 to 240 per 1000 dying in their first year of life. The average expectation of life at birth was possibly about 35 years or less (compared with, in 1970, 68·5 for males and 74·7 for females), though this was significantly lower in towns and higher during the comparatively 'healthy' periods which signalled population growth. The greatest killers, keeping the population low, were various infectious diseases, of which bubonic or pneumonic plague was only the most dreaded and most spectacular in its effects. Death was a much more common phenomenon in family life than in the experience of most of us who live in modern industrialized societies; the death of brothers and sisters, parents or friends was part of the early experience of life for many young persons. Recovery of the population from the Black Death and other plagues in the later fourteenth century was retarded by further outbreaks in the fifteenth; though many outbreaks were confined to towns and were far from being like that which Sir John Paston in 1471 called 'the most universal death that ever I wist in England'.[4] But there are plenty of records of other outbreaks, some localized, some more general, in 1563, 1579, 1593, 1597, 1603, 1610, 1625, and so on before the Great Plague of 1665–6. A simple harvest failure could be serious, though not necessarily fatal, to people living close to subsistence; but a series of such failures could and did bring death from famine and starvation. In the bad years of 1594–7 much of the country was thus affected, especially in poor and remote areas, such as in Cumbria, where famine was also followed by outbreaks of plague in the local towns in 1598.

Because of these determinants of death, population tended to fluctuate fairly violently, and sometimes locally, in the short run. Periods of good harvests, a recession in the virulence of disease, perhaps an increase in fertility or earlier marriage: these could have been the causes of the upward movement of the sixteenth century. Age at marriage demands our attention. English women, like western European women generally, seem to have married rather later than their Asiatic or even eastern European counterparts. In the sixteenth and early seventeenth centuries, the average age of first marriage for women in England was probably within the range 23 to 26. Any variations, up or down, in this age, could have affected population. We do not know precisely what social or economic, religious or ritualistic factors may have influenced age of marriage, nor can we be certain of its wider results. As we shall see later (see Chapter 6), a rise in the average age at first marriage for women may have been important in the slackening of population growth after 1640–50. But much has yet to be discovered about both the rise in population and the check to it

(iii)

We are on rather safer ground about some of the economic and social consequences of the upswing in population. Consider what happened in the conditions of the pre-industrialized economy which was Tudor England. As more survived in the village, only some of the increased numbers could be absorbed into the local economy in agriculture or even in labour-intensive industries for which cheap labour was thus provided. Some therefore migrated in search of work, some became vagrants, some swelled the ranks of landless workers in the towns. Not every sixteenth-century beggar should be glibly presented as just a demographic phenomenon; there were plenty before the population started to grow. But the great increase of 'rogues, vagabonds and thieves' complained of in 1573 or the 'multitude of beggars' grumbled about in the House of Commons in 1593—to take but two examples[5] of many such comments—do testify to an economy failing to provide employment opportunities in the face of population growth.

There were other demographic influences behind the social and economic responses of the day. A further characteristic of the population was an age-structure with a high proportion of young people. That this was so can be inferred from what is known about the mortality rates of the time and from our knowledge of the structure of similar populations in certain countries today; it also receives confirmation from the pioneer calculations made by John Graunt and Gregory King in the 1660s and 1690s respectively. At that time about 38 per cent of the population of England and Wales was under 15 (as compared with 23 per cent in the U.K. today and about 40 per cent in some modern underdeveloped economies with high rates of population growth). The percentage would have varied in space and time with the short-term fluctuations in numbers, but the general consequence is evident enough: an intensification of the continuing problem of how to feed and employ a high proportion of young persons in a pre-industrialized economy. This is the demographic background to child labour and the contemporary attitude to juvenile work. So far from thinking it morally wrong, contemporaries thought it wholly right that children, especially those of the poor, should be put to work and kept out of mischief by being given employment, preferably by doing useful jobs within their capabilities in such home-based industries as woollen manufacture. A further consequence of this age-structure was that a smaller percentage of the population lay within the effective working age of adults. If we assume that maximum productive efficiency is reached within the age-range of, say, 15–60, then in the later seventeenth century there would have been about 50 per cent in that range as compared with over 60 per cent today. Put another way, the 'dependency-ratio', that is, the numbers of young and old dependent on the producers in the economy could at times have been very high. This, again, is an aspect—but only an aspect—of the evolving Tudor and Stuart poor law and its attempts to separate the treatment of the able-bodied pauper and that of the aged and infirm. This does not 'explain' the actions of contemporaries; but it should help us to see into the nature of the problems with which they grappled even though they saw them differently, as manifestations of God's ways to man.

One other feature of the country's population at the time needs some consideration: its distribution and density. Here again, the great contrast with today is apparent. In 1450 there were about 15 persons per square kilometre; the 6 million or so people of 1750 lived at a density of 43. In 1970 the 49 million population of England and Wales implied a density of 328 per square kilometre. These overall figures give no more than impressions of difference, for then as now they conceal great variations. But two overriding facts stand out. One was the existence of a moving frontier of settlement and cultivation, retreating in the earlier fifteenth century and then expanding, as it did in Tudor and early Stuart times, to accommodate the growing numbers. The other was the disproportionate growth of the one great urban centre, London. Around 1500 it had a population estimated at about 33,000; by 1650, it had perhaps grown to some 400,000, reaching over 500,000 by the end of the seventeenth century, by which time it had overhauled Paris to become the biggest city in western Europe. Yet for most of our period England was far less urbanized than the Low Countries or Italy, just as it also had a lower average population density. Tudor London was still a long way behind the great cities of continental Europe in size and wealth, but its exceptional growth soon made it into a unique urban entity in England, the next biggest towns, Norwich and Bristol, being very much smaller. Today, a quarter of the English population live in four great cities— London, Birmingham, Manchester, and Liverpool; then, fewer people had much contact with such metropolitan life, although growing numbers were moving into London. Just as we are ignorant of the precise mechanism of the population upsurge so we are not certain where it was mainly concentrated. It seems likely that many people moved from rural areas either to other rural areas which offered jobs and facilitated settlement, or to the towns, above all to London. There, because its death-rates were not only higher than in the countryside but also normally higher than its own birth-rates, much of the increase must have come from immigration. So London became increasingly both a focal point and a centre of diffusion for urban values—to be copied or rejected.

(iv)

The rise in population was paralleled by another great rise: in the level of prices. Did the one cause the other? Before starting to examine the causes and consequences of a long-sustained price inflation—which to a generation of historians not yet inured to the inflation rates of today seemed so remarkable that it used to be called 'the price revolution' —we must look at the evidence.

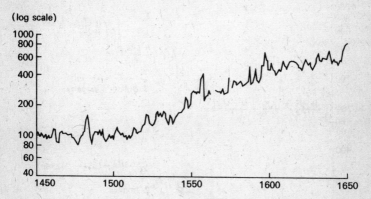

FIG. 2   Price index of a composite unit of consumer goods in southern England, 1450–1650 (1451–75 = 100)

Source: E. H. Phelps Brown and Sheila V. Hopkins, 'Seven Centuries of the Prices of Consumables Compared with Builders' Wage-rates', *Economica*, November, 1956.

Fig. 2 illustrates, for the period 1450–1650, a widely-used index of general prices. It covers a basketful of goods selected and weighted, as far as the evidence allows, to represent the purchases of the ordinary householder; the prices are drawn very largely from southern England, not from choice but because they have happened to survive in the records. The average level around 1650 was six times higher than that around 1450. Most of that increase, however, had taken place after about 1540. From 1450 to 1515 prices were virtually stationary, except for short-term fluctuations; they started their upward move and then rose particularly rapidly between 1540 and 1560 and again between 1570 and 1600; thereafter the rise continued at a slower pace to a high point at the end of the 1640s. In order to explain this occurrence, the general index must be broken down into some of its constituents and comparisons made. The three lines in Fig. 3 are similar indices of: (1) cereals and peas; (2) textiles; and (3) building wages. The divergences are very obvious. To

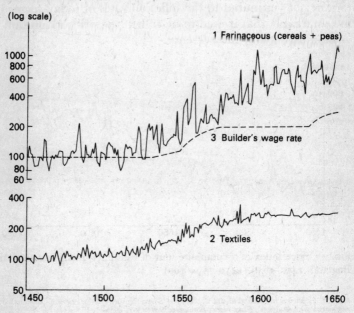

FIG. 3   Index of (1) Prices of farinaceous products (cereals and peas); (2) Prices of textiles; (3) Wage-rate of building craftsman (1451–75 = 100)

Source: E. H. Phelps Brown and Sheila V. Hopkins, 'Seven Centuries of Building Wages', Economica, August, 1955 and 'Seven Centuries of the Prices . . .' Economica, November, 1956.
   (Unpublished annual figures for (1) and (2) kindly supplied by Prof. Phelps Brown.)

bring the message home and to appeal to those readers who find graphs uncongenial, Table 3 offers a confirmatory picture using more figures, some identical in origin, some different.* In brief, while the prices of industrial products, like the price of labour—assuming that the wages of builders and agricultural labourers in southern England can be used as a proxy for English wages generally—multiplied about threefold in 150 years, the products of the soil rose in price far more, cereals leading in the race with a sevenfold rise.

TABLE 3

Index of prices and wages, 1450–1650

1450–99 = 100

	Av. all grains	Av. all livestock	Timber	Industrial Products	Day wages of agricultural labourers in S. England
1450–69	99	100	102	101	101
1470–89	104	102	101	102	98
1490–1509	105	105	88	98	101
1510–29	135	128	98	106	104
1530–49	174	164	108	119	114
1550–69	332	270	176	202	169
1570–89	412	344	227	227	205
1590–1609	575	433	312	247	219
1610–29	649	516	424	269	241
1630–49	788	649	500	294	296

Source: Averaged for 20-year periods from P. Bowden, 'Statistical Appendix' in J. Thirsk (ed.), *The Agrarian History of England and Wales*, IV, (Cambridge, 1967).

Ever since this happened, there have been discussions about why it happened. More than one explanation is available. It is a highly complex issue, full of technicalities which

* *Note:* In the Phelps Brown index used in Figs. 2, 3, and 6 and in Tables 8 and 10, the 'years' are harvest years running from Michaelmas to Michaelmas and dated by the calendar year in which the harvest was mainly consumed, for example 1575 means the harvest year Mich. 1574–Mich. 1575. The Bowden index used in Tables 3, 4, and 5 and the Hoskins index in Table 9 use harvest years dated by the calendar year in which the harvest was reaped, for example 1575 means the harvest year Mich. 1575–Mich. 1576. The use of averages in the Tables lessens the dangers in making comparisons, but readers should beware when attempting to compare single years.

will not be pursued in detail here. Suffice to say that there were three main forces at work, operating in different ways and at different times. They were: debasement of the coinage; an inflow of bullion; and the rise in the population.

The first of these was a short-term force and it was essentially a result of a fact of politico-economic life which will reappear on several occasions in the course of this book: the Crown's need for money in order to wage war. A small debasement in 1526–7 was followed by the 'Great Debasement' of 1544–51, which was on such a large scale that it is estimated to have doubled the size of the circulating medium (whilst bringing a substantial profit to the Crown). Prices did not rise exactly in proportion. They never do, whatever the cause, because elasticities of supply and demand vary from commodity to commodity. Nor did they rise simply because of debasement, for the 1550s also experienced bad harvests which pushed up grain prices. Although we cannot precisely evaluate the role of debasement in the price rise, we can note its coincidence in time with the highest rate of growth of all prices, that is, between 1540 and 1560.

Like debasement, an inflow of bullion could also have the effect of increasing the money supply. In the coinage system of the time, directly based as it was on precious metals, there was a continuous need for replenishment. Coins wore out, were clipped, lost, hoarded, or exported, mainly to Asia. Gold and silver were also in demand for other purposes, mainly for plate or for ornament, religious or secular. Was the new inflow so big as to do far more than replenish the money supply? The influx is assumed to have come largely from the massive recorded imports into Seville of American silver, as a result of the Spanish conquest and the discovery of silver in Peru and Mexico. There is no doubt about the imports into Spain, but there is some doubt about precisely how they influenced prices in England, at any rate before the later sixteenth century. Imports into Spain did not rise significantly until after the 1550s, reaching a high point in the 1590s. Did Spanish bullion begin to affect English prices after, say, the 1560s, and if so, how? We do not really know, though it may have done. It seems at least likely that the momentum of inflation was maintained by an increase in money supply, provided by an inflow of Spanish bullion from the 1590s onwards into the early seventeenth century. Certainly there were substantial increases in coinage at the English mint, notably around 1600 and in the 1640s.

Neither of the two monetary forces bearing upon English prices, debasement and bullion inflow, can be quantified any more than can the third possible explanation, population increase.

. . . a redundancy of population was acknowledged at the end of the sixteenth [century]. And it was this change in the state of population, and not the discovery of the American mines, which occasioned so marked a fall in the corn wages of labour [i.e. a fall in the amount of grain that money wages would buy].[6]

So wrote Malthus in the 1820s. His explanation got buried under that of the monetary enthusiasts. We need not accept it as an alternative argument to bullion—or debasement—but it does have the advantage of providing rather better answers to questions posed by certain characteristic features of this Tudor and Stuart inflation, namely, its length, and the marked discrepancies between food prices and industrial prices. How, given the nature of the pre-industrialized economy of the time, was food to be supplied to the increased numbers in the villages? Some of the population increment remained and could extend the area under cultivation; others became landless labourers in local agriculture, industry, trade, or service; some migrated to become landless workers in the towns. Those in the latter two categories thus came on the market for foodstuffs without directly contributing to their production. Therefore there was both an overall increase in the demand for cereals and, specifically, an increase in the demand for those sold in the market, as distinct from those consumed as subsistence production; and there was a rise in rents. But in the agricultural circumstances of the time (see Chapter 3) there was little chance of securing much in the way of increased productivity at least in the short or even medium term. Therefore the supply of foodstuffs was markedly inelastic. Hence they rose sharply in price. Conversely, the supply of manufactured goods was markedly more elastic (see Chapter 4). In a few industries there were technical advances which helped to restrain real costs as output increased. Far more important, however, was the highly labour-intensive nature of much industrial production, often susceptible to reductions in real costs by organizational changes, notably an extension of 'putting-out' techniques. A substantial increase in population thus came as a great economic blessing to producers, especially of such goods as textiles. Their price consequently did not rise nearly so much as did the price of the land-intensive agricultural products.

So it may be that the population rise was the vital force in sustaining the length of the price rise, but that debasement earlier, and Spanish-American bullion later, contributed in their different ways to push up the level and to keep up the momentum of inflation. Harvest failures would jerk up food prices; continuing population pressure would prevent them from falling back to their old levels; increasing money supply, especially from the 1590s, coming into the towns and then gradually reducing the surviving non-monetized sections of the economy, maintained the momentum.

(v)

Before going on to consider some of its general consequences, something needs to be said about the European dimensions of population and its increase as well as of the price inflation. Despite many regional variations, changes in both population and prices were such as to suggest some common elements in causation. English population structure was, as suggested earlier, merely a regional example of a wider, western European phenomenon; it had similarly high birth- and death-rates, low expectation of life, and high infant mortality; it had a similar age-structure and similar ages at marriage; it was open to the same agents of mortality and they often struck or receded at about the same time. Much of our information naturally comes from towns and there is ample evidence of their growth; but there is also

more evidence coming to light to confirm the rural growth
without which the urban growth could hardly have proceeded, because of the high urban death-rates. Cities like
Naples or Florence, Augsburg or Antwerp, Madrid or Seville,
all expanded rapidly. Estimates of territorial population
show similar trends: the population of the area we now call
Italy is estimated to have risen from about 10 million to 12
million in the course of the sixteenth century; the French
population, around 12 or 13 million in the mid-fifteenth
century, grew fairly rapidly from about the 1520s until the
1630s or 1650s to reach about 19 million. Then came the
same killers. The harvest failures of the 1590s and the ravages
of plague were Europe-wide; plague came, for example, to
Andalusia and Castille as well as to England and Germany;
starvation hit some Swedes and some Frenchmen, as well as
some Englishmen. And so again in the 1630s and 1650s
epidemic disease struck fiercely in Italy as well as in Amsterdam and London; and between 1648 and 1652 the crops
failed in one country after another.

So it is reasonable to assume that if population increase
was an important agent in pushing up prices in England it
was also operating all over Europe. And here again the
evidence is Europe-wide. A great number of prices from
Poland to Spain, from Italy to England, have been assem-
bled, collated, analysed, infinitely processed, plotted on
graphs, and mapped. The result is a single theme with many
regional variations. Seville was the main doorway through
which the bullion came to supplement exiguous supplies of
African gold and central European silver, and thus to influence the money supply. Much of it left Spain almost as
rapidly as it came in, in part to pay for the Spanish Hapsburgs' boundless military and dynastic ambitions. But again
we are left with the unresolved problem of the timing and
method of transmission into the English price level. In continental Europe, too, there are indications of the same disparity between agricultural and industrial prices. As in
southern England, so in Vienna and Valencia, Augsburg and
Alsace, there have been found these disparities at the same
time as population rose. The Tudor and Stuart price

inflation was not a peculiarly English phenomenon—any more than is the mid-twentieth century inflation in industrialized economies. It was part of a wider inflation affecting a complex of pre-industrialized economies.

(vi)

Much has been laid at the door of the so-called 'price revolution', varying from the onset of capitalism to the Tudor poor law. One feature seems to be clear. So far from being a wage-cost inflation of the type which has been seen in modern times, in this one money wage rates lagged well behind the prices of foodstuffs, which were themselves major determinants of the cost of living. But did the wage-earner really suffer so badly as would seem evident from Table 3 and Fig. 3? Furthermore, if he did experience the large fall in real disposable income which those figures would imply, how is this compatible with the increase in aggregate demand which must have existed in order to sustain the expansion of economic activity which apparently characterized this period? Who, in short, bought the goods?

In attempting to answer such questions, it is salutary to try to avoid being blinded by numbers and to consider what all these prices do not tell us. They do not tell us to what extent that great majority of ordinary persons who lived in the country and worked on the land were in various ways insulated from the full impact of the inflation. They do not tell us about payments in kind, in food and drink and accommodation, all of which were common in employment arrangements at the time, especially for agricultural workers. They do not tell us about the elements of a subsistence economy still surviving in varying degrees in parts of the country, though almost certainly diminishing over the period. If they tell us a good deal about wheat prices in such places as Winchester and Oxford they tell us very little about what those prices meant to Lancashire peasants or Northumbrian shepherds. And though informative on single male workers' money wage rates, they tell us nothing about real family earnings. In case any reader should consider these matters to be marginal trifles, little affecting the great and obvious issues, let him bear in mind that two authorities on the period come up with utterly contrasting views of the ordinary Englishman's experience at this time. According to one, 'standards of living improved for the population as a whole', and 'as they now produced more, English people now consumed more. Production mounted steadily and people in all walks of life were able to enjoy new comforts and little extras in the happy security of the knowledge that there was plenty more where that came from.'[7] According to another, 'the living standards of men and women of the lower classes fell catastrophically' and 'the mass of the population were forced down to a diet of black bread.'[8]

There can be no doubt that the inflation put in a relatively advantageous position anyone who had enough land to produce a marketable surplus of food which could be sold on a consistently rising market (see Chapter 3, pages 44-7). It also put a premium on economic enterprise. The adventurous or the lucky, the ruthless or the greedy did better than those who, for reasons of laziness, inertia, or misfortune, were unwilling or unable to depart from old ways. The losers were certainly most to be found amongst the landless or the least-landed, the poor, the dispossessed, those least well-placed to take advantage of what to others were 'stirring times'. The gainers were to be found in all ranks of life but more especially amongst enterprising yeomen and landowning gentry, amongst traders, merchants, and lawyers. Before concluding that this reveals the location of increased aggregate demand in the economy, it is worth remembering that the statistics also suggest that money wage rates rose as much as the prices of manufactures; some of the latter therefore became cheaper in terms of foodstuffs. Consequently any disposable surpluses accruing could have helped to stimulate industrial production which in turn created employment for the growing population—at least in some areas. Aggregate demand from wage-earners would indeed have risen if their numbers actually employed increased faster than real earnings fell. Industrial employment could, however, be a dubious blessing, for the family's standard of life became dependent on work which was probably part-time and also peculiarly open to the fluctuations of trade, thus adding an additional hazard to the unpredictable effects of harvest weather.

Perhaps the two most important characteristics of the Tudor and early Stuart inflation were: its dependence upon cereal prices; and its length rather than its severity. It took a general index heavily weighted with cereals roughly a century and a half, from 1500 to 1650, to rise sixfold. In the present century the U.K. retail price index, with a lower cereal weighting, has risen over sevenfold in a mere 70 years, with much of that rise concentrated in the last 30 years. We are now living with general inflation and know it. When the contemporaries of the earlier inflation grumbled, although alarmed by rises in customary rents and in prices which had long remained stable, their concern was not so much at the general phenomenon as at the immediate reality of the 'excessive price of victuals'.

3

Agriculture and Rural Society, 1450–1650

(i)

If it is correct that during this period the population of England approximately doubled in size and that the prices of grains multiplied about sevenfold, then two big questions present themselves: how did the country's agriculture adapt itself to these phenomena; and what consequences followed from this adaptation? In seeking answers to these questions let it be emphasized, once again, that we cannot put any figures to such facts as total output, or sales, of any agricultural products; acreage planted with different crops; volume or rate of farming profits; distribution by size of farms or estates; or amounts of land held under different sorts of tenure. Only prices come in relative profusion though in uneven geographical distribution. But their very availability ensures their use. Moreover, we are encouraged to believe that, as in other peasant societies at other times, most men readily responded to the stimuli of changing prices, that they really were moved as some contemporaries said they were. For example:

... the price of corn would rise [and] ... that price would provoke every man to set plough in the ground, to husband waste grounds, yea to turn the lands which be enclosed from pasture to arable land; for every man will the gladder follow that wherein they see the more profit and gain. (*circa* 1549)[1]

Or, in 1607:

. . for corn being dearer than cloth or meat comparatively, then only will the husbandman plough, since his only end is profit.[2]
Remarks like these better testify to contemporary motivation

than the inertia which an Italian visitor attributed to English farmers in 1497:

. . . The farmers are so lazy and slow that they do not bother to sow more wheat than is necessary for their own consumption; they prefer to let the ground be transformed into pasture for the use of the sheep that they breed in large numbers. [3]

It is possible, of course, that the price rise had itself helped to stimulate the very responses which were noted at the later dates. But medieval history does not suggest that peasants consistently failed to behave like economic men. In brief, they showed a fairly high responsiveness to changes in the price of alternative products of the land they occupied.

Even when we have made this assumption a further difficulty looms: the extreme diversity both in agrarian practices and in patterns of land tenure. One authority distinguishes no less than 40 different 'farming countries of England'; another is content with 10 main regions, though stressing the variations within them. [4] In the quest for order and classification three main sorts of farming types have been distinguished, and these in turn have been separated out into two big regions. The dividing line between the two regions is the familiar south-west to north-east line, this time roughly joining Weymouth to Teesmouth and separating a zone of mainly pastoral and high land in the North and West, and a zone of mainly mixed farming with an emphasis on arable in the lower lands of the South East. The three chief farming types to be found within these areas were as follows. (1) Various sorts of mixed farming primarily for the growing of cereals but also involving the rearing of livestock. This type of cultivation was to be found on many of the lighter soils as well as in clay vales; and it was the dominant pattern in the south-eastern zone, though also existing in some of the lower lands of the North East and parts of the west Midlands. (2) Pasture farming of sundry sorts, such as dairy farming, stock-rearing or pig-keeping, sometimes combined with some grain-growing but all generally characteristic of rather heavier soils and more wooded areas—hence generally classifiable as woodland pasture. Many such areas were dotted about in the south-eastern zone, for example, the Weald of Kent and Sussex, parts of southern Suffolk and northern Essex, or the cheese-making and dairying areas of Wiltshire. (3) Cattle or sheep rearing carried on in the higher moorland zones, and other pastoral activities such as horse-breeding or fowling, as in the Fenlands. This general category of open pasture farming was characteristic of much of the higher western zone, stretching from Northumberland to Devon. It also covered much of the Celtic and Gaelic areas of the British Isles with which this book is not concerned, viz. Wales, Ireland and the Scottish Highlands and Lowlands, though not the central valley of Scotland.

These farming regions, as will be evident, were not co-terminous with county boundaries any more than were different types of land tenure and field systems. The 'classical' manorial system of open-field husbandry was far from ubiquitous. Its very characteristics suggest the broad type of farming with which it was likely to have been associated. The intermixture of arable holdings in strips, divided roughly equally between two or three or more large fields, and the annual use of one of those fields as a common fallow pasture, suggests a pattern of mixed farming with an emphasis on grain growing; for the common rights, and the rules to enforce them, were crucial for the pasturage of beasts needed to provide manure for the arable fields. The system—if it can be so called, for it was neither uniform nor unchanging—was concentrated largely in the predominantly grain-growing areas of the Midlands and the South East. In the woodland pasture areas within this zone, however, many of these open-field arrangements had either disappeared by the beginning of the sixteenth century or had never been known on lands drawn in piecemeal from woodland and waste. So substantial parts of Essex, Kent, and Suffolk were already enclosed, although common pasturage arrangements often survived and these were interspersed with open fields here and there— some of them surviving well into the eighteenth century despite London's commercial pull. The survival or dis- appearance of open fields was thus not just a function of proximity to market forces, because in the remoter western and northern highland zone the classical pattern hardly existed at all. There, for the most part, lands were enclosed and common rights not the subject of elaborate manorial regulation, though once again there was diversity within the zone. Devon, for instance, was a largely enclosed county but it had certainly known strip cultivation. In very rough terms, however, one can say that where pasture was both predominant and plentiful there were fewer rules and more flexible systems; where tillage was predominant and expansion less easy, there were more rules and a less flexible system. The pattern, at the end of the fifteenth century, alike of farming arrangements, field systems, and manorial significance, was thus a complex result of settlement, soil, and climate as well as of law, custom, and local power.

(ii)

What happened, then, in these diverse circumstances, in response to changing economic stimuli? The substantial fall in population and prices after the mid-fourteenth century had brought about a reduction in the area under cultivation. Because labour thus became dearer in terms of land, this had led to some increase in the less labour-intensive activity of sheep-rearing instead of cereal-growing; and many landlords had parted with land to peasant proprietors, of one sort or another. By the mid-fifteenth century the long, fluctuating decline in the prices of agricultural products had just about reached its lowest point; real wages, in contrast, were at a relatively high point; and, despite signs of depression and stagnation in some sectors of the economy, many workers, agricultural and urban, were probably better off than they were to be a century or more later. In the absence of all the data desirable in a quantitative paradise, relative price movements can be used as proxies to indicate change. On these criteria two broad phases can be distinguished in the first two centuries of our period. One runs from about 1450 to the 1520s, the second from the 1520s to about 1650. Table 4 suggests (though it does not prove) that until the 1520s a current of demand for wool to feed the expanding cloth industry (see below, pages 50 and 75–81) was running more rapidly than that for grain to feed the population.

TABLE 4
Index of prices and 'wool' exports, 1450–1519

1450–59 = 100

Decade	Average all grain prices*	Average wool prices*	Average export (by volume) of raw wool and woollen cloth†
1450–9	100	100	100
60–9	101	132	98
70–9	95	121	—‡
80–9	116	138	130
90–9	99	117	128
1500–9	114	113	158
10–19	117	145	168
1520–9	157	135	155

Sources: * Re-calculated on 1450–9 = 100 base from Bowden, 'Statistical Appendix', loc. cit. Use of T. H. Lloyd's wool price series (*The Movement of Wool Prices in Medieval England*, Supplement No. 6 to the *Econ. Hist. Rev.*, Cambridge 1973), which ends in 1500, shows a similar, though less marked, difference between grain and wool prices from 1450–9 to 1490–9.

† Calculated from *England's Export Trade, 1275–1547*, ed. E. M. Carus-Wilson and O. Coleman (Oxford, 1963), assuming 4¼ cloths = 1 sack of wool.

‡ Complete annual figures for cloth and wool exports survive for only three years in this decade.

This first phase is also that associated with enclosure for sheep-farming, a process which has become well known because it sometimes resulted in the depopulation of villages and thus attracted critical comment from contemporaries and historians alike. Before too readily claiming that the relative movements shown in Table 4 point to this growing demand as the cause of the enclosures, it is worth emphasizing three points: that the total amount of wool exported, either raw or as cloth, may still not have been as large even in the 1510s as in the 1350s; that the divergence between wool and grain prices was not large; and that the evidence on land enclosed for sheep farming shows it to have been small in extent and regionally localized. In brief, the figures do not support the idea of any sort of massive enclosure movement; they point merely to adaptation at the margin.

What such figures cannot reveal is the outcry to which

some of the events lying behind the figures gave rise. There was a petition against enclosers in 1459; the first of a number of statutes against enclosure and depopulation was passed in 1489; there were a series of enquiries and commissions starting in 1517; and a substantial literary agitation of which the most famous document was Thomas More's *Utopia*, in which the encloser was labelled as a 'covetous and insatiable cormorant' and a famous phrase complained that sheep did 'eat up and swallow down the very men themselves'. Although most of this sort of enclosure was probably over by the 1520s, some further examples of it certainly occurred both in the 1540s and in the early seventeenth century, culminating in the so-called 'Midland revolt' of 1607. Enactments and printed complaints likewise continued, the most explicitly titled of the latter being an anonymous pamphlet of the 1550s called *The Decay of England only by the Great Multitude of Sheep*.

Patently it was a topic arousing strong feelings; and such outbursts are a good guide to feelings but a doubtful guide to events. Surviving figures of areas affected are too incomplete to be meaningful but one fact seems to be reasonably clear: the whole phenomenon was largely, though not wholly, confined to the Midlands—*in umbelico regni* as a contemporary put it in about 1486—and especially the counties of Northhamptonshire, Leicestershire, Warwickshire, Buckinghamshire, Bedfordshire, and Lincolnshire. As already noted, this was precisely the area with the least flexible type of openfield system, and it bore the burden of change without ease of adaptation. When the growing profitability of sheep farming initiated a trend towards the creation of larger farms from smaller farms (called 'engrossing' by contemporaries) and the substitution of land for labour, such changes, in this sort of grain-growing area, could and did cause disruption, hardship, and complaint, as they did not when they occurred in areas where there were more flexible arrangements and ample room for expansion to find pasture.

As the economic effects of the population growth began to make themselves felt by about the 1520s, so did the second main phase of this early period become evident. Using material similar to that in Table 4, but recasting the index to show changes compared with the 1520s, we can see that the figures in Table 5 show this longer period to have been dominated not just by the massive general increase of agricultural prices but also by that of grain prices relative to wool prices. Animal products as a whole, though not rising quite as much as grains, moved far ahead of wool prices.

TABLE 5
Index of prices and 'wool' exports, 1520–1649

1520–9 = 100

Decade	Av. all grain prices*	Av. all animal products*	Av. wool prices*	Av. export (by volume) of 'cloths' from London†
1520–9	100	100	100	100
30–9	105	121	110	125
40–9	121	151	138	164
50–9	226	203	186	167
60–9	205	225	185	124
70–9	240	245	211	136
80–9	295	281	203	148
90–9	383	354	284	148
1600–9	363	369	314	166
10–19	425	427	318	151
20–9	417	406	319	136
30–9	513	433	367	131
40–9	510	436	357	—

Sources: * As in Table 4, but re-calculated on an index base 1520–9 = 100.

† Carus-Wilson and Coleman, op. cit; J. D. Gould, *The Great Debasement* (Oxford, 1970) Appendix C; F. J. Fisher, 'Commercial Trends and Policy in Sixteenth Century England', *Econ. Hist. Rev.* X (1940) (the annual figures corresponding to the triennial averages there published were kindly supplied by Prof. Fisher); and 'London's Export Trade in the Early Seventeenth Century', *Econ. Hist. Rev.*, 2nd Ser. III (1950). The shortcomings of this index of demand for wool as represented by textile exports will be evident from what is said in Chapter 4 (see especially Fig. 5 and pp. 63–4). For a note on 'cloths', see Fig. 4.

Even with all the limitations of the price evidence already discussed, an admission that there may be a substantial margin of error, and a reservation that the London cloth export statistics certainly underestimate the total exports of wool in all its forms, the complete reversal of the trend shown in Table 4 is evident enough, especially after the 1540s. What, then, do these figures suggest might have occurred in the agricultural sector?

The most obvious probability would be an extension of the total area under cultivation. Specifically, one would expect to see more land under the plough and less, relatively though not absolutely, devoted to sheep-rearing. It would be reasonable to suppose that there would be an increased amount of enclosure for all sorts of purposes including both livestock-rearing and grain-growing. And there might also be some increases in productivity as a result of farming innovations, in techniques or in organization, or as a consequence of greater specialization, by region, soil, or product. But, unless the inflation can be shown to have been entirely a monetary phenomenon, it is reasonable to deduce that the very rise in agricultural prices is itself an indication that such productivity gains as were achieved must have been insufficient to offset the increase in real costs incurred in the process of increasing output.

For all these suppositions from prices, we have no supporting or refuting evidence of an aggregate nature. General statements by contemporaries show an awareness of the problem, as in this plea by a correspondent of Burghley's in 1576:

. . . For the people are increased and ground for ploughs doth want. Corn and other victual is scant . . . People would labour if they knew whereon, the husbandman would be glad to have ground to set his plough to work if he knew where. [5]

The patient work of scholars has, however, brought to light a great and growing amount of local evidence, and it is upon this that we must rely. All sorts of examples of men pushing out the margin of cultivation can be found. From about the 1560s onwards the drainage of low-lying marsh land went on apace in many areas—salt-marshes around the East Anglian coasts, the Thames and Medway estuaries, mosses in Lancashire and Cheshire, as well as the more famous works put in hand by such local landowners as the Earl of Bedford in the Fenland around the Wash between the 1590s and 1650s. Not all of these were successful in a process which reclaimed land for new farming at the cost of sometimes destroying an ancient local way of life. The comment in a manorial survey of a Shropshire village in 1563 that 'the many enclosures . . . are like to destroy the woods'[6] could have been echoed all over the country as woodlands were being cleared; the plough was pushed into downlands, in Wiltshire and Kent alike, into sheep pastures, heaths and even some of the parks and game preserves which provided status-pastimes for landowners. As wool prices sagged, so farmers in the North and West and on the heavier soils elsewhere turned more to cattle-raising and fattening, to dairying and meat. The hunger for land and the long upward movement in prices pulled up rents, but again evidence is local. On the estates of the Earls of Pembroke in Wiltshire, rents rose about fourfold between the 1530s and 1640, perhaps eightfold over the whole period from 1500 to 1650. The rent of arable land in Norfolk and Suffolk rose sixfold between the 1550s and 1640s, that of pasture and meadow rose by double or treble. The gap widened between the rents of enclosed and of open-field land. Yet we must be careful about assuming too great an extension of enclosure. It has been estimated that even in Leicestershire, a county at the heart of the Midland movements, only 10 per cent of the open-field arable land of the county had been enclosed by 1607; the real switch to grazing there came later and especially after the mid-seventeenth century. All the time, specialization by region and product increased; it was reflected in the evidence of growing quantities of grain shipped by coastal trade, for example, from Kentish or East Anglian ports to London, in the growth of cattle-droving from the North and West to the fattening areas of the Midlands and South, and in increased activity in market towns all over the country. Before any further multiplying of local examples, certain points demand emphasis.

First, the course of change in the English countryside cannot be evaluated in terms of enclosure. The word itself has become an omnibus in meaning and emotive by usage. The mere act of putting hedges or fences around land was no guarantee of improved farming. What mattered was the extinction of common rights, whether over the fallow arable fields or over common pasture; and the greater *possibility* of the introduction of new methods, improved organization, or specialization which separate individual ownership permitted. Many troubles arose over the loss of common rights. Resentment, hardship, a sense or a reality of injustice came by various channels. Sometimes it was the pasturing on the commons of large numbers of cattle or sheep, by bigger farmers, thus making life more difficult for the smaller husbandman; sometimes it was the loss of ancient rights in the woodlands—to cut underwood, to run pigs. Although the agitation against the big sheep-masters died down, bad harvests and high prices, as in the 1590s, in 1607, or the 1630s, stimulated grain riots which often took the form (sometimes as symbolic acts of protest against unpopular local figures) of the pulling down of enclosing hedges or fences around arable land.

What could be done on enclosed land, however, brings us to the second point to be emphasized. Because of the essentially mixed nature of English farming at the time, an increase in pasture was an essential part of an effective increase in arable land. They were not just two alternative uses of land. And the major possibility of increased productivity came with the development of what was variously known as 'convertible', 'alternate', or 'up-and-down' husbandry or 'ley farming'. The essence of this was that every few years the main lands of the farm alternated between tillage and pasture, instead of being permanent arable or permanent grass. A survey of a Warwickshire parish in the 1650s recorded the practice in terms which held good for other areas: '. . . it being a usual course with the inhabitants thereabouts . . . to plough their pasture ground for two or three years together and then to let it lie for ten or twelve years and so to plough it again.'⁷ Such procedures were known in the early sixteenth century, especially in the North West where they fitted in with the more flexible field system, but they spread in the Midlands and elsewhere particularly from the 1590s and onwards, thus introducing greater flexibility into these areas.

Enclosure could obviously expedite these developments, though it did not necessarily bring them about; grass leys were already being used in the sixteenth century along with the open-field cultivation, to increase the area of available pasturage. These convertible husbandry practices raised the quality of the grass land; allowed more livestock to be reared, thus making more dung available for manuring the arable land; and also improved the cereal output by resting the land from time to time. What is not known, however, is how extensively these methods were practised and therefore how much they contributed to the main task of feeding the increased numbers. This same qualification holds for the evidence which has been gathered for other innovations. For example, the floating of water-meadows—a device for flooding and draining low-lying land, thereby turning it into rich meadow—was expensive of capital; it was used especially in parts of the West Country, but mainly from the early seventeenth century onwards. What all these changes did was to operate indirectly, not directly, on the task of growing more grains, still the main food of the people. The calculation that there was a 30 per cent increase in the yield of wheat between 1450 and 1650 may be correct, though its foundations are shaky. But it still seems very likely that, before the mid-seventeenth century, more land and more specialization by region, rather than improved techniques, were the chief means by which the increased numbers were fed, and that the real pay-off came later.

(iii)

Just what happened to the various strata of rural society in the period of later medieval decline (if it was a period of decline) is still a matter of debate among medievalists. But with the customary reservation demanded by the presence of learned debate, it seems probable that a long-term decline of both population and prices between approximately the 1370s and 1470s brought with it certain general tendencies in land holding. Faced with scarcer and dearer labour, landlords tended to abandon the direct cultivation of manorial demesnes and to lease them to tenants; the value of land, as exhibited in the level of rents or of fines payable on entry to manorial holdings, declined, though rents as a proportion of a landlord's total income often rose; some land went out of cultivation, some found its way into the hands of peasants, demesne farmers, or prospering townsmen on comparatively easy terms. In many cases, the economic lease was already the crucial element in the landlord's income, sundry feudal and manorial rights and dues being of lesser consequence. By the end of the fifteenth century, serfdom, villeinage, and labour services were largely defunct in England, though some examples of the survival of villeinage can be found throughout the sixteenth century. The manor, the essential unit of feudal landholding, continued in being and served to delineate the legal position of many classes of tenant—freeholders, copyholders, or tenants-at-will. Manorial customs varied enormously. Broadly speaking, freeholders could do what they liked with their land, though still having to pay certain fixed dues or fines or quit-rents. Copyholders were mainly customary tenants holding their lands by inheritance or for various terms—for life, for two or three lives, for specified periods of years—all with fines, fixed or variable, payable to the manorial lord on entrance to the tenancy. Tenants-at-will, holding entirely at the will of the lord, were usually to be found amongst the poorest of cottagers and squatters on the waste lands. Then there were the leasehold tenants, holding lands at economic rents for lives or terms of years—anything from seven to ninety-nine—and ultimately dependent not upon manorial custom but upon the common law. Although the manor survived, it was in a variety of ways being by-passed. Lands held by tenants of the manor, copyhold or freehold, were often let at an economic rent to someone else—a sub-tenant whose existence was not in the cognizance of the manorial system.

It was upon this complex, shifting, weakening structure that there broke the long rises in prices and population. The reversal of the trends in prices and wages, evident after 1500, meant that land became dearer, rents and entry fines rose, leases were shortened; everywhere the terms of tenancies

were under stress if they prevented the ambitious, the enterprising, or the greedy from acquiring land to farm or increasing their return for letting it. There was a boom, especially
after the 1540s, in the land market; a great amount of land
changed hands. What had emerged at the end? Did any
particular social strata, classes, groups, or institutions significantly rise or fall in the process?

Two landowning institutions unquestionably lost—the
Church and the Crown. At the beginning of the period the
Church owned perhaps 20–25 per cent of the country's land.
Many monastic houses had become rentiers; some took part
during the first phase of change, *circa* 1450–1520, in the
movements towards enclosure for sheep farming. But their
activities were soon cut short by that first great act of
nationalization in pursuit of war finance, the dissolution of
the monasteries, and the subsequent sale of their lands by
the Crown. The survey of the Church's income, the *Valor
Ecclesiasticus*, was carried out in 1535; dissolution in 1536 was
followed by financial crisis, and an urgent need for hard cash
evident by 1540; sales followed rapidly through the 1540s,
continuing thereafter so that by the accession of Elizabeth I
in 1558 well over three-quarters of all the former monastic
lands had been sold off, the rest going between then and
1640. For the same reason that the Crown grabbed and sold
the Church land so did it have to sell its own lands and thus,
in its own right, join the ranks of the losers. Owning perhaps
about 5 per cent of the land in the mid-fifteenth century, the
Crown, in the persons of Edward IV and Henry VII, for a
while extended and improved its position, by forfeitures, by
administrative skills, and by keeping out of expensive warfare.
But Henry VIII and his successors soon reversed matters,
reducing the Crown lands to insignificance by the time of
the Civil War (see below, pages 189–90).

To define and come to even rough conclusions about other
groups is more difficult. Peers are distinguishable enough in
their possession of titles, some legal privileges, and their
common membership of the House of Lords. But as landowners they were heterogeneous; not all big landowners were
peers; not all peers were big landowners. The composition of

the peerage changed radically between 1450 and 1640—by attainders, by failure in the male line, by a surge of new creations by James I. A total of some 50 peers at the beginning of the period had grown to 120 at the end. A few, a very few, rose on the strength of successful farming, like the Spencers, fifteenth-century Warwickshire graziers who entered the peerage in 1603; more, like such famous examples as the Cecils and the Russells, Wriothesley and Cranfield, rose through high office and Court favour; many rose through a series of fortunate or skilful marriages; others fell through extravagance or stupidity. Estimates of the total and average incomes of the peerage between 1558 and 1641 do not suggest that as landowners their relative position changed very strikingly: although their average holdings of manors fell, their average landed income is calculated to have roughly doubled in monetary terms, though remaining at about the same level when allowance is made for the rise in prices. Of course, the peerage may well have been losers in power and prestige, as some contemporaries thought, but it is not immediately evident that this was due to loss of income as a group. Indeed, it is not clear that their economic experience as a group, or their share of total land or of the spoils of the land market is very meaningful, if only because of their lack of economic homogeneity. Another sort of guess is that the share of the land owned by larger landowners generally remained at about 15–20 per cent for much of the period as a whole, although the composition of that group undoubtedly changed.

If the Church and Crown were significantly losers, and the bigger landowners, including much of the peerage, retained about the same share, despite internal changes, the gainers must have been found amongst the other strata of rural society, notably the gentry and yeomanry, best placed for taking advantage of the market. No really effective way has yet been discovered to quantify the almost certain rise in the share of land owned by the gentry and yeomanry, or of the incomes derived thereby. The counting of manors held by different social groups has been practised and found wanting for a variety of reasons; the significance of the manor as an indicator of control over landed wealth was not only variable, because manors were merely heterogeneous collections of rights, but almost certainly diminishing over the period. For what they are worth, however, some calculations for the period 1561–1640 have shown a fall in the numbers of manors held by the Crown and the peerage and a rise in those held by the gentry. And, however inadequate its statistical basis, the contention that the thrusting and ambitious members of the gentry and upper yeomanry were those who did best in this battle for landed wealth remains plausible and not disproved. They were joined, as they had been at other times in the past by lawyers, merchants, burgesses who wanted land, not only or principally for the possible profits of farming but also for its prestige and security; and by successful office-holders whose numbers undoubtedly rose as the Tudor and Stuart governments offered a wider range of attractive plums.

One of the results was a rise in the numbers of the armigerous gentry mirrored both in claims to the College of Heralds for coats of arms and in detections of bogus pedigrees by the heraldic visitations carried out between 1530 and 1686. There was a particularly large increase in grants of arms between the 1560s and 1680s and the results can be seen in the counties. Between the visitations of 1562 and 1634 in Lincolnshire, for example, there was an increase of 78 gentry families many of whom had risen from the yeomanry; of all the gentry families of Yorkshire in 1642, 23 per cent were new since 1558, some having risen from the yeomanry, some from business or professions, some having arrived by marriage. In county after county the numbers were rising of those who laid claim to gentry status—though not all got it. Another mirror of the rising prosperity of these broad classes of society was the great amount of building and rebuilding which went on in rural England between roughly 1570 and 1640. For every grand new house built by a Cecil or a Howard there were dozens of solid farmhouses of the upper yeomanry or gentry built or improved. New cottages testified to the rising rural population; but bigger and better farmhouses and country seats, whether the stone rebuildings of the Cotswolds or the timber-framed and pargeted houses of Suffolk, meant more money. When Robert Loder, a Berkshire yeoman, wrote in his farm accounts in 1618 of 'money laid out about my chimney . . . in making my stairs, my window and ceiling and plastering, etc.',[8] he was recording expenditure on a type of improvement of which many signs still remain all over England. And it was the owners or occupiers of these houses, big and small, whose aggregate incomes contributed much to sustaining the internal demand for industrial goods or imports during this period.

Though Church and Crown were the main institutional losers, they were not the only individual losers. Some were peers, some were gentry—the less enterprising or provident, the more extravagant—but many were also the smaller farmers—lesser yeomanry, minor husbandmen, smaller copyholders—whose disability was to have had too small a holding from which to profit by the rising market and no resources to increase it. Evictions of tenants certainly occurred, especially those with the weakest sorts of tenancies, such as copyholders on the demesne land, various tenants-at-will, or the occasional surviving serf; and certainly there were many disputes over rights, as landlords showed their eagerness to acquire more land, to enclose land or to jack up their rent-rolls. Many a tenant of small resources could not afford legal redress against such pressures; or, squeezed between rising prices and inadequate land to provide a consistent saleable surplus, sold out to neighbours with larger holdings or to landlords eager to consolidate their estates. In this way, such men went down the social ladder to swell the growing number either of wholly landless agricultural labourers or of that familiar stratum of the pre-industrialized society, the struggling husbandman, the small peasant with just enough land to feed his family in good times but forever at the mercy of a bad harvest and often in debt to local tradesmen. Nor did the times help such men, for the later sixteenth and early seventeenth centuries seem to have had more bad harvests—in 1555–6, 1586, 1595–7, 1629–30, 1636–7, and 1647–9—bringing dearth, hardship, and even starvation, than in either the preceding or succeeding centuries. Rich farmers sometimes benefited by such times, but if they did not they could bear with them; the small peasants and the poor could not. At the bottom of the social scale poverty probably worsened. Beggars and squatters multiplied—ignorant and feckless, alienated from ordered society.

4

Commerce and Expansion, 1450–1650

(i)

In the mid-fifteenth century English fortunes were not at their best. Political woes—instability and unrest periodically bursting into active warfare at home, losses in the last stages of the Hundred Years War abroad—did not, of course, produce exact reflections in the economy. Nevertheless, all that is known of the country's overseas trade suggests that this indicator of the generation of wealth was at a very low ebb in the 1450s and '60s. Furthermore, even when recovery was under way from the 1480s onwards, England was still a country on the near-fringes of the European world, economically and culturally as well as geographically. The dominant economies were in the Mediterranean lands, especially in Italy; in South Germany; in the commercial and industrial cities of Flanders; and the north German towns of the commercial empire of the Hanseatic League. Indeed Hansards and other aliens, mainly Italian, still controlled about 40 per cent of English overseas trade. The English mercantile marine, though showing healthy signs of expansion in the later fifteenth and early sixteenth centuries, was of small significance. England's one substantial commercial city, London, was overshadowed in wealth and size as well as in political and cultural consequence by the great cities of continental Europe. It was of about the same rank as Verona or Zurich; it did not compare with the greatest seaport in Europe, Venice; and nothing in England even began to match such a manifestation of wealth and power as the Medici family controlling the biggest financial organization in Europe, with its base in Florence, and branches and related enterprises in Venice, Milan, Geneva, Avignon, Bruges, and London.

In the course of the fifteenth century, the structure of England's export trade had undergone an important transition. No longer simply a supplier of primary products, as it had been for much of the fourteenth century, England had become a major exporter of a manufactured product. Although English cloth had achieved some export renown in the twelfth and thirteenth centuries, the country's export trade had long been dominated by raw wool, supplemented by other raw materials, notably tin and lead, as well as skins and hides. By the middle of the fifteenth century the switch was evident: as much, or more, wool was being exported in the form of manufactured cloth than as sacks of raw wool. Cloth exports averaged 55,000 cloths per annum *circa* 1438–48; wool exports only about 9000 sacks per annum. In value, cloth probably accounted for about two-thirds of total exports. In the 1450s and '60s however, bad times pushed down even the cloth export figures to an annual average of only about 30–40,000; whilst wool exports, running at less than 8000 sacks and long declining since their heyday in the early fourteenth century, were little more than half their level at the beginning of the fifteenth century. Other indicators, too, testify to this mid-fifteenth century depression in English commercial fortunes. Exports of tin almost certainly fell, following the sharp drop in English production registered in the half-century from 1415 to 1465. Wine imports fell from a high level in the 1410s and '20s to the lowest figures of the century in the 1450s and '60s. Imports and exports of miscellaneous other wares all fell markedly from the early years of the century to low points in the 1460s. The general picture of gloom needs a word of qualification. For various reasons, the Customs figures from which these data are drawn may exaggerate the depth, though not the reality, of the depression.

After the 1460s trade recovered. Despite some short-term fluctuations, the upward trend was unmistakeable and continuous, culminating in a high point in the 1550s. It was dominated by the sustained rise in cloth exports, shown in

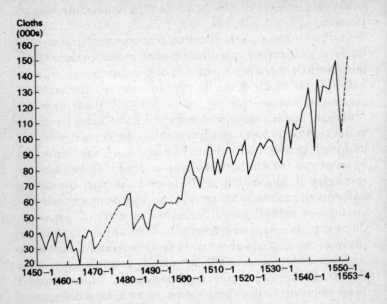

FIG. 4   English cloth exports, 1450/1-1553/4

Source: E. M. Carus-Wilson and Olive Coleman, *England's Export Trade, 1275-1547* (Oxford, 1963) and J. D. Gould, *The Great Debasement* (Oxford, 1970).

Note: A 'cloth' was a notional standard cloth to which the various types were reduced for accounting purposes by the contemporary Customs' authorities.
The years ran from Michaelmas to Michaelmas.

Fig. 4. Cloth exports multiplied about three-fold, averaging some 130,000 cloths per annum in the period 1547-53. Such an increase in a century may not seem much by the standards of achievement in the industrializing economies of a later era. Moreover, exports of raw wool revealed an opposite trend, continuing their downward slide, despite a temporary recovery in the 1470s and '80s, to an average of less than 3-4000 sacks a year by the mid-sixteenth century. For the pre-industrialized economy, however, this long-sustained growth in one particular sort of manufactured export commodity had a significance for economic and social change far beyond the mere numerical indicator of a three-fold rise. Tin exports increased by approximately 120 per cent between 1477 and 1547, though reaching much higher levels in the first decade of the sixteenth century. Exports of hides, of minor importance in the fifteenth century, boomed, especially in the 1530s; and wine imports showed a significant recovery, though the increasing consumption of home-produced beer meant that total wine imports in the mid-sixteenth century were almost certainly well below their peak in the early fourteenth century.

How had this commercial growth come about?

As soon as answers to this question are sought, one fact about this long boom has to be made clear at the outset. A great part of it was heavily concentrated on London. In the mid-fifteenth century, London accounted for rather less than 50 per cent of the cloth export trade, itself, as already mentioned, worth about two-thirds of total exports. In the mid-sixteenth century, London had attracted to itself about 90 per cent of those exports, and cloth accounted for 75–80 per cent of the value of all exports. London's own trade in the country's main export had thus increased at roughly twice the rate for the country as a whole. This development was part of a wider, European phenomenon: the remarkable rise of Antwerp to a position of commercial and financial pre-eminence. Between approximately 1490 and 1520 Antwerp emerged as the commercial metropolis of Europe and its main money market; it sustained that position, though not without some crises in the 1520s and 1550s, until war, famine, and emigration brought the role to an end in the 1570s and 1580s. For the English economy it meant the creation of a London–Antwerp commercial axis. It acted, to change the metaphor, as a funnel. Through it were poured both exports and imports, and a larger share of the increasing volume of total business.

This remarkable process was to have important consequences. It emphasized the existing tendency for southern and especially south-eastern England to be the richer and more active area of the economy, sucking in people, goods, and trade. The commerce of the old and important port of Bristol declined, its annual cloth exports in the 1550s, for example, averaging 2312 cloths as compared with 3355 a century earlier, a drop of 31 per cent, and a very long way behind London in its share of the total. A similar fate befell such ports as Hull, Boston, and Sandwich, although some developed other types of trade, for example the coastwise export of cereals, often, again, to help feed the growing number of hungry Londoners. Many provincial traders found themselves unable to compete against that powerful predator, the rich London merchant. It was not a continuous, unbroken trend throughout the period. Some outports participated in the earlier phases of the boom, the most striking example being Southampton. An important centre for Italian trade to England, its safe harbour received many Venetian galleys bringing wines, oil, silks, and other Mediterranean wares in exchange for cloth, wool, and tin. In the mid-fifteenth century, it was certainly the biggest cloth-shipping port outside London and probably had the largest share of the country's tin exports. After declining in the 1470s and '80s, it then enjoyed so remarkable a boom in the thirty years between approximately 1495 and 1525 that London's share of total trade even fell for a time. But it was short-lived. The town's tin export trade had not shared in the boom; it went to the ports of Devon and Cornwall and to London. The Italians gave way to the Londoners who, in any event, already controlled much of Southampton's trade during its early Tudor expansion. In the 1550s its cloth exports averaged only about 1600 cloths per annum, a fall of 86 per cent on its heyday in 1515–25. The only outports to increase their share of the cloth trade during this century of growth were, significantly, two outlets for cloth-producing hinterlands: Ipswich (including Colchester) and Exeter, though the total trade of both together was still less than 5 per cent of London's share.

In this whole development an important and interlocking dual role was played by the government and the trading organization known as the Merchant Adventurers. During the fifteenth century the latter emerged as a recognizable and separate entity, coalescing from a number of groups of merchants trading to the Low Countries but dominated by members of the Mercers Company of London. They fused into a separate body to obtain privileges from the king; to secure royal support in their trading relations in the Low Countries, especially when, as so often happened, a trade prohibition was in force as a lever in some political or dynastic dispute; or to present a united front in their rivalry with other groups, notably the Hansards and the English Merchants of the Staple, the much older organization which controlled the wool trade, with the Staple or market town at Calais. Conversely, monarchs, especially Henry VII, found the Merchant Adventurers a useful weapon in the conduct of political relations with the rulers of Burgundy, Brabant, and Flanders. Formal recognition of the Fellowship of the Merchant Adventurers of London came in 1486 and 1505. The negotiation by Henry of successive commercial treaties, in 1496 and 1506, substantially improved and strengthened the English trading position in the Low Countries and served to consolidate the gains of the Merchant Adventurers. They operated as a 'regulated' company, a guild-like organization which regulated the conduct of the trade but did not operate a common joint-stock fund of capital, individual merchants trading separately or in partnership. It soon became the most powerful English business organization of the time. From its joint headquarters in London and Antwerp, it controlled entry into the trade, chartered ships and arranged for them to sail in convoy, kept out 'interlopers', and earned the substantial resentment of its much less powerful provincial counterparts in Newcastle and York.

Antwerp was, above all, an international entrepôt. The colonies of merchants there—Italians, Germans, Spaniards, Portuguese, Frenchmen, and Englishmen—conducted the business of the town; they brought wealth to it, by importing and re-exporting an immense range of wares; and in so doing all stimulated local processing industries of which the most important for the English was that of cloth dyeing and finishing. Much—but just how much is not known—of this expansion in English textile exports consisted of unfinished and undyed cloths. Although the renowned English broadcloths, some white, some coloured, continued to be in demand, cheaper and lighter fabrics of only medium quality, especially those known as 'kerseys', featured notably amongst the cloths which overseas customers evidently wanted, particularly in the later stages of the boom. Via the Antwerp mart, sometimes by sea but often by the land routes across Europe, large numbers of kerseys and other English cloths, some of them finished and dyed in the Low Countries, went to Italy and other parts of the Mediterranean; others found their way to Hamburg and ports in northern Germany and the Baltic, to Nuremberg and towns in south Germany; and more to eastern Europe, to Silesia, Poland, and Hungary. *Carisez, kersie, karazja, karasia, karazsia,* . . . English kerseys were internationally known. But only rarely were they, at this stage, taken to their ultimate destination by English merchants.

For much of the export boom, there had been no increase in the share of the trade in English mercantile hands. Indeed as more of it was concentrated in London cloth exports, the share even fell slightly; during Henry VII's reign about 53 per cent of total cloth exports was in English hands, the remainder being roughly equally distributed between Hansards and other alien merchants; by the early 1540s, the native share had fallen to just below 50 per cent. Then change began to set in. The leverage which the Merchant Adventurers could exert was strengthened as they became more useful as sources of loans to the Crown; in conjunction with the varying posture of English political relations with the Hapsburgs, it operated to ensure that the privileges accorded to the Hanseatic merchant colony in London were increasingly in jeopardy. In the 1550s the share of London cloth exports controlled by native merchants rose to over 70 per cent. Nor did the concentration of trade upon Antwerp mean that English merchants were excluded from direct trade with more distant places. Many of the southern and eastern ports, from Bristol round to Hull, conducted trade, albeit small in total volume, with Iberian, French, Dutch, and even Baltic ports, with interests stretching northwards to the fisheries of Iceland. There was an increasing penetration by English merchants into the Mediterranean, notably from Bristol; short-distance trade went on between south-coast ports and France; small west-coast ports, from Barnstable to

Chester, traded with Ireland. Yet, in total, English merchants before the 1550s took only a very small part in the longer-distance trade of the day. After the crises of the 1550s the pattern of English participation began to change radically.

(ii)

The English role in the drama of early European expansion was minimal. Portugal was the pioneer, its seamen and merchants exploring into the Atlantic and down the west coasts of Africa in the fifteenth century, preparatory to Diaz rounding the Cape in 1489 and da Gama reaching India in 1497. Columbus, a Genoese in Spanish service, had available to him the fruits of Portuguese knowledge and methods when he made his famous voyage of 1492—discovering America whilst in search of Asia—and opened the way to Spanish America. By 1520 a Portuguese trading empire in the East—with outposts in Africa and Brazil—had turned Lisbon, temporarily, into the main port for Asiatic produce brought by the sea route; by the 1540s the activities of Cortes and Pizarro had created a Spanish empire in the West, from Peru to Mexico, and made of Seville the great port of the Spanish New World trade. From Bristol, meanwhile, another Italian, the Venetian John Cabot, had sailed in 1497 and reached what was probably Newfoundland; twelve years later, his son Sebastian sailed to the area later to be known as Hudson's Bay. But the subsequent European interest in cod fisheries and furs had little or no immediate consequences for English mercantile endeavour any more than had the voyages of odd traders from Bristol, Southampton, or Plymouth, putting their ships into Iberian preserves, in Africa, Brazil, or the Caribbean. Too many energies and resources were devoted to the London–Antwerp axis.

In the second half of the sixteenth century, however, change was rapid and often violent. It was a product of political, religious, and economic forces in so explosive a mixture that economic abstraction is meaningless. War between Spain and France and its attendant financial problems came to a head with the bankruptcies of both states in 1557, with drastic consequences for the money market of Antwerp. To difficulties in Spanish-American trade were added Europe-wide harvest failures and grain crises. In the early 1550s, the English cloth export boom, perhaps made more unstable in its later stages by debasement of the coinage at home, col-lapsed; there were complaints of over-production and decay of trade, with corresponding appeals for regulation of both industry and commerce. Then, and in the ensuing decades, the Crown's advisers showed great concern about the balance of trade and the inflow of bullion, about gathering of informa-tion on trade, and devising sundry ways to harness economic power and political advantage. A series of attacks and reprisals, part of worsening relations between England and the Hapsburgs, led to stoppages of trade between London and the Netherlands, culminating in the Merchant Adven-turers leaving Antwerp in 1564 and spending the next thirty years settling variously in Emden, Hamburg, Stade, until in 1597 mutual reprisals brought their expulsion from Stade and that of the Hansards from London. Despite recovery in Antwerp after the Franco-Spanish peace of Cateau-Cambrésis in 1559, the outbreak of religious revolts in the 1560s and the ferocity of the ensuing Spanish repression smashed Antwerp's commercial pre-eminence, with the enforced closure in 1585 of its vital trading artery, the river Scheldt, sealing its decline, and famine adding its horrors in 1586–7.

Such events did not in themselves cause the first big phase of English maritime expansion which, in the course of a century, was to lay the foundations of the first British empire. But they went far to influence its timing and form. The isolated endeavours or the occasional tracts, like Robert Thorne's *Declaration of the Indes* of 1527, urging that the English should develop a route across the North Pole to the riches of 'Cathaio Orientall', could hardly hope for much effect, not simply because of the concentration on Antwerp but because of the power of Spain. The English rupture with Rome, the unleashed momentum of the European Reforma-tion, and the inability of the Iberian powers to control their fantastic empires so suddenly created, let in the Dutch, the English, and the French, as Hansards and Italians alike found themselves ill-placed and ill-equipped for this new and expansive world. English voyaging proceeded apace. Sir Hugh Willoughby and Richard Chancellor in 1553 vainly sought a north-east passage, but in so doing opened up English commerce with Russia via Archangel. The notorious plundering activities of John Hawkins and Francis Drake in the Spanish West Indies were followed by Drake's circumnavigation of 1577–80 and Thomas Cavendish's in 1586–8. Martin Frobisher's and John Davis's various voyages in continued search for the north-west passage to eastern riches were overshadowed, in their great significance for the future, by the deliberate efforts to plant colonies in America by Humphrey Gilbert, Walter Raleigh, and others in the 1580s. By this time a tide of writings, advocating English colonizing and expansion was flowing fast and continued to do so until the 1630s. Its most famous product was Richard Hakluyt's *Princpal Voyages*. Publications of this sort made stirring reading, as they were intended to. Their practical influence was probably not great; nor do they tell us much about the motives of individual emigrants. But they do reveal something of contemporary views on colonization.

The arguments for it defy ready classification. Spain could be bridled, the Christian religion planted, seamanship encouraged, the Newfoundland fisheries exploited, markets developed, raw materials supplied. Philosophically-minded writers, such as Francis Bacon, saw colonies as part of the reproductive process of ancient kingdoms; theologically-disposed enthusiasts presented them as possessing 'their warrant from God's direction and command'.[1] Amongst the economic arguments, hopes for greater self-sufficiency loomed high, as did the merits of colonies as devices for promoting the much desired exchange of imported raw materials or precious metals against exports of domestic manufacture. Thus would national wealth be increased and home employment encouraged. The refrain of providing work at home or opportunities for emigration to endless land abroad was played with unsurprising gusto in this era of population growth. 'So great a body of many millions which yearly do increase amongst us':[2] this phrase of a writer of 1612 was echoed by similar comments, plentiful from the 1580s to the 1630s. And colonization was perenially lauded as a strategic move in a perpetual commercial strife between emergent nations. With supplies of goods from her colonies, wrote Hakluyt in 1584, England would overcome her commercial rivals and 'drive them out of trade to idleness'.

Political aspiration was an integral part of the whole process, not just of colonization but of aggressive, nationalistic commerce everywhere. Whatever lay behind the initiative of individuals—whether land-hungry younger sons of gentry families, the adventurous or the disenchanted, moved by religious discontent or by clamorous greed—the State found reason to encourage and support as English governments equipped themselves to battle with Spain or Holland or France. The English State rarely initiated; still less did it impose the centralized control favoured by Portguese and Spanish governments; its actions did not add up to a far-sighted plan for national expansion. But Tudors and Stuarts alike, though bowing to political expediency, now this way, now that, gave their imprimatur to English commercial expansion and aggression as an integral part of the pursuit of power. This linkage was made manifest in the creation of a network of royally chartered trading companies, enjoying monopolies over English commerce in their specified areas of operation. Some were 'regulated' companies, like the Merchant Adventurers and the Merchants of the Staple; others took the form of joint-stock companies, thus creating the first faint beginnings in England of a market for stocks and shares. Whatever the financial form, however, it was the collection of rights and privileges which reflected the deal between the State and the merchants. The latter got the official backing of the government in opening negotiations with the rulers of a new area of trade; a monopoly of an area; control of entry and thus, it was hoped, the ability to maintain profits; the right to keep out retailers, thus adding a cherished social distinction to reinforce the economic advantages of exclusiveness; and the creation of a corporate entity to lobby for the interests of the group. The State, for its part, got something which war and inflation made it want in ever-growing amounts: a source which it could tap for money and especially for loans of cash. Not all companies were thus tapped but some were, notably the Merchant Adventurers and the East India Company. Incorporation by charter had long been made to yield money, as the ancient guilds and companies of the City of London knew to their cost. But the 'livery' companies—Mercers, Merchant Taylors, Haberdashers, and the rest—bore less and less relevance to the conduct of trade. The new companies could run it and pay the State for the privilege. The State, too, got a series of readily identifiable bodies to negotiate with or to use in the conduct of the politico-economic battle of commerce, thereby facilitating the task of government in commercial as in political matters, for nobody, as yet, had conceived the extraordinary notion that trade might be best left to its own devices.

And so there came upon the English economic scene the Muscovy (or Russia) Company (1553), an important new charter for the Merchant Adventurers (1564), the Spanish Company (1577), the Eastland Company (1579), the Levant Company (1581), the East India Company (1600), the Virginia Company (1606), the New Plantation of Ulster (1609), the French Company (1611), the Somers Island or Bermuda Company (1612), the Plymouth Adventurers to New England (1620), the Massachusetts Bay Company (1628), and the Providence Island Company (1629)—to name only some of the more important or notorious or enduring. Some, for varying reasons, were ineffectual or short-lived, like the French Company and the Spanish Company. Some, so far from being adventurous became increasingly restrictive. The Merchant Adventurers provided the classic example of this in their attempts to limit trade geographically to the appointed mart town and quantitatively by seniority of membership. Some effectively established trade, like the Russia Company, or maintained relations with distant powers, as did the Levant Company with the Turks. Some helped to bring settlement and trade and then lost their initial raison d'être as companies, as happened to a number of the American and Caribbean ventures. Some changed their form from time to time, as did the Levant Company, which had a sequence of charters. One, the East India Company, was later to grow into the most powerful mercantile corporation in the country. Nearly all had their roots in London and were dominated by London businessmen. All, at one time or another, attracted the opposition of three main groups. First, their existence greatly exacerbated the resentment felt by provincial merchants against their London brethren.

. . . by means of the said Companies (the Government whereof is ruled only in the City of London) all the whole trade of merchandize is in a manner brought to the City of London . . . and other ports hath in a manner no traffic but falleth to great decay, the smart whereof we feel in our port of Kingston-upon-Hull.[3]

This Hull complaint, of about 1575, was echoed and expanded in a larger debate in 1604 about 'free trade' (a phrase which, it should be noted, did not then carry the same meaning as it did to nineteenth-century 'free traders') when it was complained, no doubt with some exaggeration, that the 'whole trade of all the realm is in the hands of some two hundred persons at the most.'[4] Secondly, they attracted the odium of the producers, especially the clothiers, who complained of the low prices paid by the monopolistic merchants. Such complaints were particularly loud at times of depressed trade, as in the 1550s and 1620s. And, thirdly, the companies were under continuous attack from the outsiders, the independent traders, the 'interlopers'. Singly or in partnership, merchants had long traded wherever suitable contacts could be had and profits made, unmoved by the behest of rulers or the ambitions of dynasties. They continued to do so, raising capital by the simple process of dividing enterprises into shares for particular voyages, just as the ownership of ships had long been divided into shares, two or three parts for small coasting vessels, eighths, sixteenths, or thirty-seconds for bigger ships. By the middle of the seventeenth century, several 'trades'—to use the terminology of the day—were virtually free of company control, notably the commerce with the American continent, Ireland, France, and the Iberian powers.

(iii)

How, then, did these developments affect the volume and growth, nature, and direction of English trade in the century from 1550 to 1650?

The short answer to such a question is that nobody knows, at least with any of the precision which measurement can give. The period from the 1550s to 1697 (when a new series of trade returns was started, see below, pages 135–6) is the most barren of continuous commercial statistics for any time in English history since before 1275. The reason, significantly enough, lies with the pressure upon the finances of the State. The data from which Fig. 4 was constructed were not kept by contemporaries to tell them about the course of trade, but as records of royal revenue from the Customs duties. Sundry administrative changes in the collection of the Customs, made at various times from 1558 onwards, render the use of these records for obtaining trade statistics difficult, misleading, or sometimes completely impossible. Although other records of trade, both overseas and coastwise, start in 1565, in the shape of the 'Port Books', many have been lost or destroyed, notably during the crucial period of the Interregnum, and others have still to attract research. So we are forced back on fragmentary figures, some of them arising from attempts by contemporaries themselves to find out more about the state of the country's commerce. The scope for guess-work is large.

Some contemporary estimates of the value of English trade in the 1560s may serve as a starting point. They reveal the continuance, perhaps even the high-point, of English overseas trade as an exchange, conducted largely through London, of woollen textiles against a wide range of imported wares. Woollens of one sort or another still comprised over 80 per cent of all exports, with raw wool down to a mere 6 per cent. The value of the country's total exports in normal years at this time was perhaps about £750,000 per annum. Among imports, available data for London only show that non-woollen textiles were the most important: linen, canvas and fustians (see below, page 162) accounting for around 18 per cent of the value of London's total imports, raw flax and thread for another 4 per cent or thereabouts, and sundry silk fabrics for around 6 per cent. Raw materials for the woollen industry—oil and dyestuffs—accounted for about 12 per cent, wine for 10 per cent, iron and miscellaneous metalwares for about 6 per cent; the remainder comprised a very wide variety of other goods, including salt, spices, and Mediterranean foodstuffs. Taking these exports and imports together, it is noteworthy how remarkably important textiles and textile raw materials were in the foreign trade of the day, accounting all told for about 86 per cent of exports and 40 per cent of imports. The geography of English trade shows that most of it was still conducted in European waters, from Holland to southern Spain, with various northern French ports, such as Rouen and La Rochelle, following Antwerp as the main sources and destinations. The English mercantile marine was still of small consequence, perhaps about 50,000 tons, far smaller than those of the Hansards, the Dutch, and the Spaniards, and much of the country's foreign trade, even when handled by English merchants, was carried in foreign vessels.

When one turns to the mid-seventeenth century—or more exactly to about 1640—surviving evidence points both to considerable change and also to some elements of continuity. Some statistics are available for the export from London of the same sorts of cloth as in the earlier period. They are plotted on the graph in Fig. 5. Their scantiness for the later decades is only too evident. They depict a fairly stagnant level of trade for most of Elizabeth's reign, followed by revival to 1614. They fit in with what is known about a depression in 1616, brought on by a foolish scheme designed to force the export of finished rather than unfinished cloth, and with what is known about a worse depression in 1620–22, associated with severe difficulties in overseas markets. However, this picture of a long-term trend of decline throughout the half-century from, roughly, 1590 to 1640 is almost certainly grossly misleading. Indeed, the graph can be represented as an interesting example of how such quantification can falsify reality. For alongside the exports of these traditional

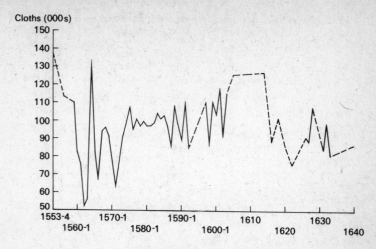

Cloths (000s)

FIG. 5   London's cloth exports, 1553/4–1640

Source: F. J. Fisher, 'Commercial Trends and Policy in Sixteenth Century England', *Economic History Review* X (1940) (unpublished annual figures kindly supplied by Prof. Fisher); and 'London's Export Trade in the early Seventeenth Century', *Economic History Review*, 2nd Ser. III (1950).

Note: After 1606 the years in which the data were recorded changed from Michaelmas–Michaelmas to Christmas–Christmas.

sorts of woollen cloth there had developed the production and sale of different sorts which, for administrative reasons, were not recorded in this way. These were known to contemporaries as the 'new draperies'. Their manufacture will be discussed in Chapter 5 (pages 80–1). Plenty of literary evidence has been generated about them but their export can be quantified only in value and not in amounts. On certain assumptions about the values to be assigned to 'cloth', the following rough estimates can be made:

TABLE 6

Estimates of total textile exports, early seventeenth century

		(£000s) London	Outports	Total
Circa 1606/14	cloth	880	313	1,193
	new draperies	267	80	347
	Total	1,147	393	1,540
Circa 1640	cloth	580	267	847
	new draperies	515	90	605
	Total	1,095	357	1,452

Source: J. D. Gould, 'Cloth Exports, 1600–40', *Econ. Hist. Rev.*, 2nd Ser. XXIV (1971).

Little weight should be put on the difference between the two dates. But two points need stressing: the new types of textiles were approaching the importance of the old sorts; and the outports had regained some of the headway lost in the previous century, accounting for about 25 per cent of total textile exports at both dates. For the new drapery totals to have reached these figures there must have been considerable export growth going on since the later sixteenth century, thus modifying the picture of stagnation and depression given by the London cloth statistics. The new draperies went to different markets; by the 1630s and '40s about two-thirds of them were going to Spanish, African, and Mediterranean ports, and moreover were carried there directly by English merchants. Nor was this process of expansion confined to the new fabrics. The kerseys which had earlier gone via Antwerp and overland to the Mediterranean were replaced or supplemented by coloured Suffolk broadcloths, shipped by merchants of the Levant Company, and outselling in Turkey the products of the decaying Venetian industry.

But textiles and Europe still dominated the pattern of English trade. The following figures afford a poor base for generalizations in that they apply to only one year, for one port, and for English merchants only:

TABLE 7

Exports from London by English merchants in 1640

	£000s	%	
Cloth (old draperies)	580	48·7	86·9
New draperies (and hosiery)	455	38·2	
Other English manufactures	27	2·3	
Minerals	35	3·0	
Agricultural produce	17	1·4	
Re-exports	76	6·4	
	1,190	100·0	

Source: J. D. Gould, 'Cloth Exports, 1600-40', loc. cit. and F. J. Fisher, 'London's Export Trade in the early Seventeenth Century', loc. cit.

Despite these deficiencies, the distribution is unlikely to be very misleading for the country as a whole. Inclusion of the outports would probably have increased the proportion of minerals and agricultural produce (including fish). By this time alien merchants were responsible for too small a share of total exports significantly to have altered the distribution. Re-exports demand a word of explanation. About 1 per cent (over the country as a whole) in an estimate of 1565 and 6·4 per cent in this list, in 1640 they may have temporarily accounted for about 17 per cent of total English exports and re-exports, if the short-lived Dover 'composition' trade (see below page 68 and Table 11, page 133) were included. It is unlikely, however, that that part of the re-export trade which sprang from English expansion, East or West, yet accounted for more than a very small share of total English trade.

The East India Company had made a number of voyages to the area of what is now Indonesia, then known as the Spice Islands or East Indies. Some of the voyages had been highly successful, some complete losses. In general, however, although the Company had established trading posts at Bantam in Java and at Surat on the Indian mainland and done some trade in spices, drugs, and Indian textiles, they were still overshadowed by their Dutch rivals. The Dutch had emerged as the most powerful European trading nation, its East India company ousting the crumbling Portuguese presence from much of Asia, its mercantile marine dominating the carrying trade of Europe, and Amsterdam becoming the new financial and commercial entrepôt. The English company, under-financed and poorly organized by comparison, had made only slow progress by the 1640s, though its great potential was attracting increasing amounts of capital. Westwards, the English had tried out their colonizing enthusiasm in the testing ground which was Ireland. Early Protestant settlements—including many ex-soldiers as well as adventurous gentry—were made in Ulster and Munster from the 1570s and '80s onwards, thus laying seeds both for expanded trade and for future rancour. Beyond Ireland, across the Atlantic, English merchants and settlers, like their Dutch counterparts, had come to understand that economic returns demanded a pattern of endeavour totally different from that necessary for success in Asia. In the East the Europeans made their way into the trading networks of existing economies; America, after the great looting and mining bonanza of the Spaniards in Mexico and Peru was over, demanded settlement and cultivation. French, Dutch, and English all began it effectively with the waning of Spanish power and the end of the long war with Spain in 1604. English settlement in St. Kitts and Barbados and other West Indian islands, as well as in Virginia and Maryland on the American mainland, was completed within the three decades before 1640; but it was to be made effective only by the development of plantation economies—sugar in the Caribbean, tobacco on the mainland—worked increasingly by imported negro slave labour. The settlement of New England—aided by the religious disaffection which drove out Puritan settlers especially during the intolerant years of Charles I and Laud between 1629 and 1640—proceeded on the quite different basis of agriculture, lumbering, fishing, and trading.

Certain crucial points demand emphasis. By the time that civil war broke out in England, the country's colonial expansion had brought little or no *net* increase in markets for English produce. The 50,000 or so transatlantic emigrants would have to grow into a population—along with the imported slaves—which would constitute an economically significant demand before that could happen. Moreover, neither from the West nor from the East was the flow of imports yet big enough to make any radical differences to the structure of English trade. An analysis of London's imports in 1621 shows a distribution by origin and value very similar to that of the 1560s. Sundry non-woollen textiles were the dominant imports, followed by wines and spirits; 63 per cent of total imports still came from northern and north-western Europe, 31 per cent from the Mediterranean, and only 6 per cent from Asia and America. Nevertheless, by the 1640s the process of expansion was beginning to project the European commercial struggle on to a wider stage. The eclipse of the Iberian powers did not mean the eclipse of their American empires, from Peru and Brazil to Mexico and Florida. England, Holland, and France were warming up for their long struggle over this commercial prize. It was a struggle over both the production of and the trade in sugar, tobacco, and slaves; over Asiatic spices and textiles; and over the carrying trade and the supply of manufactures. Much of the combat in its varying forms was made manifest only in the second half of the seventeenth century; its origins lay in the first half. Meanwhile, however, English preparedness in this 'combat perpétuel' (as the French statesman, Jean-Baptiste Colbert, was later to call it) was improved by the growth of the country's mercantile marine. From the mere 50,000 or so tons of the 1570s it had grown to an estimated 115,000 in 1629 and about 150,000 in 1640. This was not only generally useful in the sharpening Anglo-Dutch struggle for the international carrying trade. It was specifically valuable when the 1609–21 truce between Spain and Holland ended with renewed war; during the long phase of England's virtual neutrality in the Thirty Years War; and especially after the outbreak of Franco-Spanish war in 1635. The commercial advantages of neutrality whilst rivals squabbled was succinctly put in a speech to Parliament in 1641:

. . . our great trade depends upon the troubles of our neighbours, and we enjoy almost the trade of Christendom; but if a peace happen betwixt France, Spain and the United Provinces, all these will share what we now possess alone.[5]

It was a temporary glory brought to an end by the Treaty of Westphalia in 1648. But whilst it lasted English shipping had been in great demand, carrying Spanish silver to Flanders, developing a re-export trade in all sorts of European products (based on Dover—the 'composition' trade—and reaching a high point in 1638), taking an active part in the Spanish-American commerce, and even doing well in that great Dutch preserve, the Baltic. It brought a substantial accretion of wealth and experience to individual English merchants and to the nation's invisible earnings.

5

Occupations and Industries, 1450–1650

(i)

Because of the survival and use by historians of the cloth export statistics, and because of the concern by contemporary statesmen with trade as a weapon in an international battle, it is easy to impute to the woollen industry a significance for the Tudor economy greater than, or at any rate different from, that which it probably had in reality. Three main guides to realism need to be followed when trying to assess the place of industry in the England of this time.

First, despite the shift to being an exporter of cloth rather than wool, industry in Tudor England remained technically backward in comparison with the best practices of continental Europe. From about the middle of the sixteenth century it started to catch up, but the results of that overhauling process were not evident until later. Woollen cloth aside, English exports were still those of a primary producer, with virtually no other manufactured wares in the export list. The nature and variety of English imports show how much the economy was dependent on other countries' industries, sometimes for manufactured wares which were not made in England, more commonly for the better quality goods. Over a range of industries—paper, linen, silk, leather-working, hosiery, iron-founding, glass-making—English inferiority to French, Spanish, Italian, Flemish, or German products was manifest. In mining and metallurgy the Germans were the masters; in shipbuilding, first the Iberian powers and then the Dutch were well ahead of English methods. The import of continental skills and techniques, via immigrant labour and, in some cases, capital, is one of the major themes of

Tudor and Stuart industrial history. Even in woollen textiles, English dyeing and finishing seem, in some respects at least, to have lagged behind the best continental practice. Nor was it all a matter of supply. English demand for many manufactured wares was limited largely because levels of wealth and income, as of culture, sophistication, and urban achievement, were inferior to those of the great towns of Europe.

Second, despite the dual-purpose favour accorded by the State to cloth exporters—as legionaries in the commercial combat and as potential milch-cows for the Exchequer—contemporary opinion came only very slowly to look upon the industry which fed that trade as an economic plant to be cherished, a source of wealth in itself. William Camden's enconium of English cloth as 'one of the pillars of the State' belonged, in sentiment and chronology alike, to the end of the sixteenth century. But neither of his near contemporaries, William Harrison and Thomas Wilson, in their accounts of the country saw reason to refer to it in any such terms; indeed they barely referred to it at all. Far more common was another, earlier, but long-enduring view. This saw the spreading, rural, cloth industry as 'the greatest occupation and living of the poor commons of this land'[1] (1454); as a desirable source of employment for the poor who, in the words of a tract of 1549, 'working a little in summer be more than half idle all the residue of the year'.[2] It was seen as a useful sponge to mop up what the jargon of our age would call the endemic underemployment of the pre-industrialized economy. And it is well, to recall that in 1555 the so-called Weavers Act (see below, pages 180-1) sought to curtail the entrepreneurial doings of the richer clothiers, 'ingrossing . . . looms into their hands', in the interests of the poor weavers.[3] Although out-working became a feature of various industries, the woollen industry provided a particularly striking example of the combination of extensive division of labour and the use of the workers' own households to provide work for men, women, and children. It performed a socio-economic role within the community even more important than its exporting function.

Third, this picture of an English woollen industry raising

the nation's commercial importance, as well as providing much rural employment must not be allowed to obscure the realities of this pre-industrialized economy. Many industrial jobs—indeed many non-agrarian occupations generally— were part-time activities, shared with agricultural work. Moreover, much industrial work consisted of the direct processing, with little capital equipment beyond simple hand tools, of agricultural products in order to meet the basic needs of life—food and drink, shelter and clothing. The arable economy provided the raw materials for milling and baking, for malting, brewing, and distilling; from home-reared sheep and cattle came those for making woollen textiles and leather, as well as for the preparation of soap and candles; the woodlands provided timber for shipbuilding and house-building as well as coppice wood for charcoal, the common fuel of numerous industrial processes, or for the domestic hearth. Many productive activities were thereby closely geared to the seasonality of crops and at the mercy of the weather. Consequently, industrial jobs were often seasonal or intermittent; and there was no readily definable and separate 'industrial sector'. Labour and capital were rarely as specific and particular as today: a water-mill might be used for a variety of purposes, a weaver would work in the fields at harvest time, fishing was combined with various land-based jobs, a clothier might be a grocer or an innkeeper, a yeoman farmer also a tanner of leather

Finally, for much of the period most manufacturing activity was still carried out by a multitude of small artisans and craftsmen in town and village. Self-financed, because of their small capital needs, though often dependent on some credit arrangement for raw materials or upon cash advances, they rarely worked with more than an apprentice or a day labourer at most. Alongside them were the increasing army of dependent or only semi-independent workers in the putting-out system, of which woollen textiles was the prime though not the sole example. And, from about the mid-sixteenth century onwards, they were joined by a growing, but still very small, number who worked in centralized establishments with some concentration of capital equipment.

(ii)

With these warnings in mind, it may be useful to start by looking at some characteristic patterns of non-agrarian occupations, mainly urban crafts; and then to consider how they were affected by the population rise and the commercial development of the English economy.

In 1525 Norwich—then the second city of the kingdom—listed about 80 different crafts or trades; at the same time the equivalent number for another, though much smaller East Anglian town, Sudbury, with a population of only about 1200 people was about 46; in the early seventeenth century, Southampton, a town intermediate in size but quite different in character had about 72. Not surprisingly, the larger the town the more varied its occupational structure, with London having 160 or more crafts, including many catering for the fashionable, or merely diverse, wants of the metropolis, varying from jewellers and broderers to spectacle-makers and paviors. But over a wide range such non-agrarian occupations fell into ten fairly clear groups. The victualling trades (bakers, brewers, innkeepers, etc.) and the building trades (masons, brickmakers, thatchers, etc.) supplied food and shelter. The textile workers (weavers, dyers, fullers, etc.) and the clothing workers (tailors, cappers, hosiers, etc.) supplied the other necessities of life. Three groups are distinguishable by the materials used by their members: wood-workers (carpenters, joiners, shipwrights, etc.); metal-workers (blacksmiths, plumbers, goldsmiths, etc.) and leather-workers (tanners, cordwainers, glovers, etc.) The distributive trades (merchants, grocers, etc), transport (carriers, sailors, etc.) and sundry professions (surgeons, scriveners, musicians, etc.) all provided services of one sort or another. And a miscellaneous category necessarily covers everything from cardmakers to horse-leeches.

The importance of these craft occupations can be illustrated in a variety of ways. In the 1520s in four towns of varying size—Coventry, Northampton, Leicester, and Norwich—the six groups of victualling, building, textile, clothing, leather, and metals accounted for 70–85 per cent of all crafts. Naturally there were variations according to local specialities: textiles accounted for about a third in both Coventry and Norwich; leather-workers predominated in the pastoral regions of Northampton and Leicester. The distributive trades were more important in a big town such as Norwich, and naturally dominated a port: in Southampton, of 400 apprentices bound to trades between 1610 and 1648, over 40 per cent went to merchants, mercers, dealers, or the like, though even there textile and clothing accounted for nearly 33 per cent of the remaining indentures. Although these concentrations of industrial artisans were normally associated with the towns, a scattering of such occupations was to be found in many villages throughout the land. In the wholly rural Shropshire parish of Myddle, for instance, with a total population of around 350 in the mid-sixteenth century, about 11 per cent of its adult male population were craftsmen—blacksmiths, carpenters, coopers, tailors, shoemakers—though, as was normal, many such men were small husbandmen as well. Or, again, in the Suffolk hundred of Babergh, the heart of the woollen industry of that area, many of the settlements outside the main towns of Sudbury and Lavenham—themselves quite small—had their quota of non-textile crafts: tailors, carpenters, shoemakers, bakers, tilers, millers, and carriers.

Historically, the crafts have been linked with the guilds; and the decline of the latter has figured as a well-worn theme of English economic change. Many guilds did indeed exist in corporate towns, sometimes with as many guilds as there were crafts and trades. It is important to understand their nature and functions. They were not units of industrial organization; they were methods of association and control. They did not, in themselves, finance production, though ties of kinship or brotherhood might shape the flow of credit. They did not busy themselves with industrial innovation; they were the guardians of craft tradition. Their purpose was to promote the welfare of their members, and only to a limited extent did they attempt to do so by strictly or directly economic means. In this period their role became increasingly social rather than economic. They were fraternities, sometimes with a religious flavour, sometimes with religious possessions, foci of local craft endeavour and pride, of civil ritual and ceremony. Although in some towns the guilds decayed, changed their nature, or lost their significance, in others they long endured, providing for important groups of burgesses and artisans both elements of social cohesion and paths to power in local administration.

Their most potent economic function was to control entry into the craft or 'mystery', thereby preserving a local monopoly and, by the enforcement of apprenticeship, maintaining both the standards of work and the level of wages. Full membership of the guild then became a formal path to the 'freedom' of the town and thus the right to carry on business there. In a national context, there can be little doubt that the economic—though not necessarily the social—importance of guilds declined in the course of the sixteenth and seventeenth centuries. Increasing labour supply, changing patterns of demand and expanding trade; the growth of new industries and the considerable extension of rural industry organized on the putting-out system: such developments tended to disrupt or simply to bypass the guilds which, with a few exceptions, were unable to impose authority on rural manufacture or new industries. But it was not a rapid or country-wide movement, proceeding at an even pace. In many provincial towns changes came only in the later sixteenth century; in some, as in York, their powers and numbers remained much the same into the early Stuart times. But often there were conflicts. Guilds enroached upon each other as crafts overlapped; or amalgamated in the face of decay or competition. In London, craft guilds came under the domination of mercantile guilds whose members, richer and thus economically more powerful, controlled either the markets or the raw materials of the craftsmen. Thus, for example, did the London leather workers, at various dates between 1479 and 1517, come under the power of the Leathersellers Company. The big London companies— Grocers, Merchant Tailors, Haberdashers, Goldsmiths, and the like, the majority of them incorporated by royal charter in the later fifteenth century, itself an expensive process dependent on a wealthy group in the guild—survived to typify the guild structure of the capital and to mark out the paths to power in the government of the City, dominated as it was by the richest merchants of the land.

The gradual decline in the guilds' economic power and their slide towards a social and ornamental function was assisted in England by the attitude of Tudors and early Stuarts in their perennial search for cash. A bite at their religious possessions by Protector Somerset and the sale by Elizabeth I and James I of grants of incorporation to sundry trivial crafts in London were small aids to change. Nor did the English State, unlike some of its continental counter-parts, seek to rejuvenate guilds or to endow them with powers of control on the new national scale which the times seemed to demand. Yet this slow change and decay of an institution must not be confused with the very real persistence of the artisans and craftsmen themselves—in little towns and growing villages all over the country.

(iii)

Whether English wool was exported raw, in sacks, or manufactured, in bales of cloth, made some but not perhaps very much difference to the country's agriculture. But it made, and was increasingly seen to make, a big difference to trade, wealth, and employment. In the absence of output data, exports are the only guide to the course of national production, although after 1570 they can be supplemented by data derived from the 'hallage' duties payable on cloth sales at the London cloth market of Blackwell Hall. Between the 1450s and 1640s, the value of English textile exports possibly multiplied about fifteen- to sixteen-fold in monetary terms; allowing for the price rise this meant perhaps five- or sixfold in real terms. Assuming that the population had meanwhile rather more than doubled, and that the ratio between exports and home consumption had remained con-stant, then there must have been an increase in output, per head of population, of roughly two- to threefold. Further-more, textile prices rose by only about half as much as the prices of cereals and other foodstuffs. For producers and sellers of foodstuffs, therefore, their real price fell. Such indices of increasing productivity are inevitably very rough; but the non-quantitative evidence points in the same direction. How, then, did it come about? What did the industry produce? And where?

The primary answer is that the main route to this increase in productivity lay through the extension of the putting-out system, thus using greater division of labour to take advantage of the rising population. The secondary answer is that it was greatly facilitated by the diversification of the products manufactured by the industry, a diversification owing much to skills brought by alien immigrants.

The growth of the woollen industry in Tudor times was effectively a continuation of trends already evident in the fourteenth century, impeded in the decades following the Black Death, and then undergoing expansion again during the second half of the fifteenth century. Thereafter the upsurge of population provided an increase in labour supply peculiarly useful to so labour-intensive an industry, in which the processes of manufacture fitted into the family economy to an unparalleled extent—and indeed had long done so. Children carded the wool; women spun it with spindle or spinning wheel; men wove the fabric and did the finishing processes. Only for fulling, dyeing and, sometimes, for finishing did it have to leave the domestic circle. Consequently the fixed costs of some central establishment were not normally worth incurring, though one or two much-publicized but untypical and short-lived examples of such enterprises were to be found during the early sixteenth-century boom. In a fully-fledged system of putting-out capitalism the central figure, the clothier, so organized and financed the processes of production that the out-workers were dependent upon him for their livelihood. But such a situation was far from ubiquitous, particularly in the earlier part of the period.

Many independent weavers, with little more than their family unit of labour, were at work in their stone houses and cottages in the West Riding of Yorkshire, one of the three major areas of the industry's expansion, making their 'penistones' and 'northern dozens' or 'kerseys'. The putting-out arrangements were more evident—and strengthened their hold—in the two other big producing areas: East Anglia and the West Country. The former encompassed parts of Norfolk especially around Norwich, but was particularly concentrated in southern Suffolk and northern Essex, an old-established and important area of coloured broadcloth and kersey making (including the village of Kersey). The towns and villages in and around the valley of the Stour and its tributaries—where today tourists come to wonder at the great churches built (or, more accurately, rebuilt) from the profits of the cloth trade and to peer at timber-framed 'weavers cottages'—constituted one of the most densely populated industrial regions of early Tudor England. The third major area was that of the West Country, stretching from Gloucestershire through Wiltshire and parts of Somerset, down into Devonshire. Gloucestershire and Wiltshire were famous for broadcloths and fine woollens; although dyed cloths were made in some parts, it was from this area, as from Yorkshire, that came many of the white and 'undressed' cloth exported to the dyers and finishers of the Low Countries. The area developed the full range of the characteristic structure of the industry. At one end was the small quasi-independent weaver, struggling and often in debt to the wool or yarn merchants who supplied his raw material; at the other end, the rich clothier, operating on an increasingly large scale, putting out wool to be carded and spun in the local villages, supplying yarn to the weavers, and seeing the cloth fulled and sometimes sheared, before sending it up for sale at Blackwell Hall in London. Such men climbed the social scale by the money made in their business, and married into the local gentry. As well as in these three main areas, active cloth making on similar lines went on elsewhere in the country: in parts of Lancashire, the Welsh borders, the West Midlands, in Hampshire, Surrey, and Berkshire, notably around Guildford and Reading, and in the Weald of Kent. This last area indeed reached its zenith of importance in the early seventeenth century, exporting heavy, coloured cloths,

and maintaining, as was commonly said of all such manufacturing districts, an abnormally dense population.

The reasons for the location of the industry and for the rise
and fall of particular regions are complex, but are of two
main sorts: the great dependence upon abundance of labour;
and the demand for the particular sorts of fabric made in
particular regions. In the Yorkshire branch of the industry
in the 1580s, for example, it took about fifteen persons—with
five or six spinners and carders needed to keep one weaver at
work—one week to make a short broadcloth (the 'northern
dozen', measuring 12 yards by $1\frac{3}{4}$ yards); or, in the same
time, six persons to make a narrow cloth such as a kersey
(18 yards by 1 yard). These were relatively simple, undyed
cloths. More complex products raised the labour intensity.
To keep one weaver going at his loom could mean work for
anything from, say, twelve to forty persons according to the
nature of the fabric. As a contemporary put it in the 1620s,
about the Suffolk industry, 'he which maketh ordinarily
twenty broad cloths every week cannot set so few a-work as
five hundred persons.'[4] Mild exaggeration, perhaps, but it is
easy to see why direct labour costs accounted for about 55–65
per cent of total production costs. Consequently the location
of the industry was dependent more on labour supply than
on raw material supply, on families of underemployed workers rather than on local wool. This in turn was linked to the
amount of employment or underemployment generated by
the type of agriculture practised in a particular region; and
with the sorts of customary local land inheritance systems,
aiding or hampering the subdivision of holdings and hence
the ease or otherwise with which a settlement might be
gained. It seems likely, though not certain, that those regions
where arable farming was subordinated to dairying, where
much land was enclosed, and where holdings were small and
readily obtainable, offered favourable havens for such industrial development. The dairying areas of Wiltshire, the
Kentish Weald, or south-central Suffolk provide some examples of this conjuncture. Population multiplied, by natural
increase and by immigration; the earnings of industrial
labour became vital supports to the community. The clothiers

got a cheap labour force and, like those of Gloucestershire in 1577, could parade their virtues as providers of employment to an expanding population:

... there is builded in this county above five hundred cottages, for the poor to inhabit in, more than was within this 30 years, which for the most part are only relieved by the clothemen, them and their families.[5]

Nevertheless, it was almost certainly the nature of local wools which had originally determined the sort of fabrics made in particular areas. In the gradual commercialization of peasant activities, such as spinning and weaving, traditional ways of using local materials crystallized into the production of items identifiable by regional names and ordered thus by merchants selling in distant markets. So wool was moved into, say, Devon or Suffolk, from such sheep-rearing counties as Lincolnshire. And merchants wrote, as did Lionel Cranfield in 1604 to his correspondent in Antwerp, thus:

Of them [fine white cloths] there be also three several countries making. The best are called Worcesters and contain 31 yards ... Then there are Gloucestershire cloths and Wiltshire which contain but 28 yards ... all prices from £8 to £30 sterling. ... For white kersies there be of several kinds as devonshires, northerns and westerns ... For mingled coloured kersies there be of them only two sorts, devonshires and hampshires ...[6]

In such a system, feeding distant markets, shifts in demand could and did have serious consequences. Just as booms sustained employment and prosperity, so slumps spread unemployment and poverty over an ever-widening area of the countryside, with reduced incomes affecting the consumption and production of other goods; it only needed the coincidence of such a depression with a harvest failure or, worse still, a run of bad harvests, for depression to become crisis, for poverty to lead into starvation. Such short-term crises punctuated the long process of expansion, notably in the 1520s, in 1586–7, 1614–16, and 1641–2. But some had more enduring effects, notably those of the 1550s and of 1620–4, merging as they did into the long-term changes affecting the

industry. These posed the problem of how the system adap-
ted itself to a decline in the demand—whether induced by
changes in tastes or incomes or by successful competition
from elsewhere—for the particular products of particular
regions. To reduce costs was difficult. The pressure on wages
certainly intensified but they were already so low in the
conditions of ample population as to provoke an Act in 1604
regulating minimum wages in textile manufacture; and there
was a rising chorus of complaints about reductions in standards, as short cuts to cost-saving (or wage-supplementing)
made themselves manifest. The real answer came through
the diversification of the product, sometimes initiated by
merchants trying to induce imitation of successfully competing fabrics, and certainly stimulated by the dissemination of
skills from other lands which came with successive waves of
alien immigrants into England.

The innovation of what contemporaries called the 'new
draperies' was largely, though not solely, a product of the
migration into England in the 1560s and '70s of Protestants
fleeing from the Spanish Catholic persecution in the Netherlands. 'Much wool', it was reported in the 1590s 'is turned
into bayes, sayes, grograines, rash, and other kinds of foreign
wares of late years made here by divers workmen strangers
that are come over and do inhabit here.'[7] The refugees
settled mainly in eastern and southern England, in Norwich,
Colchester, Canterbury, and other towns. They brought with
them continental European techniques of woollen textile
manufactures which helped to transform the fabrics made in
various parts of England. The older sorts of cloth—which in
turn came to be known as 'old draperies'—were mainly pure
woollens, that is, both in warp and weft, and made of carded
wool; the 'new draperies' were either worsteds, made from
combed longer-stapled wools, or more commonly mixtures of
woollen and worsted yarns or even of worsted and silk. They
were generally lighter, more colourful, often cheaper and
sometimes less durable, thus bringing a bigger replacement
demand. Under sundry names they were naturalized to the
English industry: bays and says in northern Essex, with
Colchester and its 'Dutch Bay Hall' as a thriving centre;

serges and perpetuanas in Devon and western Somerset; and a great revival was brought to the old Norwich worsted industry which turned to camlets, grograines, callimancoes, and other 'Norwich stuffs'. None of these changes was based on major technical innovations. They were essentially mutations, variations on an old theme. They may well have been helped along by changes in the nature of English wool; some of the new fabrics doubtless owed their existence to the ingenuity of English weavers. But demand plus immigration— mainly induced by religious persecution—were probably the most important forces bringing the changes to the English industry. These changes then, as we have seen in Chapter 4, helped the export trade to greater successes in the Mediterranean areas in the early seventeenth century, and the 'new draperies' came to equal the value of the old amongst the country's textile exports.

Although the making of woollen fabrics in some form— old draperies and new—continued to dominate the English textile industry throughout the first two centuries of the period, other sorts of production were to be found in sundry parts of the country. In sixteenth-century Lancashire, alongside its manufacture of coarse woollens (some of which bore such confusing names as 'cottons' and 'rugs') was a growing linen industry, drawing on local flax but mainly dependent on imports of Irish yarn to make its output of the cheaper and coarser linen fabrics. Both manufactures were still mainly carried on, as in Yorkshire, by independent weavers also engaged in agriculture; though buying the raw materials on credit, they were not part of a putting-out system. Small-scale linen making was also carried on elsewhere in the country; so too was hand-knitting, producing hosiery of various qualities and types in regions of England ranging from the Lake District to the Cotswolds. With the invention by William Lee during the 1590s of the knitting frame, an important step had been taken towards the growth of a putting-out system in the hosiery industry, gradually replacing the older pattern of work which, for most of this earlier part of the period, essentially comprised a by-employment for small-holding peasants. Finally, the most expensive and prestigious of all textiles, silk, had but a very minor foothold in England. There had long been some silk weaving carried on in London and a company of silk throwsters ('throwing' in silk is the approximate equivalent of spinning in other textiles) was incorporated there in 1629; other centres which had some participation in silk weaving included Coventry, as well as Norwich and Canterbury, where Protestant refugee workers provided some stimulus in the course of the sixteenth century. But, in general, quality was low and output very small despite James I's characteristic—and useless—instruction that Lords-Lieutenant of counties should encourage the planting of mulberry trees (upon whose leaves the silk worm feeds with notable gusto).

(iv)

Apart from trading and carrying and fishing, a number of other non-agrarian occupations were to be found in the Tudor and early Stuart scene; and some of them have been singled out for particular attention by historians because they seem to embody features which make them progenitors of the industrialized world of our own day. This anticipation of the future has revolved around two commodities and one economic characteristic: coal, iron, and capital intensiveness. Since they have been the subject of some notable exaggeration, they demand a careful scrutiny.

Tin mining and lead mining, feeding the export trade (already noted in Chapter 4), as well as the home market, were industries of great antiquity in England. Various parts of the Pennines, from Northumberland to Derby, north and central Wales, the Mendips and Cornwall were the main areas of lead mining; Devon and Cornwall, mainly the latter, formed the great tin-mining region, its high-quality raw products enjoying a near-monopoly of European markets for most of the sixteenth and early seventeenth centuries. Copper may have been mined in medieval England, though only from the 1560s are there records of successful exploitation, initially in Cumberland and later in Cornwall and Wales. Together with the extraction of zinc ore (calamine) found in the Mendips, it formed the basis of a brass-making industry which owed a good deal to the deliberate importation of German metallurgical skills.

The mining, and more particularly the smelting, of iron received a new stimulus by a radical innovation of this period. The introduction into England, towards the end of the fifteenth century, of the water-powered, charcoal-fuelled blast furnace provides another example of England catching up with foreign industrial techniques, for it seems certain that this improved method of smelting, which produced what was in effect a new product, cast iron, was earlier developed in continental Europe. The new device spread rapidly in the Weald of Sussex and Kent, where iron ore of a low grade had long been exploited and was found in conjunction with the necessary streams to operate the water-powered bellows, and the woodlands to provide the charcoal. From three furnaces known to have been at work before 1530, the total rose rapidly to 26 in the 1550s, still all in the Weald; thereafter blast furnaces were also being erected in similar areas elsewhere in the country—the Forest of Dean, south Wales, the west Midlands, south Yorkshire—and by the 1650s it is estimated that some 86 furnaces were at work in England and Wales, about half of which were outside the Wealden area. Their total annual output was probably around 23–24,000 tons of iron. Some of this was made directly into various cast products of which cannon and shot attracted the most attention (and State support). Some, probably most of it, was cast into pig-iron which was then converted in a particular sort of forge, also using charcoal and water-power, called a 'finery', into bar iron; this in turn formed the raw material of the wrought-iron branch of the industry, bar iron being turned by numerous smiths into such small objects as bolts, nails, tools, or locks. This metal-working part of the industry, because of its quite different technical base, developed on a labour-intensive, putting-out system, like textiles, and grew up especially in Staffordshire and other parts of the west Midlands in the early seventeenth century. Despite the important innovation of the blast furnace, the output of the home industry did not meet total demand, and bar iron was imported (at least 3000 tons per annum in the 1630s), especially the higher quality iron needed for making the very small quantity of steel produced at the time.

The blast furnace and its concomitant forge were both prodigious consumers of charcoal, fuel accounting for some 60–75 per cent of total costs in the whole process of smelting and conversion to bar iron. Soon there were complaints of destruction of timber in the interests of the furnaces. There can be little doubt that in the early years of the process in the Weald some reckless cutting went on; and the noise of protest began to rival that of the axes. Heeded by some historians, it has been turned into an all-embracing theory of England's 'fuel-famine' or, more mildly, 'timber shortage', causing 'exhaustion' of the woods, in turn leading to a huge expansion in English coal-mining and thus, via the eighteenth-century discovery of how to smelt iron with coked coal, to the coal-and-iron world of the nineteenth-century industrial revolution. It is a neat sequence with all the allure of cause and effect, challenge and response. The reality was more complex and less neat. Of the course of the iron industry more will be said later (see below, pages 153, 165–6). Coal, meanwhile, demands attention.

Coal had been known in England certainly since the thirteenth century, and small consignments of it were shipped overseas in the fourteenth and fifteenth centuries. Although it was extracted from most of the currently used coalfields in Britain, the greatest source of it in Tudor and early Stuart times was the Northumberland and Durham field. Moreover, figures of the sea-borne shipments from Newcastle are almost the only significant early data usable as a pointer to coal production; estimates of mid-sixteenth century national output, necessarily entailing figures from the other fields, are guesses with hardly any visible means of support. Before the 1590s there are only scattered figures for odd years, mainly, though not solely, for the small overseas exports between 1377 and 1574. Continuous figures do not start until the early 1590s and these show that Newcastle was then shipping coast-wise an average of 111,000 tons a year; the corresponding figure had risen to 298,000 in the early 1620s (an increase of 168 per cent) and 412,000 in the later 1650s (an increase of 38 per cent). What the data suggest—no more—is that some time between the later fifteenth century and, say, the 1580s a very rapid *rate* of increase in output set in although, of course, absolute amounts were at first very small; as amounts got bigger so the rate of advance slowed down— the normal behaviour of an output curve. A similar course of expansion may have been found in some other coalfields.

What caused this upsurge in coal production? Three main uses for coal existed at that time: for any process involving the heating of a liquid, for example, in a dye vat; for the ordinary smith in his forge (though *not* at the iron 'finery' or furnace); and for domestic heating. Whether coal or charcoal was used depended almost entirely on transport costs. As the population increased, woodlands were grubbed up for the plough and timber was felled to build houses and ships. So local shortages of wood for all purposes, including making charcoal, were created, exacerbated in a few areas by the local consumption of the iron works. There was no *national* exhaustion of timber, nor was there a *national* fuel crisis; but there were certainly areas in which timber and charcoal were so scarce and expensive—because, like coal, they were bulky and costly to move about—that it was cheaper to bring in coal, provided that it could be brought by water transport. Here are Harrison's comments in his *Description of England* about just such a problem at Cambridge in the 1580s:

Only wood is the chief want to such as study there, wherefore this kind of provision is brought them either from Essex and other places thereabouts, as is also their coal . . . and sea coal, whereof they have great plenty, led thither by the Grant [i.e. river Granta or Cam].[8]

The crucial elements are evident: sea transport and river transport, the supply of both 'coal' (charcoal) and 'sea coal' (coal) from other areas to relieve the local shortage. For Londoners, and especially the poor, coal was becoming a vital fuel to warm their hearths; and any rise in its price brought protest, as in the 1590s, against the monopolistic control exercised by the body known as the Hostmen of Newcastle. Had there been a national timber crisis one would have expected timber prices to rise accordingly; in fact the best available price index shows timber prices between 1450–9 and 1640–9 rising by only 395 per cent whilst those of all agricultural products rose by 571 per cent. These are national averages; they conceal the local variations. But it was precisely those variations which determined the substitution of coal for charcoal according to accessibility. Likewise it was local availability and transport costs which affected the price of charcoal fuel at the blast furnaces—not a national exhaustion of woodlands.

Although the main destinations for coal in this period almost certainly remained the domestic hearth and the smithy, some other industrial uses also developed. In those limited circumstances in which it could be used, it is reasonable to suppose—though difficult to prove—that its use lowered costs below what they would have been in the same location and dependent on charcoal. Where this occurred it may well have been to the advantage of England relative to equivalent continental industries. Amongst such industries were salt-making by the evaporation of brine; this was an old process, but in the course of the sixteenth century a number of coal-using plants were set up mainly around the mouths of the rivers Tyne and Wear. From the later sixteenth century onwards the treating of agricultural land with lime was aided by coal-using furnaces for lime-burning—at least in areas where sea-borne or neighbouring coal was cheaper than charcoal. The preparation of alum, employed as a mordant in dyeing and in leather manufacture, made use of coal when alum-making was first started in England in the early seventeenth century; soap-boilers, starch-makers, and brewers began to use it; so did those who prepared saltpetre, which was needed more and more as the armies and navies of the time became gunpowder-hungry. Glass-making provides an interesting example of a struggling native industry which was first revivified by foreign immigrants, from France and Italy, in the second half of the sixteenth century, and then given a further boost by a successful English patent for the use of coal in the glass furnace. First established in the Wealden area, the industry spread from there to areas where coal was available, so that by the 1630s Newcastle and the west Midlands were the main producing regions. Glass was becoming more common in windows as well as in utensils; and its real price fell.

All these various activities—mining, smelting, the making of glass, salt, lime, alum, gunpowder, and the like—were to some extent centralized in the sense that they required some fixed plant. They could not therefore be carried on under the arrangements of a putting-out capitalism. And in so far as they demanded fixed plant beyond that of the ordinary artisan and his tools, they represented a move in the direction of capital intensiveness in industry. The same holds true of some other industries unrelated to coal use, which were either expanded or introduced during this period. Shipbuilding provides an example of the first category. The growth of the English mercantile marine, especially after the mid-sixteenth century, led to a corresponding growth in native shipbuilding, particularly in a number of east-coast ports such as Newcastle (much stimulated by the needs of the coal trade), Ipswich, Woodbridge, and, of course, London. The paper industry offers another instance of an innovation from continental Europe where paper making had long been practised. An unsuccessful first English paper mill of 1495 was followed by the effective establishment of the industry in the later sixteenth century, so that by 1650 some 30–40 water-powered paper mills had been set up, mainly in southern and south-eastern England.

There can be no doubt that these new or expanded centralized industries, with their mines or mills or furnaces, could, and sometimes did, make demands for capital investment and finance on a scale quite outside the scope of the small man who was still the characteristic producer in textiles or in sundry craft activities. The ease of entry into cloth making, which allowed the yeoman clothiers of the West Riding to flourish as they did, could not readily be copied in iron smelting, or copper mining or alum manufacture. The search for copper and brass, partly for armament needs, brought into being in the 1560s the first English industrial joint-stock companies, the Mines Royal and the Mineral and Battery Works, corporate entities with royal charters and with share capitals which between them totalled nearly £30,000. They were probably over-capitalized, wasteful, and inappropriate in structure for what they were trying to achieve. Nevertheless, they represented a scale and type of undertaking quite unknown in the England of a century earlier. The same is true of the iron industry in which the establishment of an integrated plant, with furnace, forge, water-course, and water-wheel, could demand investment on a scale open only to landowners, merchants, and others with ready access to finance. The Earl of Rutland, for example, was adding to his landed revenues, between 1600 and the 1630s, net annual profits of around £1000-£1500 from his iron furnace and forge in Yorkshire, producing some 150-200 tons per year and fed with both iron ore and charcoal from his own estate. Coal mining in the Northumberland and Durham area brought into being, as in the iron industry and in overseas trade, investment by businessmen, both merchants and landowners, in the form of unincorporated partnerships. And so these illustrations could be multiplied, to sketch an impression of these new fields of capitalistic endeavour which brought a new face to English industry in this period.

But now a note of caution needs to be sounded. The temptation to resort to hyperbole, to scatter one's pages with such words as 'vast', 'large-scale', 'highly capitalistic'; to detect in sixteenth- and seventeenth-century England an 'industrial revolution'; or to feel oneself present at the unearthing of the roots of modern, materialistic industrial civilization: such delights need to be resisted. To some extent it was simply that the English were catching up industrially with continental Europe, and using more coal in the process; so much so indeed that England had probably become the biggest coal producer in Europe. More important, however, is the simple fact that the technical circumstances which demanded centralization of production do not in themselves tell us anything about the optimum economic size or scale of plant in the economic and social circumstances of the time. The exceptional must not be confused with the typical. And there can be little doubt that in this period the typical unit in centralized production, whether for soap-boiling or ship-building, in paper mills or salt works, for iron making or even in coal mining, at least outside the North-East, was small in size. It employed not hundreds or thousands of wage-workers but numbers which fluctuated sharply between a handful and a few score, varying with the state of demand, according to the seasons, or at the mercy of water power affected by drought or floods. The casual labour which found work at such enterprises, aiding a small hard-core of skilled men, may indeed be seen as an early part of the industrial proletariat of the future. But it was also a tiny fraction of that growing population which, overwhelmingly, found its livelihood in agriculture, textiles, and sundry trades and crafts, from fishing to shoe-making. The many thousands of out-working textile makers were a far more significant germ of a future industrial proletariat; and their presence probably had more important social and demographic consequences for their communities than that exercised by the much smaller number employed at this time in centralized establishments.

By 1650 the new industries had made little impact on England's export trade. The biggest achievement was probably in iron and other metals, for without the advance of these home industries, imports would have had to have been greater in order to meet domestic demand; import-substitution was likewise achieved in alum, salt, and some other manufactures. By far the biggest objects of investments, however, for farmer, landowner, merchant, lawyer, or anyone else who had accumulated profits from expanding trade, rising prices, or growing population, were land and houses for those with an eye to safety or prestige; and ships, trade or colonial ventures for the venturesome. The biggest private acts of investment were the vast houses built by great landowners— Howards, Cecils, Russells, and the like who had done well out of Court office, State finance, the spoils of the monasteries, or simply by the skilful exploitation of the land market and the marriage market. Moreover, compared with the sort of building which was going on in 1450, such Elizabethan and Jacobean acts of conspicuous investment as Hatfield House and Audley End, or lesser examples like Wollaton, Blickling, or Hardwick, were, in their own way, just as new or 'revolutionary' as a bigger coal-mine or a different sort of ironworks. The one represented the consolidation of power—economic, social, and political—of the landed classes; the pay-off was then and there. The other was merely a small beginning, a seed, it is true, but the pay-off was in the future.

6

The New Context

One of the most difficult problems in presenting the economic and social past is that posed by the need to balance change and continuity. Change is the greater temptress; continuity appears as the bore to be avoided. The effort to reveal the shifting patterns in the complex texture of a whole economy and society only too often results in an over-emphasis on dramatic movement, an under-emphasis on the quieter, less obvious mutations which lie concealed beneath the screen of continuity. So the two centuries between 1450 and 1650 secure the centre of the stage for European economic historians, offering as they do the powerful drama made up by the voyages of discovery, commercial expansion, and conquest, the upsurge of population, and the sustained inflation of prices. Eager to note the incentives to change posed by the geographical extension of trade or the increasing wealth of merchants or rulers, we do not always, or with equal dispatch, heed the non-inducement to change provided by the very expansion of numbers. The drama of rising prices is readily translated into rising profits, expanding cities, bigger and better buildings; that of falling prices into loss, unemployment, poverty, decay. We know that neither is wholly true; that for most people in such pre-industrialized economies real consumption per head may well have fallen in the former period, risen in the latter. We seek, with varying degrees of bias or success, to balance gain and loss to different groups in society. But what happens when the drama is missing? Does seeming stagnation of prices or population mean that nothing is happening?

Or does this sort of continuity conceal another sort of change?

In recent years, the seventeenth century has provoked a miscellany of lugubrious noises from economic historians, especially, though not exclusively, from French historians writing about continental Europe. A dark century, *siècle de malheur*; a century of stagnation and prolonged economic depression; an age of recession after the expanding activity and revolutionary change of the sixteenth; an age, above all, of crisis—economic, social, political, intellectual: the pursuit of such seductive visions of historical classification has, not surprisingly, led to sundry versions of when the seventeenth century was. Measured against the criteria of movements in prices or trade the old dates are patently meaningless. So, according to what part of Europe is under discussion, the gloomy, depressed, crisis-laden seventeenth century succeeds the 'long sixteenth century' in 1610, 1620, 1650, 1660 and ends at various dates between, roughly 1680 and 1750. This contraction and expansion of a 'century' seems a poor aid to clarity and makes no more sense than does the effort to impose a common, simultaneous experience of crisis or depression on Europe as a whole. English experience—or Dutch —is notably difficult to fit into the schema. Yet we need not throw out the baby with the bath water. Just as there was a real continuity in the fundamentals of the pre-industrialized economy, so there was also, within this continuing economic and social order, real change taking place in England as elsewhere. It has no precisely dateable beginning or end, nor any single definable cause, not even a clear precipitating crisis. It did not start in 1622 or 1630 or 1648. For convenience sake the new context can be seen as bounded very approximately by the dates 1650 and 1750. It was a context definable neither as boom nor slump; it was far from being an age of sustained depression in England; its contours were undramatic. But the indigenous responses to the problems created by these new economic circumstances are of peculiar importance, for they were to be followed, uniquely in the Europe of the day, by the first termination of the very pre-industrialized economy in which they were conceived.

Absence of the possibilities of experiment inhibits, as usual in the social sciences, any test of whether these responses were 'pre-conditions'—causes, necessary or sufficient—of the subsequent industrialization. They inevitably drew upon the expansion of the preceding period; we cannot isolate one age or another, one reaction or another, as alone embodying a crucial piece of causation. In the new context, there were changes of climate—intellectual, political, and social—as well as of demographic and economic indices. It will be convenient to start with people and prices; and, first, to pick up the threads of population change where they were left in Chapter 2.

(ii)

The ending of the period of population growth was signalled by a dire sequence of outbreaks of plague. In London, in the three successive visitations of 1603, 1625, and 1665–6, the numbers dying of the plague were recorded as 33,000, 41,000, and 69,000 respectively. These figures are undoubtedly underestimates; the true totals must have been appreciably higher. The Great Plague of 1665–6 was the last big outbreak in England, its grim reappearance in the Marseilles epidemic of 1720–2 its last in western Europe. Meanwhile, the toll of death which it and its predecessors took was formidable. At least 2,300 died in Exeter, for example, in 1625–6; the West Riding, to take a quite different part of the country, suffered in 1644–5, especially such rising cloth-making centres as Leeds, Bradford, and Halifax; Leeds itself possibly lost, from all sorts of causes, about one-third of its population between 1640 and 1650. Such infectious epidemics were, of course, the especial scourge of towns. Many areas of the countryside often went unaffected. To take one example: while nearly 900 people out of a total population of about 3,000 died of plague in the crowded dockyard town of Chatham in 1665–6, much of rural Kent, despite its proximity to London, remained virtually untouched by the epidemic. The unhealthy reputation of the times did not arise simply from these visitations of the plague. The too-vigorous guzzling of cheap gin, especially by Londoners, in the 1730s and '40s may have helped quite a few people to a quicker death, as Hogarth's famous drawings suggested, but is unlikely to have had major demographic consequence. Severe outbreaks of typhus did far more than gin to increase mortality. It was abroad in Devonshire in the mid-1640s; it contributed to heavy mortality in the Midlands in the 1680s. More or less endemic in crowded and insanitary towns, its intensity worsened and brought many deaths in 1728–9 and 1741–2; on both of these occasions, though not on others, it was linked with bad harvests and high prices. Sundry other fevers, variously described by contemporaries as 'agues' or 'sweating sicknesses' but which included influenza and malaria, also burst into malignant outbreaks, for example, in the 1640s and in 1678–80. Smallpox, like typhus virtually endemic in London and other large towns, seems to have acquired a new virulence during this period. A particularly infectious disease, it sometimes appeared in epidemic form and when it did so, then, in the words of an eighteenth-century observer, 'entire villages are depopulated, markets ruined, and the face of distress spread over the whole country.'[1] In the first half of the eighteenth century it *may* have been responsible, on average, for as much as 15 per cent of all recorded burials.

The links between all these powerful killers and that other determinant of survival in the pre-industrialized economy— the state of the harvest—became more complex in this particular period. The first half of the seventeenth century in England came to an end with one of the worst sequences of bad harvests, rivalling that of the 1590s. Behind the rocketing food prices (see below, Table 8, page 101), lay the realities so graphically depicted in the diary of an Essex clergyman, Ralph Josselin:

[Oct. 1646] . . . a wonderful, sad, wet season, much corn in many places . . . rotted and spoiled in the fields. [Nov. '46] . . . this week the wetness of the season continued with little or no intermission & so it hath continued for above two months . . . [June '48] . . . floods every week, hay rotted abroad . . . corn laid, pulled down with weeds; we never had the like in my memory . . . [Aug. '48] continual rain to the spoiling of much grass, and threatening

of the harvest . . . [Sept. '48] . . . the season very sad both in
reference to corn and unto fallows, very few lands being fit to be
sown upon; some say that divers cattle that feed in the meadows
die, their bowels being eaten out with gravel & dirt.[2]

Amongst a people of whom many lived around the level of
bare subsistence, such catastrophic weather—and there are
suggestions of a general worsening of climate in northern and
north-western Europe in the late sixteenth and early seventeenth centuries—brought scarcities which could hardly have
failed to exacerbate the results of chronic malnutrition. For
England, though not for other European countries, it was the
last of the really bad long series of harvest failures. Although
there were failures again in 1661, 1693, 1697–8, a bad
sequence in 1708–10 which brought near-famine conditions
in some areas but not in others, and poor years in 1727–8 and
1740, none of them seems to have brought demographic
consequences clearly attributable to high food prices. Indeed,
the correlation between high food prices and high mortality
seems, in England though certainly not everywhere in
Europe, to have become less close. This is not to say that it
had disappeared. The combination of epidemic disease,
worsening weather, and a very bad harvest could still wreak
havoc, as, for example, in parts of rural Worcestershire in
1725–9. Whatever the causes, various parish registers up and
down the country show a fall in the ratio of baptisms to
burials, a trend usually, though not invariably, becoming
evident in the early seventeenth century. The duration of the
phase varied greatly. In some areas burials exceed baptisms
until the 1730s; in others the 1690s seem a crucial turning
point when both baptisms and marriages rise and burials
fall, only to suffer a reverse in the 1720s and '30s (see Fig. 1).
The pattern and timing of stagnation and renewal varied
not only from area to area but according to types of community. In Nottinghamshire, for example, between 1674 and
1743 the population of 62 wholly agricultural villages increased by only about 13 per cent; that of 40 villages having
some significant amount of industrial activity grew by nearly
48 per cent.

As already noted, the ending of the population upsurge was a Europe-wide phenomenon. The ferocity and virulence of the killing agents seem, however, to have been greater in parts of continental Europe, especially in its many towns, than in England. England, too, was spared the worst of the sustained land wars, notably the Thirty Years War which brought death and destruction to many parts of Germany, not so much directly by the sword as indirectly by the stimuli given to the spread of disease and the dislocation of trade and agriculture, bringing deserted farmhouses and starvation. Agrarian depression and economic stagnation seem to have lasted longer in Spain, Italy, France, and Germany than in England

We do not know what the total population of England was in the mid-seventeenth century. It may not have been much different from the reasonably well-supported estimate of 5·2 million in 1695. So if the other estimate of 6·3 million in 1750 (for England and Wales) is roughly accurate, it may be that no more than about one million persons were added to total numbers in this curious century from 1650 to 1750. But how and why and when and where? This period has rather more beacons to help relieve the demographic darkness. In addition to the original work, in the late seventeenth century, of Gregory King and John Graunt there are a number of contemporary lists of local populations; some new and demographically useful taxes, for example, the hearth tax of 1660–89; an ecclesiastical census of 1676; and more surviving parish registers. Subjected to the increasingly sophisticated analysis of historical demographers, they add up to a picture of English population marked not simply by this slower growth but by complex changes of structure and distribution. It is possible that men and women were marrying later, returning again to earlier marriage in the later eighteenth century, when population was again rising sharply. But the evidence is localized and variable. There also seems to have been a drop in average family size during this same period; and there is some, inferential, evidence, to suggest deliberate family limitation. If these phenomena prove to have had some fairly general existence they pose very difficult questions of explanation. Were they in some sense the instinctive re-actions of a society striving to palliate the near-Malthusian situation generated by the population pressure of the preceding century or so? Were such reactions economically motivated in that they were related to real or perceived difficulties in earning a livelihood, securing a settlement in a village, taking up a holding?

For the present such questions must remain unanswered. There is much surer evidence, however, for a different sort of trend in the demographic development of this period: a notable growth of towns. During the preceding two centuries of expansion London's growth was wholly exceptional as it multiplied some twelve- or thirteen-fold to reach its size of about 400,000 in 1650. In the century that followed, London's rate of growth was, not surprisingly, much slower; its population increased by about 70 per cent to reach an approximate total of 675,000 in 1750. But it was accompanied by the more rapid growth of a number of other towns. In the 1660s and '70s, there were probably not more than three or four towns outside London with populations of 10,000. By the mid-eighteenth century there were not less than fourteen, with a total population of 250–260,000, which represented at least a doubling of the size of those same towns in the decades immediately after the Restoration. Put another way, in the mid-eighteenth century whilst London contained around 12 per cent of the total population, nearly 17 per cent lived in towns of 10,000 inhabitants and over. It was still a long way from an urban society but it represents a significant move in that direction. Amongst the newly important towns were three which grew at rates which rivalled London's earlier progress; Liverpool, Manchester, and Birmingham all reached well over 20,000 by the mid-eighteenth century, to join Norwich and Bristol, still the only others in that category outside London.

The higher urban death-rates which, even in the earlier period of general growth, had meant that London's expansion was dependent on substantial rural-urban migration, continued into the period of slackened growth. It has indeed been estimated that to provide the additional 275,000 from

1650 to 1750, an average net annual immigration into London of 8,000 persons would have been necessary. In smaller towns the gap between birth- and death-rates was probably not as high as in London, but many of those with populations around 10,000 would have been similarly failing to reproduce themselves by natural growth. Nottingham, for instance, which rose from about 5,000 in the 1670s to about 12,000 in 1750 derived nearly the whole of its growth in this period from immigration; and this in a town which in the 1730s had been spoken of as unusually healthy and much improved from its past state. The net annual inflow necessary to provide for all the provincial towns with populations of 10,000 and over in 1750 may have added another 4,000 per annum to the 8,000 migrating into London. These are only rough estimates. But they force the obvious question: where did they all come from? Some older, medium-sized towns, with populations in the 3–6,000 range, for example, Bury St. Edmunds, Lincoln, Gloucester, and Southampton changed very little in size; a few places declined. But if the total population increased by not much more than one million there must have been both a substantial rural growth in some areas and a great increase in internal migration. Yet the evidence on migration into London points to a decrease in the distances whence the migrant came. Merchants' wills and records of apprenticeship suggest that in the fifteenth century London and the Home Counties may have provided only some 25–30 per cent of the City's businessmen and their apprentices, the remainder coming from far and wide; in 1690, however, London and the same group of Home Counties provided 49 per cent of the total of those admitted to freedom by apprenticeship. Although London's magnetism was such that it still attracted people from all parts of the country, short-distance migration was becoming increasingly common elsewhere because of the attraction exerted by the other growing towns upon the increased population of their own catchment areas. And those towns and those catchment areas were especially to be found in the North, North-West, and west Midlands. It was here that the population was probably growing at its fastest in the early eighteenth century; it was from the countryside in those areas that people were moving, not now so much to London, but rather to Bristol, Birmingham, Coventry, Leeds, Liverpool, Manchester, Newcastle, Nottingham, Sheffield, or Whitehaven. They came from the woodlands and uplands; from forest villages, already growing faster than others in the sixteenth and seventeenth centuries, like those of Northamptonshire, on the very edge of the Severn–Wash line; from Sherwood forest and the Pennines; from the Lake District and Lancashire; from the North and West Ridings of Yorkshire. Despite the increased mortality of the 1720s and '30s, the northern and north-western counties showed a consistently higher ratio of baptisms to burials. For that part of England which between 1450 and 1650 had seemed almost a backwater compared with London and the South-East, the new century was both demographically and economically a vital period of expansion and change—the true prelude to its pioneering age of industrialization to follow.

(iii)

Fig. 6 continues for 1650–1750 what Fig. 2 showed for 1450–1650: a general weighted index of the prices of goods bought by ordinary persons in the society of the time. Utterly unlike that for the previous period it shows what is almost an horizontal line, with the usual short-term fluctuations. The trend is in fact slightly downwards, the average for 1740–60 being 3 per cent lower than 1640–60. Just as the long inflation calls for explanation, so does this mildly tilted price plateau. The monetary explanation in terms of the supply of American bullion is, again, of only partial use in accounting for the English experience, as it was for the upward phase. After their high point in the 1590s recorded bullion imports into Seville began to decline, despite a temporary revival around 1620. Total output from Spanish America, however, was maintained at a much higher level; it began to fall significantly only in the last decades of the seventeenth century, and rose again early in the eighteenth century. So although some short-term difficulties appeared, there was obtainable by various routes a plentiful supply of bullion to finance the great increase in European trade with Asia (see below, pages 141–2). Within Europe, and specifically in England, the effective supply of money for transaction purposes was much increased by the development and increased use of many forms of paper—bills, bonds, notes, cheques— emerging from banks and various financial intermediaries. They certainly did not solve all the problems of ensuring a supply of cash for the increasing volume of economic business; and acute difficulties forced a recoinage in 1696. In general, although some slackening of the inflow of bullion may have made some contribution to ending the price rise, English economic experience in this period does not show any serious signs of sustained monetary deflation.

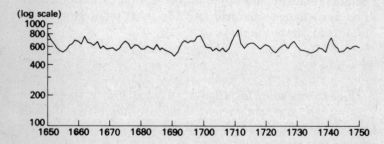

FIG. 6   Price index of a composite unit of consumer goods in southern England, 1650–1750 (1451–75 = 100)

Source: As for Fig. 2.

The withdrawal of population pressure upon the means of subsistence probably contributed more to bringing the price rise to an end. Naturally, it made itself felt only gradually; and it did so in a slowing down of the rate of increase which became apparent during the first half of the seventeenth century and went into long-term reverse after the 1630s and '40s. Again, support for this contention comes from a comparison of food prices and industrial prices. The figures in

Table 8 show how the ratio between the two began to change in this crucial mid-century period. The serious trade depression of the 1620s is manifest in some set-back to the gradual upward movement of industrial prices; but despite the trouble and dislocation of the Civil War there is no evidence of any continuing, all-important national economic crisis; nor is there of a crisis in the supply of money which would have affected both series in the same direction.

TABLE 8

Index of prices and wages, 1611–80

1451–75 = 100

Decade	(a) Price of a composite unit of foodstuffs	(b) Price of a sample of industrial products	(c) $\frac{(b)}{(a)} \times 100$	(d) Index of 'real' wage rates of building craftsman
1611–20	583	274	47	39
21–30	585	264	45	39
31–40	687	281	41	—
41–50	723	306	42	—
51–60	687	327	48	49
61–70	702	343	49	48
71–80	675	351	52	49

Sources: (a), (b), and (c) E. H. Phelps Brown and Sheila V. Hopkins, 'Wages and Prices: evidence for population pressure in the sixteenth century', *Economica*, Nov. 1957.

(d) Phelps Brown and Hopkins, 'Seven Centuries of the Prices of Consumables', loc. cit.

What is happening is that the terms of trade between foodstuffs and industrial products are just beginning to move in favour of the latter, as the prices of foodstuffs fall from the high level of 1641–50, while those of industrial products continue to rise. At the same time the real value of wages is starting to rise from the very low level it had reached in the early seventeenth century. Such a conjuncture is compatible with a slackening in the rate of growth of population, even a temporary absolute fall in numbers, but also with the maintenance of effective demand for industrial products. This new and important trend constitutes a crucial part of the changing context of the final century of our period. To look at it more closely a rather different set of prices and wages is exhibited in Table 9. They are expressed on different base years so are *not* comparable with those in Table 8.

TABLE 9

Index of prices and wages, 1650–1749

1680–9 = 100

	(a)	(b)		(c)		(d)	(e)	(f)
		Industrial products		$\frac{(b)}{(a)} \times 100$		'Real' wage rates of building craftsman	Real wages in London	Real wages in Lancashire
Decade	Wheat	(i)	(ii)	(i)	(ii)			
1650–9	124	109	—	88	—	96		
60–9	124	120	119	97	78	90		
70–9	120	107	108	89	74	94		
80–9	100	100	100	100	100	100		
90–9	138	103	108	75	78	—		
1700–19	104	100	83	96	80	110	108	99
10–9	113	89	85	79	75	111	106	103
20–9	112	98	98	88	88	117	110	123
30–9	94	93	99	99	105	134	127	145
40–9	91	90	93	99	102	129	123	138

Sources: (a) 'General average wheat prices' from W. G. Hoskins, 'Harvest Fluctuations and English Economic History, 1620–1759', *Agricultural History Review* XVI (1968).

(b) (i) An unweighted average of prices of kersey, thrums, leather, bricks, lead, anchors and copper, purchased as naval stores, calculated from W. Beveridge, *Prices and Wages in England from the Twelfth to the Nineteenth Centuries* (London, 1939). (ii) An unweighted average of prices of broadcloth and lead exported by the East India Company—annual figures from the Company's accounts in the India Office Library, kindly made available to me by Dr. K. N. Chaudhuri.

(d) 1680–7 = 100, recalculated from Phelps Brown and Hopkins, 'Seven Centuries of the Prices . . .', loc. cit.

(e) and (f) 1700 = 100, recalculated from E. W. Gilboy, 'The Cost of Living and Real Wages in Eighteenth-century England', *Review of Economic Statistics* (1936).

The rise in real wages is evident enough here, though it must be stressed that just as the price data have a limited geographical range, the number of observations on which the wage series is based is not nearly so large as would be desirable. The statistical evidence, in short, is shaky; but it is suggestive. The apparently favourable movement of real wages sprang from the fall in food prices combined with an increase in money wages, induced by the slackening in the supply of labour; the money wages of building workers, for example, rose by some 45–50 per cent between the mid-seventeenth and mid-eighteenth centuries whilst the general index of prices of consumer goods (see Fig. 6) fell by about 3 per cent. Over the same period, industrial products fell in price, though not so much as foodstuffs. Consequently although the terms of trade between the two continued to move in industry's favour, the move was small and not as great as the rise in real wages. The implication of all this is that despite short-term reversals, for example, in the 1690s and 1709–11, there was probably a moderate, long-term increase in disposable income for many wage-earners. It was combined, as will be shown later, with a similar long-term increase in the output of industrial and other consumer goods, available at lower prices.

Such a shift in the position of the wage-earner, even though gradual, piecemeal, and unevenly distributed over the country as a whole, induced corresponding shifts in the attitudes of employers and employees alike. The rapidly enlarging pool of labour, which had earlier facilitated expansion of output with low wages and a minimum of technical innovation, could no longer be dipped into with such ease and speed: Complaints of 'want of hands' could be heard; and the inducement to invest in labour-saving, productivity-increasing innovations enjoyed a corresponding boost. Conversely, workers freed from the worst pressures of dearth and chronic poverty, found themselves periodically able to choose between more work and more leisure. So to the endemic underemployment of the pre-industrialized economy is added some increased tendency to that voluntary underemployment which provoked shouts of dismay from employers of the time:

The men have just so much more to spend in tipple, and remain now poorer than when their wages were less . . . They work so much the fewer days by how much the more they exact in their wages.[3]

Complaints similar to this example from the 1660s abound

over the next century or so. They were made about agricultural workers and urban craftsmen, about the cloth workers
of the South, the framework knitters of the Midlands, the
linen yarn spinners of Scotland. They achieved their starkest
and most generalized form in Arthur Young's famous utter-
ance of the 1770s: 'Everyone but an idiot knows that the
lower classes must be kept poor or they will never be industrious.'[4] Such remarks stimulate the adoption by some
twentieth-century readers of fixed moral or ideological pos-
tures. Before taking them up, it is well to bear in mind two
relevant considerations.

First, there is no particular evidence to suggest that any
but a few exceptional people have ever positively wanted, or
want today, to work to a regular timetable, hour-by-hour,
day-by-day, week-by-week, smoothly and automatically
working longer in response to the offer of higher wages,
consistently eschewing leisure in favour of higher earnings.
That great majority of historical men and women with
limited horizons of consumption or of social movement have
long behaved rationally enough, and happily continue to do
so, in preferring more leisure. So in this sense the specific
economic context of this period merely added force and
weight to customary patterns of behaviour which were
especially evident in an agrarian economy ruled by sunrise
and sunset, and by the rhythm of the seasons. Meanwhile,
the consciousness of clock time, aided by the increasing public
use of clocks and watches, had been notably advancing
throughout England during the sixteenth and seventeenth
centuries. Such perceptions were thus nicely poised in time
to interact with economic circumstances, thereby to stimulate
employers in their demand for more regular labour just
when their workers were finding better opportunities for the
joys of being less regular.

Second, it is important not to believe that frequency of
complaint signifies ubiquity of performance. The observations tell one as much about the persistence in the attitudes
of governors to governed, of the political nation to the poor,
as about the behaviour of workers. That the happenings
complained of happened we need not doubt. But it would be

absurd to suppose that, although they may have been true of some of the people for some of the time, they were necessarily true of all of the people for all of the time. Patently they could not have been, because otherwise the advances in output which we know did occur in the eighteenth century before the Industrial Revolution could have come about only or mainly as a result of very substantial increases in productivity, compensating for a lack of increase in hours worked. And although there is evidence of some real increase in productivity, both in agriculture and industry, it seems very unlikely that they alone were responsible for expansion. What we are witnessing is in reality no more than an economic context different from that of the preceding period but likewise providing stimuli for the ambitious and the persistent. The immediate manifestations varied but the results were familiar. And, as a comment of the 1680s indicates, contemporary limitations upon an unending pursuit of gain were not confined to a single economic category:

The rich merchant or tradesman commonly knocks off, and reckons it his glory to be a gentleman: and the generality of poor manufacturers believe they shall never be worth ten pounds, therefore they seldom strive to get ten shillings beforehand; and if it so be they can provide for themselves sufficient to maintain their manner of living by working only three days in the week, they will never work four days.[5]

Here is testimony not only to that world of popular morality typified by the idle and industrious apprentices, by Gin Lane and Beer Alley, but also to that widely recognized social ambition to cross the great divide of gentility rather than to amass more money. It was not new, but the context of post-Restoration England provided no lack of impetus towards such divisions of endeavour.

(iv)

The sixty years from the Petition of Right of 1628 to the Revolution of 1688 approximately delimit that sequence of upheavals in English life which no history of the period can ignore, however much it is concerned with economic and social matters rather than with political and religious. Its impact upon the economy cannot be measured with any sort of precision, if only because the chronic absence of statistics becomes particularly acute during the Interregnum, in part because of the very events of the time. We can be reasonably certain that the upheavals in themselves did little to alter the basic characteristics of the pre-industrialized English economy. Although religious intolerance certainly stimulated emigration, it is unlikely that the number of migrants was enough to have had a significant effect on general demographic development. The loss of Puritan craftsmen to America or to Holland might well have had some adverse consequences, however, for particular villages or industrial areas, for instance in East Anglia. There were, of course, a variety of short-term disturbances to economic activity. The execution of the King brought sundry commercial reprisals from states, for example, France and Portugal, which disapproved of such doings and were happy to shelter Royalist privateers; houses were ransacked by the soldiery of either side during both stages of the Civil War; crops were damaged, some rents went uncollected, and the poor sometimes took advantage of the times to plunder the rich. Yet there were none of the fierce and widespread peasant uprisings which at various times flared up in continental Europe; some of the unrest of the late 1640s was due as much to dearth after the appalling harvests as to the particular circumstances of war and regicide. Neither the rolling of some important political heads nor the sundry acts of revenge in the 1640s and 1660s alike did much to change the course of the country's economic development; and, despite some fines upon those found too obviously committed to the wrong political side at the wrong time, plenty of businessmen showed a tenacious ability to continue their profit-making careers through Protectorate, Restoration, and Revolution.

In truth, the consequences of the troubled times were more complex and more subtle; they were felt in the long-run rather than the short, affecting social attitudes and behaviour rather than having a direct influence on economic activity, and leaving their mark on economic policy because of shifts in the location of effective power.

As emphasized earlier, the concept of a society ordered by status and degree—with a modifying flexibility introduced by gradations of wealth—sustained and pervaded Tudor and Stuart life. To that concept the troubled decades of mid-seventeenth century England brought challenges, in ideas and in action. Most obviously contrary to this ordering of power and property were such actions as the execution of the King, a blow at the mystique of kingship; the fact of civil war, setting family against family, disturbing the peace of that company of county gentry which held sway over the shires; the rule of the county committees, putting responsibility into the hands of lesser men of 'mean' extraction, to the indigna-tion of those more accustomed to its exercise; and a variety of scattered agrarian uprisings which, triggered off by dearth or enclosure, especially between 1630 and 1650, acquired in the 1640s some features of the primitive agrarian communism typified by the Diggers. The ideas of the Levellers, however much their concepts of democracy excluded those at the bottom of the social pyramid, alarmed the men of the politi-cal nation who saw no reason to share power with the 'poor and middle sort of people'. Still more aimed at upsetting the prevailing order of society were the political and econo-mic ideals enshrined in the radical sects—Quakers, Ranters, and Fifth Monarchy Men. Here a variety of inner voices, prophecies, and millenarian visions promised all manner of somersaults in the social order as well as in religious obser-vance. They ranged from attacks on tithes or advocacy of a moderate redistribution of land to the anarchic communism of the Ranters, whose programme included the borrowing of money but not the repaying of it, and the notion that 'they should not only make use of a man's wife, but of his estate, goods, and chattels also, for all things were common.'[6]

It was not to be. Yet the failure or suppression of the social revolution does not mean that the happenings and ideas of that time were of no consequence for the world of the Restora-tion or of the successful political revolution wrought by the events of 1688. For it was precisely then that men turned away from many-coloured visions to a duller rationality; that revolutionary sects were transmuted into respectable Dissent; that the squabbles of Whigs and Tories took over from the fervour of religious conflict; and that ecstatic ideals of a radical, egalitarian Christianity were watered down into a serious-minded Nonconformity set in suitable antiphony to an accommodating Anglicanism. The latter truly established itself as the landowner's badge, with an unmistakable function in the social order. As Davenant put it in 1698 (typically in a work on colonial trade):

wise lawgivers have therefore endeavoured to keep the inferior rank of men within bounds, by a sense of religion, and a fear of offending that power by which they were created . . . The wiser sort had generally one religion for themselves, and another for the vulgar.[7]

For those on the other side of the gentility divide, Dissent in its various quiet and respectable forms, had its appeal—for small merchants, traders, artisans, manufacturers, and emergent industrialists. If the 'Protestant ethic' was here at work upon capitalism—and for England this was its most apparent early arena—the influence was essentially permissive rather than positive. It probably owed little to Calvin or the idea of a 'calling', or to Protestantism as such. It probably owed more to a set of socio-historic circumstances which left groups of inter-marrying families of co-religionists excluded from a ruling political nation of landowning Anglicans—socially apart, too, from the landowning Catholic dissenters—but faced with new opportunities for their more enterprising members opened up by an expanding economy. To 'keep your accounts punctual', to believe in sobriety and frugality, to worship a God who is supposed to help those most who help themselves: such creeds were unlikely to have done very much for the more spectacular acts of risk-taking and profit-making, but they may have given a helping hand to the vital substructure of capitalism which consolidated and extended the market economy.

The cooling years of post-Restoration England brought another set of changes which had their indirect and longer-term effect on English economy and society. To summarize them baldly as the decline of astrology and the rise of science would be grossly to simplify a complex interrelationship. That world of magical beliefs which had earlier played an important role in the cement of popular religion seems to have been waning in the later seventeenth century, though astrological predictions—much in demand during the Civil War—continued not only to be popular (as they are today) but to be taken seriously. But if to many contemporaries, as to John Aubrey, a pre-Civil War England of fairies, spirits, ghosts, rites, and ancient customs was passing away, a new one was emerging in which the useful, economic possibilities of the new science were worth exploring. The work of Boyle, Hooke, and Newton in England was part of a trend which included not merely Bacon, Gilbert, and Harvey in this country but Kepler, Galileo, and Descartes in continental Europe. There was nothing peculiarly English and Puritan about it, any more than was the Royal Society's socially wider membership much of a testimony to the role of artisans in the scientific revolution. Whatever the short-comings of that body in its attempts to marry science with 'trade', and its failure to demolish the social line between intellectual inquiry and practical technology, it helped to bring into being a new interest in new ways of improving the use of economic resources, at a time when a squeeze between costs and prices was providing reasons for being interested in such new methods. This is not to suggest any neat deterministic causality. It is simply to note the juxtaposition in this important century of economic change and opportunity, 1650–1750, of the scientific revolution and the Royal Society as links in schemes, proposals, projects, and institutions concerned both with the new interest in nature and with its control for economic ends. From the sundry schemes of social, educational, and economic reform publicized by Samuel Hartlib in the 1650s a line continues through various societies, established in London and in provincial towns in the eighteenth century, to study the arts and sciences and natural philosophy, to link up with the Society for the Encouragement of Arts, Sciences, and Manufactures in

Great Britain (Royal Society of Arts) founded in 1754. The teaching of natural sciences at Oxford and Cambridge expanded rapidly during the first half of the eighteenth century; dictionaries of Arts and Sciences multiplied. So, too, did works on commerce and industry. Some of the latter were essentially polemics, into which economic thought came more by accident than intent. Some showed simply an indiscriminate enthusiasm for trade as the bringer at once of national glory and international benefit. A few writers such as William Petty, Dudley North, John Locke, and David Hume exhibited an analytical insight which foreshadowed Adam Smith's analysis of economic life. In brief, although the direct linkages between exhortation and performance, between invention and innovation, between economic behaviour and economic thought, often remain obstinately concealed, the final century of our period is full of concern for 'scientific' rationality in the use of economic resources for the country's supposed benefit. Just how much it achieved we do not know; but if all the millenarian visions and radical utopias unleashed in the mid-seventeenth century decades had come to pass, it is hard to believe that it would have managed to achieve anything.

The Agrarian Sector, 1650–1750

(i)

The current tendency, mentioned in the previous chapter, to regard seventeenth-century Europe as an age of crisis and enduring economic gloom has been made manifest in the treatment of agriculture, by presenting the century from 1650 to 1750 as one of long agrarian depression. According to an eminent authority on European agriculture the chief symptoms of this malaise included falling cereal prices, the conversion of arable to pasture, some shifts towards the cultivation of fodder crops or of crops used in industry as well as 'few innovations in farming techniques and little interest in questions of an agrarian nature'.[1] Does such a picture, whatever its truth for Europe in general, hold good for England?

There seems no reason to alter the general assumption, set out earlier in this book (above, pages 31–2) that food growers responded to relative price changes. A preamble to an Act of Parliament of 1663, concerned like its predecessors of the previous century with the 'encouraging of tillage', went on to observe that the best way to do so, as in promoting any 'trade, occupation or mistery', was to render it 'profitable to the users thereof'.[2] So although prices are only a proxy for profits, we can try using them for this period as for the earlier. Table 10 shows decennial changes in an index of the prices of various foodstuffs in southern England.

Faced with such figures, and bearing in mind what has been said about European agriculture generally in these years, we might be tempted to see them as suggesting for England a switch from cereals towards livestock for meat; a contraction in the area under cultivation; a paucity of agricultural

TABLE 10

Index of agricultural prices, 1640–1749

1641–55 = 100

Decade	Farinaceous	Meat and fish	Butter and cheese
1640–9	101	93	100
50–9	96	106	100
60–9	107	103	95
70–9	101	95	99
80–9	89	98	84
90–9	104	107	94
1700–9	84	96	83
10–19	104	104	85
20–9	89	100	80
30–9	73	91	79
40–9	77	101	89

Source: Phelps Brown and Hopkins, 'Seven Centuries of the Prices . .', loc. cit. Recalculated on index base of 1641−55 = 100 from the annual figures for the three groups of commodities, kindly made available to me by Professor Phelps Brown.

innovations; and, indeed, a lack of interest in new techniques. The last three of these inferences would be almost certainly wholly wrong; and although the first may have been correct as a net phenomenon, we could also find plenty of examples, regionally, of a shift towards cereals. In brief, and as before, the available price data have to be handled with care verging on suspicion; they often help but are rarely conclusive.

(ii)

Whether there was interest, or lack of it, in new techniques may in part be gauged from the publication of works on agriculture. The late fifteenth and sixteenth centuries had seen an increasing output of printed books on farming, many of them published in Italy and deriving their ideas from classical authors. In England John Fitzherbert's *Boke of Husbandry* of 1523 and Thomas Tusser's *A Hundreth Good Pointes of Husbandrie* (1557) began a sequence of such writings, some derivative, some native and original, which soon began to multiply. A few examples must suffice:

Sir Richard Weston's *Discourse of Husbandrie used in Brabant and Flanders* (1645), Walter Blith's *The English Improver* (1649), John Worlidge's *Systema Agriculturae* (1669), and the first systematic work on forestry, *Sylva* (1664), written by the diarist John Evelyn. Although there was some slackening of the printed output in the decades that followed, John Houghton's *Letters for the Improvement of Husbandry and Trade*, published at various dates between 1681 and 1703 and re-published in 1727 by Richard Bradley, Professor of Botany at Cambridge, are an important landmark in this type of literature; and in the early eighteenth century Jethro Tull's famous *Horse-Houghing Husbandry* (1731) was far from being the only English book on agriculture.

Amongst such works there was plenty of both padding and plagiary. But those dating from the mid-seventeenth century and later, exhibit some common characteristics worthy of emphasis. The anti-enclosure sentiments of the earlier period were to be heard only very occasionally after the mid-century. Enclosure was lauded as a step towards better farming, for arable as well as pasture. A variety of technical improvements were advocated, for example, the use of leys, convertible husbandry, the floating of water meadows, better drainage, and heavier or different manuring. Most of these were not new, having originated earlier, during the period of rising prices, thus representing the repetition of older remarks or the recording of known practices. The appearance of such things in print cannot readily be correlated with price movements. Two particular advocacies were of special importance: the use of 'artificial grasses' (clover, sainfoin, lucerne) as field crops within rotations, to improve pasturage; and the use of turnips, again as a field crop within a rotation, as a fodder crop. Both owed much to the practice of the Low Countries and were given most of their publicity in Sir Richard Weston's work, subsequently reprinted and plagiarized by various other writers. Then there were sundry suggestions of mechanical improvements. All sorts of different ploughs were in use in various parts of England; and some of the writings show much concern with the design of ploughs. The idea of the seed-drill was developed by more than one writer, but Tull patented his design in 1701; and both this and his horse-hoe were publicized by him. Many of the books display an interest in non-cereal crops: vegetables and market-gardening; industrial crops such as hops, dye-plants, or hemp; and the growing of fruit trees. But, once again, none of these was especially new to this period; hop cultivation, for instance, had been given a particular boost of publicity in a book published in 1574. In general, the writings of the later period reveal a more systematic, rationalistic, and practical approach than many of their predecessors of Tudor times. Some originated in strictly practical problems. *Sylva*, for example, was written as a consequence of the Navy's worry about the supply of timber trees for naval shipbuilding. The magical remedies, still to be found in some of the works of the 1650s, gradually disappear in agricultural prescriptions as in other walks of life.

So much for some of the continuing interest and the dissemination of ideas. But how many landlords or farmers read the books or absorbed the ideas? And what was happening in practice? To the former question there can be no meaningful answer. It seems possible that with more contacts between even a small circle of landowners and the sundry advocates of economic advance, including the *literati* and gentry of the Royal Society—whose investigations into agriculture, however limited their outcome, typified the new trend of interest —the way was being opened up for that English fashion in 'improvement' which was later to fascinate foreign observers in the course of the eighteenth century. The line leads forward from Evelyn, writing in the 1650s of having, in the company of Robert Boyle ('that excellent person and great virtuoso') visited 'some new-invented ploughs',[3] to Viscount Townshend's celebrated act of turnip popularization (though certainly *not* of innovation) in the 1730s. It is reasonably certain that, so far from undergoing a period of long-term stagnation or recession, English agriculture in this century from 1650 to 1750 saw notable advances both in techniques and in specialization.

Amongst the various advocacies of the writers, those for fruit, vegetables, and hops were certainly being translated into reality. The West Country, especially in Hereford and the Vale of Evesham was the scene of much apple and pear cultivation; mid-Kent became notable for its apples and cherry orchards. Carrots, cabbages, and other vegetables featured in the market gardening which already flourished around London in the sixteenth century and continued to expand there as well as around other towns. Potatoes moved out of the kitchen garden to become a field crop in this period, particularly in Lancashire and more gradually in other areas of western England and Wales. The advance of hops was perhaps the most striking; and it can be given some precision as a result of the introduction of the hop excise in 1711. In 1729–31, there were over 20,000 acres planted with hops; the leading counties were Hereford and Worcester in the West and Kent and Sussex in the South-East; and average annual output rose from 9 million lbs in 1712–21 to 19 million in 1747–56. The growing of other industrial crops, such as hemp, flax, madder, woad, and saffron, almost certainly expanded, though by how much is not always clear. Flax and hemp cultivation had been the subject of official encouragement in the sixteenth century; the expansion of the linen industry implied some expansion of native flax production, and certainly by the 1780s (when a bounty was introduced) significant quantities were being grown in various parts of the country, including Yorkshire, Lincolnshire, and Dorset. Landowners were paying more attention to their woodlands, planting and coppicing as well as merely cutting. Here the lucrative business of selling timber to a growing tribe of timber merchants, active in supplying shipbuilders or housebuilders, for the Navy, for the growing towns or for the rebuilding of London after the fire of 1666, interacted with the urge to preserve the value of landed estates, for the maintenance and prestige of the family. The influence of new ideas on forestry was thus blessed with a receptive soil. For the most part the advocates of mechanical improvements in agriculture were answered only slowly. The seed drill and the horse-hoe were adopted in some parts of East Anglia; and the development, after the 1730s, of the so-called 'Rotherham' plough (which, despite its name, owed much to Dutch influences) was a pointer to later improvements in plough design, especially for ligher soils.

More significant for increased productivity in the main lines of agriculture during this period was the practical adoption of turnips and grasses in the extension of convertible husbandry. Turnips were already grown as a vegetable in sixteenth-century kitchen gardens, but their cultivation as a field crop, forming part of a rotation and being used as fodder for cattle, was first established in Suffolk in the 1650s and '60s. Thereafter it spread to Norfolk where, for example, they were being grown on the lands of the Walpole and Townshend estates before 1700; and, in the first half of the eighteenth century, to many other parts of the country, at first more in the South but gradually to the North as well. Again, it was from the 1650s that there can be dated the cultivation of sainfoin as a field crop to lay tillage to grass and thus again provide more pasturage in lieu of fallow. Clover had been experimented with earlier in the seventeenth century, but its cultivation, like that of trefoil, was again more rapidly disseminated after the mid-seventeenth century. It was found in East Anglia and the Midlands in the 1650s and 1660s, as well as in the South-West; and later made its way northwards, during the first half of the eighteenth century.

All these practical innovations, together with the further extension, especially in the South and West, of the earlier device of floating water meadows, had the effect of improving the supply of feed for beasts. This does not mean, however, that they had no impact on cereal cultivation; that they are to be interpreted simply as a mere move away from cereals because of their falling prices. On the contrary, they had a double, albeit indirect, effect on cereals. First, because more beasts meant more dung, and more dung meant better cereal yields. Second, because of the new possibilities of crop rotation better use could be made of the land by the extension of convertible husbandry and by further specialization according to types of soil; hence, again, better yields in cereals as well as more beasts. So we find extensive use of improved rotations on the light soils, for example, in Norfolk or the

Cotswolds, to grow grain and at the same time to keep more sheep or cattle. In contrast, on the heavy soils, in the clay vales of the Midlands, for example, more land was put down to grass for specialized dairying or fattening. Consequently, according to which part of the country an observer drew his examples from, there could be found illustrations both of apparent moves towards pasture and of apparent moves towards cereals. In Leicestershire, for instance, once part of the Midland grain-growing area, most of the enclosure for pasture farming took place between 1607 and 1730. By the 1720s, much of Leicestershire, Northamptonshire, and Lincolnshire seemed to Defoe to be taken up with 'breeding and fattening cattle'; and to be 'a vast magazine of wool' where 'most of the gentlemen are graziers, and in some places the graziers are so rich, that they grow gentlemen.'[4] Conversely, in Norfolk, or on the chalk lands of the Downs, from Kent to Wiltshire, sundry varieties of crop rotations helped forward the yields of grain as an essential part of the mixed farming of the day. Thereby came larger crops of wheat and barley, thus supplying, for the first time in English history, a significant export trade in cereals. Which brings us to the problem of demand.

Why did all these innovations spread in this period of falling prices and only slightly rising population? Whence came the demand? In trying to formulate answers to these questions we need to start with the home market; examine the overseas demand for foodstuffs; and make one crucial assumption about the behaviour of landowners and farmers.

The expansion of home demand proceeded from three interrelated causes: the rise in real wages; the growth of towns; and the expansion of industries based on the processing of agricultural products. The first two of these have already been set out in some detail (above, pages 97–9, 101–3), and there is no need to repeat the argument here. A variety of literary and other evidence offers support to the contention that during this period both agricultural output per head of the population and standards of living and food consumption were rising. Too much credence should obviously not be given to contemporary observations—which can be heard especially from the 1690s to the 1750s—to the effect that

English workers' wages were higher than those of foreigners; that they enjoyed a diet of 'beef and pudding'; indulged in excessive 'tea drinking'; and generally lived far better than those in France and elsewhere who are represented as subsisting on 'herbs and roots'.[5] Some of it was patriotic nonsense; some of it was part of protectionist arguments against cheaper imports; some of it proceeded from the employers' fear, already noted (above, pages 103–5), that higher standards for workers encouraged 'idleness 'and 'luxury'. Nevertheless, it seems probable that the scope for higher real wages was indeed used by many, though obviously not all, in buying some more food and drink as well as manufactured goods, rather than in merely purchasing leisure.

Estimates of agricultural output for this time are, inevitably, of doubtful accuracy. For what they are worth, they suggest that during the first half of the eighteenth century, grain output increased about 10 per cent; while that of two main excisable cattle products, tallow candles and soap, increased 16 per cent and 13 per cent respectively. Were such data extendable back into the mid-seventeenth century, it seems highly probable that for 1650–1750 they would show larger advances as well as falling prices. Moreover, because such population increase as occurred was apparently much more marked in industrial areas and in towns, drawing people away from agriculture, output per worker must have grown even more notably. For the imported consumables, sugar and tea, the rather more reliable (though not unimpeachable) trade statistics reveal remarkable increases. Retained imports of sugar rose approximately tenfold between the 1660s and 1750s, by which time nearly 1 million cwts (over 90 per cent of total imports) were being consumed at home—a far greater consumption per head of the population than in France. Tea imports were negligible in the mid-seventeenth century; by the 1750s, retained imports (again, about 90 per cent of the total) were running at over 3 million lbs. The prices of sugar and tea fell; their consumption per head rose, probably, indeed, more so than that of bread, meat and diary products. The rise in real incomes, however must surely have encouraged some switch towards meat consumption. The larger flocks of sheep, for which there is evidence in various parts of the country, were said to be increasingly bred for mutton rather than wool. And there is evidence, too, of a shift towards wheaten bread, away from barley and rye. John Aubrey commented in the 1680s that on the light lands of Wiltshire wheat was being grown where before the Civil War there was barley; and added that in those days the poor 'did eat only barley bread (which nowadays they would think a very hard fare).'[6] This shift continued to be commented on during the first half of the eighteenth century, though it was still largely confined to the South-East. Man was not the only consumer of cereals. The two biggest grain crops were probably barley and oats; and much of the latter went to feed an increasingly important item of capital in agriculture and transport alike—the horse. More wealth meant more horses; they multiplied in number and variety, on the farm, in the town, for coaches, or for war—and the demand for oats rose accordingly.

Of course, some part of the increase in disposable income was undoubtedly taken up by more expenditure on those two famous drugs: tobacco and alcohol. Retained imports of tobacco rose from around 4 million lbs in the 1660s to over 10 million in the 1750s; those of rum went from about 2,000 gallons in 1700–4 to over 820,000 in 1750–4. Much of the increased availability came not just from these fruits of settlement in the New World (on behalf of which, incidentally, tobacco cultivation in the West Country was stamped out by about 1700) but from bigger home supplies of beer and spirits. These in turn did much to support an increase in barley acreages, especially in East Anglia. Contemporary estimates, in 1688 and 1766, put barley as by far the biggest English cereal crop, and calculated that a proportion varying from 68 to 72 per cent was used for brewing or distilling, chiefly the former. On lighter soils in many areas, from Kent to Yorkshire, barley growing spread, numerous maltings were erected and many maltsters began prosperous careers. Though much home-brewing of unhopped ale continued, big breweries and brewers flourished in London and many market towns and ports, producing and marketing hopped beer or porter. Around 1580 there were only 26 common brewers in London and Westminster; in 1700–4 their number had risen to nearly 180. In the country as a whole, the number of brewers rose by nearly 50 per cent in the first half of the eighteenth century, most of the increase being outside London; and the quantity of malt charged with duty showed a rise of 36 per cent. The distillers used both malt and unmalted barley, and their rise in vigour and prosperity also belongs to this period. The duty on spirits reveals a rate of increase of output far greater than that of any of the other indices of home production, rivalling that for retained sugar imports by moving from an average of 533,000 gallons in 1684–8 to 5,754,000 in 1750–4, an advance of 980 per cent. To some extent those figures represent a compensation for the fall in imports of wines and brandies, thus mirroring some change in English drinking habits. But for the agricultural sector of the English economy, all this processing of its products certainly provided a further stimulus.

If these various factors—advancing real wages, urban growth, more horses, a continuing thirst for beer and an incipient one for gin—added up to increased home demand for cereals, a reinforcement of demand came from overseas markets. In the 1660s exports of grain were negligible, none of the country's ports sending overseas an average of more than 2,000 quarters. Thereafter the rise was dramatic. Quickly soaring to an average of over 300,000 quarters in 1675–7, total net cereal exports (comprising all grains, flour, and malt) reached over 900,000 in the decade 1745–54. The peak year was 1750 when 950,000 quarters of wheat and wheat flour and 331,000 quarters of malt alone were exported. The trade had very marked fluctuations, dependent on the variations of harvests at home and abroad, but the surplus continued to rise. After 1750, however, the wheel began to turn full circle; and as the new population upsurge got under way, England once again became a net importer of grain. To emphasize the position which had been reached at the mid-century, it is worth noting that in 1752–4 home-produced foodstuffs (including fish and hops) accounted for nearly 17 per cent by value of all exports (excluding re-exports).

Nevertheless, it is important to put the grain export trade into perspective. It took off only a small proportion of total output: if the contemporary guesses of total grain production were roughly correct, exports even at their mid-century peak amounted to only about 6 per cent of total output and averaged only 3 per cent over the first half of the eighteenth century.

The appearance of England as a significant exporter in the international grain market was helped into being by three different influences. First, the old policy of the State on the subject of grain supply went into reverse in the course of the 1660s and 1670s. Chapter 10 will look at this example of State policy in rather more detail (below, page 177). Meanwhile, suffice to note that the new corn laws brought protection to the producer against imported grain when prices were low; and encouragement to exports by means of bounties. Whether this policy was economically useful, damaging, or simply of no consequence soon became the subject of debate. By making certain assumptions it would doubtless be possible to calculate some numerical estimates of the economic, though not of the political, consequences of the policy. The results of such an exercise would probably be to reveal them as gratifyingly small.

The second influence, without which the grain could hardly have been lured out of the country, was the existence of a demand in Europe which could now be supplied, in part at least, more cheaply by grain from England than from the great east-European granary which had previously supplied the deficit areas of western Europe. Between 1600–49 and 1700–49, the average quantities of grain shipped westwards through the Sound from the big grain-exporting ports of the Baltic, fell by 54 per cent. The reasons for the decline are not the concern of this book: they may have ranged from falling population to the substitution of southern rice for northern cereals; certainly the whole of the shortfall was not simply made good by English exports. But those exports did go to the traditional receiving areas: to the Mediterranean, to Spain and Portugal, to France, and the granaries of Holland, as well as to the West Indies. In 1711 Davenant saw it as 'in a manner a new exportation'; he put it down to the wars which had elsewhere hindered tillage or 'from dearths or plagues, wherewith divers nations have been afflicted for these last 23 years'.[7] Whatever the reasons, it seems likely that the English agrarian sector was coming to have a sounder base than some of its continental counterparts.

Neither State action nor overseas deficits could have produced the export trade had it not been for the third and the most potent influence, the achievement of a more or less consistent grain surplus. It had come about substantially as a consequence of putting into wider use the various productivity-increasing methods already mentioned. Extension of the cultivated area, so important earlier, had been supplemented or replaced by more intensive farming. The result was that English agriculture in early Hanoverian times could feed about double the population that it could feed in Tudor times. It did not remove hardship; nor did it change the political and social position of the 'illiterate rabble', the 'voiceless multitude' at the bottom of the pyramid; but it may well have improved their nutritional standards and, still more probably, those in the next stratum above them. It did not advance without setbacks, in which dearth and want, hunger and disease sapped the poorer sections of the population. Yet it was a matter of great economic importance to England, for by imparting strength to the agricultural sector it provided a vital base for the later surge into industrialization.

To explain why all this should have come about mainly in this period of falling prices it is necessary to make one crucial assumption about the behaviour of landowners and farmers. This is simply that because they found themselves squeezed between falling prices and rising costs, they proceeded to make these cost-reducing innovations in order to safeguard or restore their profits. Such a deliberate course of action implies something more than the mere price-responsiveness already postulated. It means a cost-responsiveness sufficient, if necessary, to make changes in production methods: behaviour of much greater economic significance than the mere willingness to increase the area under cultivation and employ more cheap labour, which was the standard response to the sellers'-market situation of the preceding price-rise period. That producers should have so acted in the new post-1650 situation was not the consequence of some peculiar English-ness or of the Protestant ethic or of some new thrust of bourgeois exploitation arising from the 'Puritan revolution', but sprang directly from the landlord-tenant farmer relation-ship as it had evolved in England by this time. The landlord was primarily dependent, for the maintenance of his social and economic position, on his rent roll plus, in some cases, the produce or profits of his home farm; some, of course, were able to supplement or sustain it by non-agricultural incomes; but manorial rents or dues were now of no economic conse-quence. If he was faced with falling rents or profits he had to do something about it. The tenant farmer, meanwhile, had to be able to pay his rent and the more he could lower his costs, the more he would have over for his family, his stan-dard of life, his social advancement. The market for grain approached that of a perfect economic market: no individual producer could control prices or rents. This was less true of the more localized markets for meat, dairy products, and special crops, though farming in general rarely produced abnormal profits. But by the new methods and by increased specialization there was hope for reducing costs in both the main sectors of mixed farming.

The more the new methods were introduced, the more they contributed to lowering the quasi-rents attaching to particular qualities of land. Thus did a Kentish landowner, Sir Roger Twysden, complain in the 1660s:

When I came to my estate I found myself to have two great wants —meadow for winter keeping for cattle and land to plough . . . but now there is a newer device of clover seed that spoils all meadow land so as we are forced to abate 5s or 6s per acre of good land in Romney Marsh.[8]

Thirty years later his comment was echoed in more general terms by the observation that 'marsh and feeding grounds were abated in rent by the tenants, at least 20 or 30 per cent' as a consequence of the 'late general practice of sowing

clover, sainfoin, rye-grass and other grass seeds'. [9] The falling
rents, so much complained of in the 1660s and '70s and again
during the 'agricultural depression' of 1730–45, instead of
promoting withdrawals of capital from agriculture or lack of
interest in it (as evidently happened in some parts of continental Europe) helped to force this continuing adjustment of
costs. Without improvement, as more than one contemporary
observed, rents could not be paid; with it, farming became
profitable and grain available in larger quantities and at
lower prices. During the difficult years of 1730–45—particularly difficult for cereal producers—landlords were faced with
mounting arrears of rent. Again, they were forced to write off
such arrears, to make concessions, to provide capital for farm
buildings or improvements, in order to retain good tenants—
on whom they so much depended. A run of good harvests in
the 1730s and '40s kept prices low and still further encouraged this new elasticity in productive methods. To one near-
contemporary at least the results of improvement were
evident enough:

. . . All history cannot furnish twenty such years of fertility and
abundance as from 1730 to 1750 when the average prices were the
lowest ever known. Another reason we assign to the fall of price, is
the great improvements made in agriculture in the last fifty or
sixty years. [10]

(iii)

It has been estimated that in 1700 about half of English
arable land was still in open fields. Just how much land was
enclosed in the century after the great price-rise we do not
know; all we know conclusively is that the big phase of
enclosure by Act of Parliament did not begin until after 1750.
A tiny trickle of enclosure Acts started towards the end of the
seventeenth century, but numbers remained small whilst
grain prices stayed low: fewer than one per year on average
to 1720, moving up to rather over three per year over the
decades to 1750. Such instances as there are of enclosure by
this method occur after temporary price rises, for example,
in 1729–30 and 1742–3 immediately after the price peaks of

1727–8 and 1739–41. The enclosure of commons and wastes had earlier been a fertile source of complaint—in the 1630s and by the Diggers, for example—and there are some indications that more attempts were made in this later period to make provisions for poorer landholders or to secure enclosure by agreement. The latter method, sometimes given the force of law by actions in the Court of Chancery or by decrees of other courts, was certainly being used for enclosures in various parts of the country. It remains fairly clear, however, that the technical advances in agriculture during the 1650–1750 period were not dependent on a massive drive for enclosure, either for effecting improvements within existing open-field farms or for bringing new land under cultivation in severalty. In Oxfordshire, for example, continuing open-field cultivation in the late seventeenth and early eighteenth centuries witnessed the introduction of new crops, including sainfoin and clover, an increasing number of animals on these mixed farms, and a switch to the highest-priced crop, wheat. On the other hand, in Northamptonshire, where Defoe was so impressed by the amount of land put down to grass for specialized grazing, the greater part of the county was still in open fields, awaiting the later period for massive enclosure by private Acts.

For all the absence of enclosing noise—or complaint—changes were happening in rural society and the structure of landownership, just as they were in agrarian techniques. There was an increase in the size both of farms and of estates. Essentially a consolidating movement and not a spectacular surge of change, this was likely to have raised the position of the bigger tenant farmers as well as having brought a shift in economic and political power towards the bigger landowners, the county grandees. Parallel to this was the decline of the smaller landowners, the squeezing pressures upon freeholders and lesser gentry unable to cope with falling prices and rising taxes. The concomitant of these trends is thought to have been some drying up, though certainly not complete cessation, of the flow of upward social mobility which, in Tudor and early Stuart times, had brought the rise into the gentry, the flood of coats of arms, and the tidal wave of titles. Restoration, reaction, and 'Augustan calm' have been presented as the ensuing socio-economic sequence, creating a closed, exclusive, rural élite. This picture of 'stability and social conservatism' in 1650–1750, standing in contrast to the dislocation and change of the previous century, seems to be mirrored in the very architecture of the day. The burgeoning of the English baroque was followed by that restrained apotheosis of the settled power and tranquillity of the English landowning classes—the Queen Anne or Georgian country house. It all seems to fit easily into a century when neither population nor prices did anything spectacular. Yet, looked at in a different way, it is an odd picture for a century which saw political revolution and the most expensive wars in English history hitherto. It has elements of truth, but is more complex than such vistas would suggest.

Some changes followed, directly or indirectly, from the effects of Civil War and Interregnum. During the Interregnum there was confiscation and sale of some 'delinquent' Royalist lands, as well as those of Church and Crown; other Royalists sold or borrowed to pay fines in order to 'compound' for their support of the wrong side. But at the Restoration the sales of confiscated lands—though not other sales—were invalidated; and most Royalists regained their lands. It seems unlikely that, as a direct consequence of these forced transactions, there occurred any substantial transfer of land to lawyers, merchants, soldiers, rich citizens, and the like who were then responsible for putting into operation the improved methods of farming and estate management. Nevertheless, many former Royalists and other landowners whose lands bore heavy debt charges, whether incurred because of or before 'the troubles', found themselves in a very disadvantageous situation as rents and prices fell in the post-Restoration years. Legal developments since the earlier seventeenth century had facilitated the growth of a mortgage market; and some money-lending scriveners did very well out of this flourishing business. Sir Robert Clayton and his partner, John Morris, for example, ran a country-wide lending and estate agency, and their clients in the 1660s and '70s included many a former Royalist seeking to raise mortgages or to sell lands to pay debts. Many families lingered on, not selling until after the Revolution, nurturing a continuing grievance and, like the Yorkshire baronet, Sir William Chaytor when consigned to the Fleet prison in 1700, putting it down to 'the great incumbrances left upon his estate by his father who suffered for his loyalty to King Charles the First'.[11]

By this time, other forces were helping to keep the land market busy. A substantial boom in overseas trade and a notable stepping up of internal economic activity (see below, pages 134–5, 145–6) were creating wealth which still sought outlets in land. To those traditional purchasers, the successful merchants and lawyers, were added financiers, bankers, and contractors profiting by the State's needs during the wars; ironmasters and coal-owners; shippers, shipbuilders, and sugar planters; East India magnates; and a miscellany of professional men and place-men. Like their Tudor predecessors they acquired landed estates, built splendid new houses, married their children into the peerage or into older families, and started new landed families. Many, especially the parvenu amongst them, got themselves buried under some of the biggest pieces of memorial sculpture to be seen in English churches, almost all dating between 1650 and 1750. These men and their doings were to be found all over the country. They included the famous and the lesser-known: the Duke of Devonshire at Chatsworth; William Blaythwayt, administrator, building at Dyrham; Sir Robert Walpole at Houghton; the Foley family ascending into the peerage on their iron wealth and landed estates in the west Midlands; the Liddells and the Lowthers doing well on land and coal in the North-East and North-West; Daniel Finch, Earl of Nottingham, building at Burley, from his profits of office; Sir Gilbert Heathcote, building at Normanton from the profits of trade and banking; the Pinneys and Lascelles blossoming on sugar; and all those whose 'prodigous estates' and 'opulent foundations', Defoe so admired in 1727 sprouting in Surrey and the Home Counties. For every such success in these fields there were, of course, many who made no such family entrance into the ranks of landed society. And for every purchase by a newcomer there was a purchase by existing county families, whether long-established squires or territorial magnates like the Dukes of Bedford or the Earls of Rockingham. Perhaps there was some slackening of activity after the 1720s and the South Sea fiasco; the effective establishment of the National Debt and Consols lessened the scope for individual fortune-hunting in public finance. The agricultural depression of 1730–45 may have deterred some would-be landed purchasers; and urban building, whether in London or Newcastle, Liverpool or Bath, provided alternative and sometimes very lucrative speculative ventures.

If it was the rich who were thus buying in or consolidating their position, it was also they who could best cope both with the new burdens of taxation represented by the land tax of 1693 and with the improvements in farm and estate management which the new economic context demanded. The need to finance the wars of 1689–97 and 1702–13 (see below, pages 191–4) brought heavier and more effective taxation. On one Kentish estate, for instance, direct taxation as a percentage of gross rental income rose from around 4–5 per cent in 1658–65 to a figure varying from 16 to 27 per cent between 1689 and 1699. Meanwhile rent arrears had been rising and in 1688 amounted to no less than 24 per cent of the total rent roll. Such figures may or may not have been typical; but there is evidence that in the 1690s and 1730s alike rent arrears, low prices, and land taxes were pressing upon landlords all over the country. Sometimes landlords managed to shift the burden of the tax on to the tenants, but in general it seems clear that the landlords paid. In such circumstances, smaller landowners with a burden of debt and few resources, or freeholding farmers with farms of less than 100 or so acres, found it very difficult to continue. Conversely, the bigger men, who could invest in better farm buildings and equipment, consolidate small farms into bigger, and put into operation the new cost-saving, productivity-increasing techniques, could not only hope to survive, but also profit from rising urban demand for food and drink or from the bounties on grain exports. So the trend towards larger farms is clear in various parts of the country, and particularly in the first half of the eighteenth century. On one set of estates in

Staffordshire, for example, the number of farms over 100 acres rose by 44 per cent between 1724 and 1764. Whether the farmers were larger freeholders or tenants of big farms, it was they who put the new methods into operation. Only a few of the big landlords were actively interested in farming improvements. But all, or most of them, sought to preserve their rent rolls, their estates, their way of life, and their family status. In so doing they or their stewards performed a crucial function by providing the impetus towards creating the well-tenanted estate, with large farms of 200 acres or more, capable of 'holding the rent'.

This is neither to say that it was the most socially desirable way of effecting improvements in the agrarian sector, or to present such men as conscious social benefactors. It is simply to indicate the mechanism of change. The mechanism, moreover, was being aided by an important legal development. This was a particular method of strict settlement by which estates could be so entailed—to remain intact for the future benefit of the family through the male line—that it was very difficult to break the entail. In the later seventeenth century much more land was being thus entailed than hitherto; and the higher judiciary, itself increasingly identified with the landed classes, supported such moves. As big estates were thus built up, so they more and more became collections of socially prestigious rights upon which loans could be secured by mortgages. But all the time their rent-rolls needed the continuous vigilance which could be better maintained on the compact, well-tenanted large estate than on the smaller, straggling properties.

Beneath the elegant façade, then, there was plenty of change. Some of the seeming social stability may have been deceptive. Some of it may have been a product of temporary demographic stagnation, for detailed study of the British peerage has shown that uniquely between 1650 and 1725 it was failing to reproduce itself in the male line. Certainly, it was not a simple matter of big landowners and small, of Whigs and Tories, or even of that easy distinction, so beloved by Bolingbroke, between a virtuous 'landed interest' and a parasitic 'monied interest'. When, as early as 1709, he wrote that the whole burden of the cost for England of 'the two most expensive wars that Europe ever saw' had been borne by 'the landed interest', he was exaggerating. But when he added that 'the landed men are become poor and dispirited [and] turn arrant farmers and improve the estates they have left',[12] he was pointing to a true link, albeit distorted, between fiscal and economic realities, at once affecting the agricultural sector, rural society, and political alignments. The dispirited and indebted ex-Cavaliers of the post-Restoration decades had become the disgruntled and indebted Tory squires who followed Bolingbroke or dabbled in Jacobitism; and if Whig peers or country gentlemen prospered, it was not because of their Whiggishness but because they found tenants who could make their farms pay.

Trade Transformed, 1650–1750

(i)

In 1728, Defoe observed that the 'sum of all improvements in trade' was 'the finding out some market for the sale or vent of merchandize, where there was no sale or vent for those goods before'.[1] He went on to amplify his comment by emphasizing that he did not mean the mere creation of a fashion for English goods in existing markets, or sending goods via new routes to old markets, or the capture of trade from competitors, but the discovery of a fresh demand, hitherto untapped by the competing commercial powers of Europe. Such a remark draws to our attention one of the crucial characteristics of trade in pre-industrialized economies. Because of the slow or limited growth in aggregate income in a given market area, merchants could not normally hope for significant increases in their sales save by capturing more of the market from their rivals; and they were unlikely to achieve this by competitive reductions in price because of the comparative rarity of cost-reducing innovations in production or in transport. Of course, such innovations did occur: improvements in the design of ships, by the Portuguese and Dutch in the fifteenth and sixteenth centuries, had lowered the costs of ocean transport; the use of coal had probably helped to cut some English manufacturing costs. In general, however, such improvements were too gradual and infrequent to inform the economic attitudes of the traders of the day. Consequently to merchants and producers of internationally-traded goods, commerce seemed a continuous fight over a cake of a limited size, a prize more or less fixed in quantity and value. One's slice could normally be increased only at the expense of others' losses. There remained one distant and glorious hope: with the aid of God, Christian mercantile man might find some new markets. The great European discoveries of the fifteenth and sixteenth centuries had promised just that, however complex their original motivation. But reality had turned the promise sour. The East wanted silver rather than European manufactures; American incomes were inadequate (when their owners survived conquest) and needed supplementation by the long-term process of settlement and wealth-creation.

To the reality of these unfulfilled hopes there was added in the course of the seventeenth century that complex malaise which has seemed to some historians to justify the idea of a European-wide 'crisis'. Whatever its questionable validity for Europe as a whole and for England in particular, there is rather less doubt about some contraction in the volume of intra-European commerce. It seems to have set in at various dates in the first half of the century, coincident with, and indeed influenced by, the interruption caused by prolonged warfare, plagues and harvest failures, and the cessation of demographic buoyancy. Evidence for a down-turn comes from such widely separated foci of European commerce as Seville and the Sound. How far the contraction was a real net loss or merely another of the usual redistributions of traffic and profit remains to be shown by some indefatigable researcher. Its effect, however, can hardly have been other than to reinforce the contemporary vision of international trade as a part of international conflict. At the same time it put a premium upon the possession of the economic resources, moral tenacity, and political ruthlessness necessary to stay in the national business of extra-European expansion, just beginning, as it was, to show hopes of net returns which would outstrip the original loot. For England it was to mean the intense reality of Anglo-Dutch followed by Anglo-French commercial rivalry. The period between the onset of the first Anglo-Dutch War in 1651 and the end of the Seven Years War in 1763 was quintessentially the age of trade wars and trade treaties, of battle by tariffs and prohibitions as much as by navies and armies. And it saw the emergence of

Britain as the dominant commercial power in the extra-
European commercial world, and the possessor of the largest
mercantile marine in Europe.

(ii)

Because of the absence of any continuous overseas trade
statistics in this period before 1697, any attempt to show the
growth, or lack of it, of English mercantile activity has perforce to be insecurely based. The purpose of the calculations
in Table 11 is simply to give a very general idea of relative
magnitudes and a sequence of change which can reasonably
be described as likely, but on no account as definite. Un-
certainty and guesswork abound in the figures for *circa* 1640;

TABLE 11

Estimated total English overseas commodity trade, circa *1640–1750s*
(£000s)

	(a)	(b)	(c)	(d)	(e)	(f)	(g)
	Domes-tic exports	Re-exports	Imports	Gross total trade (a+b+c)	Net imports (c—b)	Net total trade (a+e)	Average annual compound growth rate of (f)
Circa 1640	2300	500	2700	5500	2200	4500	
1663/9	3000	900	4000	7900	3100	6100	1·2
1699–1701	4400	2000	5800	12 200	3800	8200	0·9
1722–4	5000	2700	6800	14 500	4100	9100	0·5
1752–4	8400	3500	8200	20 100	4700	13 100	1·3

Sources:

circa 1640   Estimates (or guesses) put together from F. J. Fisher, 'London's
Export Trade in the early seventeenth century', *Econ. Hist. Rev.*,
2nd Ser. III (1950); J. D. Gould, 'Cloth Exports, 1600–40, *Econ.
Hist. Rev.*, 2nd Ser. XXIV (1971); H. Taylor, 'Trade, Neutrality,
and the "English Road", 1630–48', *Econ. Hist. Rev.*, 2nd Ser.
XXV (1972); and R. Davis, *English Overseas Trade 1500–1700*
(London, 1973). The re-export figure for 1640 takes into account
the Dover re-export trade.

1663/9   R. Davis, 'English Foreign Trade, 1660–1700', *Econ. Hist. Rev.*,
2nd Ser. VI (1954). The totals for (a) and (d) are slightly less
than those given by Prof. Davis. Even so the 1663/9 figures may
still be too high, and so may the growth-rate figure of 1·2.

1699–1701
1722–4 and   R. Davis, 'English Foreign Trade, 1700–74', *Econ. Hist. Rev.*,
1752–4   2nd Ser. XV (1962).

those for 1663/9 have better but still insecure foundations;
and although the figures from 1699–1701 onwards are the
most reliable, they have other shortcomings because, for a
number of different reasons, they almost certainly underestimate the true value of England's overseas commerce.
They are derived directly from the official Customs valuations and are *not* comparable with the adjusted figures used
in Fig. 7 (see below, page 136). They are, however, roughly
comparable with the data for the earlier years.

Bearing in mind these reservations, what deductions may
be drawn from these figures? So far from being stagnant,
English overseas commercial activities may have at least
trebled in value between the mid-seventeenth and mid-
eighteenth centuries. It is possible that more rapid growth
occurred between 1640 and 1700 than between 1700 and
1750 (though the nature of the earlier figures makes this
difficult to prove; and the adjusted data as used in Fig. 7
show a slightly higher rate of growth for 1700–50 than is
evident from Table 11). Over the whole period, re-exports
were growing faster than any other variable. Less immediately obvious but equally important is that after the turn of
the century the growth in re-exports slackened markedly and
domestic exports took over as the quick grower, nearly doubling in the first half of the eighteenth century. To understand
these trends it is necessary to examine in more detail the
areas of trade and the goods which were traded. Before doing
so, however, some effort must be made to fill in the gaps
between these snapshots, to chart, however imperfectly, the
course of change.

A rough indication of total activity and fluctuations therein can be obtained from the gross receipts of Customs duties,
during periods when either the rates of duty were not significantly changed or when additional duties can be separated
and deducted. Surviving figures for 1643–58 show a markedly
rising trend, evident through a sharp drop in 1648 and a
strongly buoyant recovery during the years 1652–5. Although
there were some increases in rates they could hardly have
accounted for all this upward movement. They confirm the
tendency indicated in the high growth rate in Table 11,

without necessarily supporting a precise figure, and suggest that the civil wars and Interregnum had no enduring and damaging effect on English overseas commerce as a whole. From 1660 to 1671 the Customs were farmed out and there were significant changes in duties. The only clear indications that survive confirm the predictable sharp drop in activity in 1665–7 associated with the war, plague, and the Fire of London. From 1672 to 1688, after the abandonment of Customs farming, another series giving the gross value of the main duties again exhibits a strong upward trend, especially after 1674. These figures, indeed, support what is known from other sources to suggest that English trade and shipping underwent a substantial boom in the years after the third Anglo-Dutch war: another example of England's commercial activity prospering while Holland was engaged in war. The troubled years of war against France, from 1689 to 1697, encompassed some sharp cutbacks in the country's foreign trade, with losses of shipping by naval warfare and privateering. Yet there was an underlying buoyancy, a potential for expansion, which manifested itself in an inter-war boom, evident in the figures for 1699–1701. The return of war from 1702 to 1713 did not bring commercial depression but it seems to have postponed the revival of expansion until more settled times.

From the turn of the century, however, the availability of continuous trade statistics permits a more careful look at the course of change. In Fig. 7 are plotted the recorded components of English overseas trade for the last half-century or so of our period. Imports have here been valued c.i.f. (that is, including the cost of insurance and freight) and not at the notional prime cost as used by the contemporary authorities. An adjustment has also been made to take account of a change in the valuation of woollen exports from 1709. For these two reasons there are some differences from the figures in Table 11.

These statistics have normally been used as the first part of longer series extending into the later eighteenth and nineteenth centuries. In this role they naturally appear as indicators of a slow growth before the explosion of the Industrial

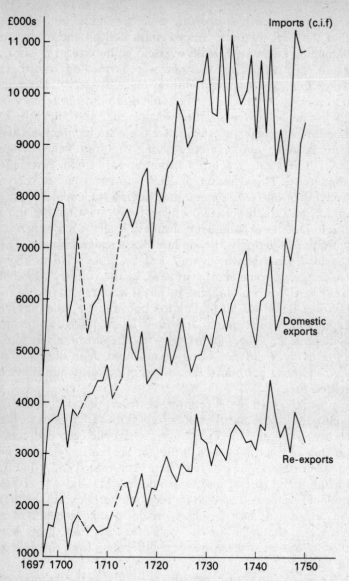

FIG. 7 English foreign trade, 1697–1750 (Imports (c.i.f.), Domestic Exports, and Re-exports).

Source: P. Deane and W. A. Cole, *British Economic Growth, 1688–1959* (Cambridge, 1962).

Revolution. If, however, they are considered in relation to what went before rather than what followed, they take on a different significance. Comparison of Fig. 7 with Fig. 4 shows that whereas cloth exports roughly trebled in the century *circa* 1450–1550, total domestic exports more than doubled in the half-century *circa* 1700–50. Although re-exports slumped during the War of the Spanish Succession, after their rapid growth in the seventeenth century, the continuing expansion of domestic exports, again evident from the 1640s, gathered momentum during the whole of the early eighteenth century. None of these figures takes into account various sources of earnings of which the net effect was almost certainly to provide an increasing flow of gains to the country over this period. Such gains included any net remittances from the slave trade between Africa and America (that is, in addition to what came in as sugar or tobacco); from the trade in fish between Newfoundland and southern Europe; from sundry branches of inter-colonial trade; and the earnings of shipping, freighting and marine insurance which markedly increased as Dutch dominance in those areas lessened. In brief, the century from 1650 to 1750 was one of considerable English mercantile advance to which the available statistics provide only partial testimony. It was certainly not so rapid as the growth after 1750; but the upward trend was sustained despite the many periods of war in which the nations of Europe engaged; and at the end of it England's trade had been transformed.

The advance had certain important characteristics. First, it was largely extra-European in origin. For all that has been so glowingly written about the expansion of Europe in the sixteenth century, it was during this 1650–1750 period that England began to reap the benefits of expansion. Second, it was an 'import-led' advance, that is, its impetus came from a surge of imports, from America and Asia. These two features are exhibited in their simplest statistical outline in Table 12. This sort of analysis can be taken a stage further by examining where English exports and re-exports went. Table 13 does so, and again brings out two clear characteristics, namely, the continuing importance of Europe as a market

TABLE 12

Sources of imports, 1622–1752–4

(Percentages by value)

	N. and NW. Europe	S. Europe and Mediterranean	America	Asia	
1622 (London only)	63	31		6	100
1663/9 (London only)	45	31		24	100
1699–1701 (England and Wales)	41	27	19	13	100
1752–4 (England and Wales)	35	19	33	13	100

Source: Calculated from the figures in R. Davis, *English Overseas Trade, 1500–1700* and 'English Foreign Trade, 1700–74', loc. cit.

for re-exports, despite its long-term decline as a market for domestic exports; and the notable increase in the importance of America as a market for both re-exports and, particularly, for exports of domestic produce. Here, at last, was the true 'new market' for English manufactures, though we must be careful at this point not to jump to the conclusion that the opening up of this captive American market was somehow a direct 'cause' of England's Industrial Revolution. Nothing of the sort can be deduced from these data for, despite the rapid growth of an overseas market thus revealed, they do

TABLE 13

Destinations of exports and re-exports 1663/9–1752–4

(Percentages by value)

	Exports				
	N. and NW. Europe	S. Europe and Mediterranean	America	Asia	
1663/9 (London only)	43	48		9	100
1699–1701 (England and Wales)	52	33	12	3	100
1752–4 (England and Wales)	38	34	20	8	100
	Re-exports				
1699–1700 (England and Wales)	72	11	16	1	100
1752–4 (England and Wales)	72	8	18	2	100

Source: Calculated from the figures in R. Davis, 'English Foreign Trade, 1660–1700', loc. cit and 'English Foreign Trade, 1700–74', loc. cit.

not in themselves say anything about the relation of that market to the growth and size of home demand. The consequences for the English economy of this transatlantic expansion made themselves felt in a more complex and indirect fashion.

A further step in the analysis may be made by examining the change or continuity in the goods featuring in this process of English overseas trade. The fall in the relative importance of woollen textiles in the exports of English produce appears very clearly in the figures of Table 14. The absolute value of woollens and worsteds continued to increase; but their share of the total—recalling that it had been around 80 per cent in the mid-sixteenth and early seventeenth centuries —evidently fell most rapidly after 1700.

TABLE 14

Commodity structure of domestic exports 1663/9–1752–4
(Percentages by value)

	Wool textiles	Other manufactures	Food-stuffs	Raw materials	
1663/9 (London only)	74	11	3	12	100
1699–1701 (England and Wales)	69	12	11	8	100
1752–4 (England and Wales)	47	29	17	7	100

Source: As in Table 13.

The corollary of this trend, and that of the falling share of raw material exports—despite the increasing value of coal, tin, and lead shipped abroad—was the marked rise in the exports of other manufactures and of foodstuffs. The basis of the latter has already been examined (above, pages 117–22); it was, as we know, to prove temporary. The growing export of other manufactures, however, points not only to the future Industrial Revolution but also to the more diverse manufacturing base of the economy which was developing during the century from 1650 to 1750. The same tendency can also be inferred from the equivalent analysis of the import trade in Table 15, showing as it does the continuously declining trend in the imports of manufactures (textiles and others), to a mere 22 per cent in the 1750s. Nevertheless, this table also reveals the continuing importance of textiles and of textile raw materials in the country's total overseas trade. Behind

TABLE 15

Commodity structure of imports, 1622–1752–4

(Percentages by value)

	Textiles	Textile raw materials	Other manu-factures	Other raw materials	Sugar and tobacco	Other food and drink	
1622 (London only)	41	14	4	15	2	24	100
1663/9 (London only)	32	17	5	18	10	18	100
1699–1701 (England and Wales)	25	21	5	14	15	20	100
1752–4 (England and Wales)	21	23	1	13	23	19	100

Source: As in Tables 12 and 13.

the aggregates lay the growth in the imports of raw silk, linen yarn, and raw cotton (still small in quantity compared with later imports); the disappearance of (legal) wool exports; and the inflow of Indian cottons, mainly for re-export, but also encouraging domestic imitations, thus helping to develop a more diversified structure of English textile manufacture. Even in absolute terms, imports of manufactured wares fell in value in the first half of the eighteenth century; but despite their falling share of the total, those of raw materials, both for textiles and for other industrial purposes, rose. These were the trading trends which bore witness to England's wider and more varied development as a manufacturing nation in the century before the Industrial Revolution and in the century after woollens had been so much in the forefront that little else was visible. The other great change in imports was provided by the rising inflow of sugar, tobacco and tea, some of it for home consumption, some for re-export. As mentioned earlier (above, page 118) their volume increased many-fold between the 1660s and the 1750s; along with Asiatic products they provided the commodity bases of London's emergent role as an entrepôt, so evident in this period.

The consequences of these developments were manifested in a drastic altering of the common sixteenth- and early-seventeenth-century pattern of commodity exchange, which had taken the form of a swap of woollen cloth against other manufactures or necessary foodstuffs. The ancient trade with the ports of the Baltic and Russia, for example, had chiefly comprised the exchange of old draperies against agricultural products, namely, grain (rye from Danzig was vital in bad harvest years in the sixteenth century), hemp, flax and, to lesser extent, potash and timber. By the end of the seventeenth century, however, grain had virtually disappeared from the list and 75 per cent by value of direct imports from that area consisted of bar iron, hemp, flax, and timber. These imports fed the domestic manufacture, for merchant marine and navy alike, of sailcloth and ropes as well as the shipbuilding industry itself, and helped to meet a rapidly growing demand for iron wares. In both the 1620s and the 1660s, over 90 per cent of English exports to the area were woollens; in the 1750s, however, the share of woollens had dropped to only 40 per cent; re-exports accounted for 25 per cent, foodstuffs and raw materials for 22 per cent, and other manufactures for 12 per cent. The older pattern of trade continued to exist in the commerce with those parts of Germany and the Low Countries which had been the traditional province of the Merchant Adventurers; but by the mid-eighteenth century the biggest market for English woollen textiles in all their forms was to be found in southern Europe —Spain, Portugal, and the Mediterranean lands taking about 50 per cent of such exports. In part this was a product of such trade agreements as the 1703 Methuen treaty with Portugal (see below, page 185); but it also reflected the successful penetration by English merchants into Mediterranean trade, especially that of the western Mediterranean which they conducted from an important base at Leghorn.

The greatest changes were in English extra-European commerce. The astonishing rise of the East India Company's trade meant that, instead of a trickle of spices arriving sporadically in exchange for reluctantly granted exports of bullion, the company's exports by the end of the seventeenth century had an average value of £500,000 a year (of which around 80 per cent was still mainly silver bullion); and these exports were securing import cargoes which accounted for about 14 per cent of total national imports. The prime-cost valuation of the imports was approximately £750,000; but they were sold in London for double that figure. By this time, moreover, 70–80 per cent (by value) of the imports were cotton textiles. In the 1750s exports to Asia were running at over £1 million per year, with bullion still accounting for about 70 per cent; imports had by then become varied in content, the share of cotton textiles having dropped to 37 per cent, to make way for tea and coffee (36 per cent) and raw silk and silk fabrics (17 per cent). The conduct of this sort of trade on this sort of scale demanded a degree of skill, sophistication, and international dealing very different from that necessary for the comparatively simple exchange pattern of the early sixteenth century London-Antwerp axis. It implied the ability to acquire substantial supplies of silver or gold bullion from specialist dealers in London and Amsterdam, or sometimes Cadiz or Hamburg; a knowledge of the changing patterns of demand both in England and in the re-export markets of Europe; an ability to keep a close control of the sources of supply in the East; to participate in trade in Oriental waters; to manoeuvre with suitable skill in eastern, as well as in western, politics. The ultimate basis of the whole business was the development of European tastes for oriental wares (but *not* the converse); the continuance of an Oriental premium on silver; and the sustained ability of the West to make that silver travel from central America via the Atlantic and Spain or via the Philippines and the Pacific. It was all very different from the commercial world of 1450.

So too was the other multilateral complex—that linking West Africa, the Caribbean islands, North America, and the British Isles, including Ireland. Some estimates of the population of the English colonial settlements in the American continent are given in Table 16. Such numbers cannot readily be translated into a quantified net increase in demand for English goods, but at least they serve to give an impression of the formidable advance in this transatlantic colonial market.

To reap the profits of European expansion, the English needed to catch up with the achievements of Spaniards,

TABLE 16

Estimated population of British North America, 1640s–1770s
(000s)

	circa 1640	1660	circa 1700	1713	1770s
Mainland colonies					
Black			?25		331
White			?225–275		2176
Total	28		?250–300		2507
West Indies					
Black		22·5		130	362
White		33		32	47
Total	20	55·5		162	409
Grand total	48				2916

Sources: Richard S. Dunn, *Sugar and Slaves* (London, 1973); J. Potter, 'The Growth of Population in America, 1700–1860', in D. V. Glass and D. E. C. Eversley (eds), *Population in History* (London, 1960); R. Davis, *The Rise of the Atlantic Economies* (London, 1973).

Dutchmen, and others who had gone before. This was done. Sugar, tobacco, or cotton was cultivated and African slave labour imported to run the plantations. In the 1670s after sundry false starts, English merchants began to get an effective grip on the slave trade, hitherto dominated by Portugal, Spain, and Holland; and extended this in 1713 by securing the formal right (*Asiento*) to supply slaves to the Spanish colonies. Africans, slave or free, provided a market for lighter fabrics, cottons, or cotton-linens, imported from India or imitated in Lancashire and shipped to West Africa. The sugar plantations gobbled up large numbers of slaves; the tobacco and cotton plantations of the southern mainland following along in the eighteenth century, though neither area imported so many as Brazil. The slave trade was stimulated by African rulers or Arab dealers and carried on by all Europeans who could get into it. Slavery was in no way peculiar to capitalism; nor was the slave trade itself peculiarly profitable. But the results, as Davenant observed in 1698, were vital for the sugar plantations:

the labour of these slaves is the principal foundation of our riches there; upon which account we should take all probable measures to bring them to us on easy terms. [2]

Whatever the profits of the odious slave trade may have contributed to the Industrial Revolution, whatever the fortunes amassed by big sugar planters, it is at least reasonably certain that without the slave trade and without the competition thereby induced between Brazilian, English, and French slave-grown sugar, English consumers, workers and rulers alike, would not have got so much cheap sugar as and when they did (see above, page 118, for quantities retained). And without the trade and shipping which brought in the sugar from the West and the tea from the East, they would not have developed so soon that taste for sweet tea which was so to horrify William Cobbett half a century later and is still with us today.

Meanwhile, the living needs for this rapidly growing population, black and white, had to be met. Income was being generated, from Jamaica to Newfoundland, and not all the demands that it represented could yet be supplied by the vigorous New Englanders. Then, too, there was New Spain: by 1700 the Spanish empire of central and southern America had a population of about 4 million. So, legally or illegally, there were profits to be made there, if only as an offshoot of trade to the West Indies. In 1699–1701 America took 13 per cent of all English exports of domestic manufactures; in 1752–4 the share had risen to 25 per cent, by which time 50 per cent of all manufactures other than woollens were going across the Atlantic, 37 per cent of all re-exported manufactures, and 90 per cent of re-exported linens. London continued to dominate both the transatlantic and the African trades, as its merchant vessels sailed along increasingly complex trading routes. Indeed, around 1700 London was still overwhelmingly the centre for trade and finance, for wealth and fashion. The biggest fortunes were made there; the

wealth of London businessmen still far exceeded that of provincial counterparts. But its *relative* importance was gradually
declining as the ports of the western seabord seized the vast
new opportunities thus opened up. Without these newly
expanding branches of commerce, especially that to America,
the fairly slow growth of Bristol would probably have been
slower, and the extremely rapid growth of Liverpool, Whitehaven, and Glasgow could hardly have taken place at all.
All these western ports enlarged their transatlantic activities
as a logical extension of their existing engagement in trade
with Ireland. Used to shipping manufactured goods, coal, or
salt to Ireland and bringing back linen yarn or foodstuffs,
their merchants moved into the transatlantic ventures, pick-
ing up salted beef and other provisions as part of their cargoes
for the Plantations and bringing back sugar, tobacco, or
cotton, which were then distributed coastwise to lesser ports
and creeks, or inland to other parts of the country. In such
ways did the country's new scale of involvement in trade
with the New World in this period help to break down the
isolation of the North-West and thereby contribute towards
the integration of the English economy.

(iii)

These changes were only particular examples of a range of
stimuli to the whole internal economy which commercial
expansion engendered. The already vigorous coastwise trade
not only grew in volume but became more diverse in its
cargoes. Tobacco and sugar from the West, tea and calicoes
from the East, Mediterranean groceries and Scandinavian
iron: a widening range of such products was redistributed
around the coasts from the main importing centres. Sundry
schemes for river improvement flowered to such an extent
that between 1660 and 1750 some 40 rivers were the subject
of new Acts to better their navigability. Such developments
derived momentum not just from overseas trade but from
industrial progress, and it is noticeable that after the 1690s
many of the new schemes related to midland and northern
rivers. The aggregate totals of private Acts passed for river

navigation, for harbour improvements, and to establish turnpike trusts for roads, can provide an index of the growing
investment and enterprise in the internal economy. In 30-
year periods the totals were:[3]

1660–89:   15
1690–1719: 59
1720–49:   130

Just as more goods moved more frequently along the country's water trading routes, so did more people and more
goods move along the country's roads. Some roads remained
badly surfaced, to await the attention of a later generation of
road builders; others were improved. Along them all passed
an increasing number of coaches and wagons as well as the
traditional pack-horses. Numerous carrier services were
advertised in contemporary guides, most of them converg-
ing upon or radiating from London. Such signs of change
did not everywhere arouse enthusiasm. During the post-
Restoration decades some traditionalists were soon busy
attacking the spread of stage coaches; bewailing what they
saw as the too frequent disappearance of gentlemen from
their country seats to sample the joys of London life and
London spending; deploring the growing profusion of hawk-
ers, pedlars, and those antecedents of 'commercial travellers'
whom contemporaries called 'Manchester men'; and snarling
at the shops and shopkeepers blossoming in many a small
town or even in villages. As people and things moved more,
so did information. The ancient dependence on the pulpit
as the broadcasting service of Tudor and early Stuart England was lessened as cheaper paper and printing facilitated
the spread of the newspaper, first in London and then, during
the first half of the eighteenth century, in various provincial
towns. This in turn brought with it the first surge of commercial advertising, thus further aiding the internal market.

Commercial expansion had other sorts of consequences: a
growth in the size of the mercantile marine, increasing
sophistication in the conduct and finance of commerce, and a
stimulus to the development of banking and insurance. More
and more of the country's trade was carried in English ships.
Total tonnage is estimated to have jumped from 115,000 in

1629 to 340,000 in the booming trade years of the 1680s and then to around 450,000 by 1750. London began to catch up Amsterdam in the finance of international trade, in the provision of shipping and freight services, and in marine insurance. As the simpler patterns of trade gave way to more complex trading, so did the mechanism of international payments evolve into an elaborate system of multilateral settlements. Such a multilateral system was in full swing by the end of the seventeenth century; bills of exchange, familiar in medieval commerce but much simplified in form, circulated throughout most of the European system and were readily discountable in London by a newly emergent group of bankers and other financial intermediaries.

Banking in England took a remarkable step forward in this period: yet another example of catching up with the better continental European practices. Before 1650 there were no English banks or bankers; what appeared thereafter were not copies of Italian or Dutch examples but home-grown variants, suited to domestic conditions. In the 1690s about 40 private banks were in existence, all in London; after the first flush of enthusiasm numbers fell to about 30 in the mid-eighteenth century. By that time they fell into two clear groups: those in the West End of London, catering for the aristocracy and gentry; and those in the City, dealing mainly with merchants and businessmen. They had evolved, not as might be supposed from the enterprise of merchants themselves, but from the work of such other intermediaries as brokers, scriveners, and goldsmiths. Their arrival owed something to the needs of State finance; that of the Bank of England owed everything to those needs (see below, pages 192–3). Their justification, however, lay in the vigorous extension of commercial activity, internally and externally; and in the very evident fact that rapidly accumulating funds needed some new institutional forms for deposit and transfer. So, from the 1650s onwards, a growing number of London merchants, financiers, and businessmen of one sort or another, as well as government officials handling monetary transactions, came to have accounts with the London bankers. Bills were discounted, cheques issued and drawn, deposit and current accounts maintained, bullion dealt in, and transfers made. The country banks, ministering to the needs of provincial trade, agriculture, and industry came later. They were set up by local traders, brewers, chandlers, iron-masters, or corn dealers. Nottingham and Bristol were amongst the earliest country towns to have banks, but even by 1750 there were not more than a dozen or so outside London.

Meanwhile, the organizational structure was also changing to meet the new shape of commerce. The earlier creation of a network of trading companies represented, it has been argued, the products of a deal between merchants and the State, seen as commending itself to both parties in specific historical circumstances (above, pages 58–60). In the final century of our period, most of these politico-commercial fruits withered; some new ones appeared, though their lives were usually brief; and one remarkable specimen grew to astonishing size.

Two of the new creations can immediately be put aside in this context. The South Sea Company (1711) had hardly anything to do with trade but a great deal to do with government finance (see below, page 194). The New East India Company (1698) represented the familiar technique of offering a group of merchants a favour in exchange for a substantial loan. Although it did conduct trade for a few years alongside the existing company—thereby providing the pretext for the publication in 1701 of a remarkable econo-mic tract on the merits of competition (*Some Considerations on the East India Trade*)—its real significance again belongs more to the political history of public finance. In contrast, the Hudson's Bay Company, formed in 1670 to pursue the Cana-dian fur trade in competition with the French, owed nothing to public finance; it had its privileges confirmed in 1690; it survived attacks on it in 1749; and it uniquely continues in business today. The Royal African Company of 1672 was the last to be chartered and the first to be successful in various efforts to establish English trade in competition with the Dutch on the West Coast of Africa. It succeeded, with royal support, in building forts, warding off Dutch attacks, and

getting a foot in the slave trade. But interloping merchants
also moved in, and the company's monopoly was ended,
partly in 1698 and wholly in 1712. Charles II granted new
charters to various companies; and the attack on corporate
trading monopolies—usually an amalgam of economic and
political rivalries—gathered force in the 1670s and '80s. It
secured a general victory with an Act of 1689 which permitted anyone to export cloth anywhere. Although a saving
clause exempted the monopolies of the Levant, Eastland,
Russia, and African companies, a breach of principle had
been made, sweeping away the ancient privileges of the
Merchant Adventurers (by this time generally known as the
Hamburg Company). In time, though only occasionally for
reasons of principle, the breach was widened. The Eastland
Company's saving clause in 1689 did not mean much because
it had already lost virtually all of its monopoly rights in 1673;
the Russia Company, which lost its privileges in Russia at the
time of the Civil War, effectively petered out in the 1690s;
the Levant Company's monopoly survived, its declining
trade finally being thrown open in 1754. The plantation
companies had performed the initial function of settlement
and had long ceased to control trade. So by *circa* 1700, it can
be said that most English foreign trade was open to all
comers, to merchants operating singly or in partnership,
raising capital for their trading voyages, chartering and
lading ships according to their personal assessment of profitability.

It all sounds like free trade; but only in a limited sense was
it so. There were two big limitations. One was an immense
apparatus of tariffs, navigation laws, and commercial treaties. If the fruits of the old deal, in the shape of the companies,
had largely withered, these were the chief forms of the new
deal. They belong to the realm of economic policy and will
be considered in Chapter 10. The other great exception
which spoils the vision of free trade was the East India
Company. In the 1650s, its trade was virtually open to all
comers; and some syndicates of London merchants did well
out of it. In 1657 subscriptions to a new 'General Stock' were
opened and the remarkable sum of £740,000 was subscribed;

only half of it was called up. After the Restoration, the company's monopolistic privileges were sustained and new charters tranted. In a period of great prosperity and expansion from 1658 to 1689 the East India Co. paid an annual average dividend of over 20 per cent (as well as paying a 100 per cent share bonus in 1682). Despite great difficulties in the 1690s, economic and political, at home and in India, it weathered the storms and survived, fusing with the New Company to form the United East India Company in 1708 with a capital of over £3 million. It survived because the circumstances of trade for Europeans in the East were still sufficiently unlike those which they encountered elsewhere that it was possible to sustain a case for monopoly—which favoured those inside it, annoyed those outside it, and gave nourishment to corruption—on grounds of politico-economic expediency. Further expansion of trade and extension of political power made it not only by far the biggest business corporation in the England of its day, but the foundation of future British rule in India.

9

Industrial Change, 1650–1750

(i)

In industry, as in agriculture, the dominating long-run
influence of this period was the combination of a mildly
downward trend in selling prices, and a mildly upward
trend in both real wages and market demand. Many producers found themselves, from time to time, in a cost-price
squeeze, and reacted to it in various interesting and significant ways. Meanwhile, shifts in fashion and taste, changes in
the patterns of overseas trade, mounting competition in
some traditional European markets, and growing urbanization in England all helped both to stimulate newer industries
and bring uncongenial pressures on those making the older
products. So the historian of industry is often faced with
seemingly contradictory evidence, of enterprise and compla-
cency, of growth and stagnation. But the long-term message
is clear: this was an age of investment and enterprise in
English industry, not manifest in any spectacular changes as
in the succeeding century, but vitally important in providing
the stronger and more flexible bases from which that later
revolution could be launched.

Perhaps the most striking feature of this century is the
appearance in manufacturing and mining of a number of
inventions, some of which became practical innovations,
designed to solve specific economic and technical problems.
Some of the innovations were still simply imports of superior
continental practices in much the same way as had happened
earlier. Examples include the introduction of the power-
driven silk-throwing machine, patented by Thomas Lombe
in 1719. His erection of a mill using it on the river Derwent,

near Derby, has been claimed as the début of the water-powered textile factory of the Industrial Revolution. In fact similar throwing mills had long been at work in Italy; his mill was not an unqualified success; and a predecessor of 1702, in the same place and using Dutch silk-throwing engines, failed. But the innovation stimulated an interest in reducing costs in silk-throwing, especially after the patent expired in 1732. By the mid-century a number of similar mills were being established; and, as in other industrial developments they were to be found in the Midlands and the North-West. The paper industry saw a number of attempts to improve the machinery used for pulping the linen rags which were then its prime raw material; and in particular to introduce the engine known, with obvious significance, as a 'Hollander'. This importation from continental practice seems to have arrived some time in the 1730s or '40s. Thereafter its use became much more common and may reasonably be thought to have brought with it the greater productivity evident in the industry from about this time.

Such examples of England continuing the catching-up process could be multiplied and some will be mentioned in other contexts. Some contemporaries even believed that the habit of borrowing and improving, rather than inventing, was so common as to be a national trait. Home-grown inventions and innovations happened, nonetheless. The use of coal was extended, for example, into malting and brick-making, and took on much greater significance with its successful introduction into lead- and tin-smelting in the late seventeenth and early eighteenth centuries; with Benjamin Huntsman's invention of the coke-fired crucible process of steel-making in the 1740s; and with Abraham Darby's experiments with the use of coked coal in iron smelting in about 1709. Although Thomas Savery's atmospheric engine, precursor of the steam engine, owed something to experimental work done in Paris and London, both he and the more successful Thomas Newcomen were setting out to solve a practical problem, the mounting costs of mine drainage as mines deepened. As a Swedish visitor who came to England in 1716 and helped Newcomen erect one of his engines, observed:

. . . a man from Dartmouth named Thomas Newcomen, without any knowledge whatever of the speculations of Captain Savery, had . . . made up his mind . . . to invent a fire-machine for drawing water from the mines. He was induced to undertake this by considering the heavy costs of lifting water by means of horses [i.e. horse-turned windlasses] which Mr. Newcomen found existing in the English tin-mines [which he] often visited in the capacity of a dealer in iron tools . . .[1]

Here, if the commentator is to be believed, is testimony to a home-grown invention proceeding from an economic problem. It was indeed fairly rapidly translated into innovations, for Newcomen-type atmospheric engines were coming into general use from the 1720s and 30s onwards in coal, tin, and other mines, especially the deeper coal mines in northern England.

Not all invention or innovation was as simply attributable to the pressure of costs and prices. Dud Dudley and others had interested themselves in the possibility of cutting the high cost of charcoal in the iron-smelting industry at various times in the seventeenth century, but there is no particular reason to suppose that Abraham Darby's success was the outcome of a deliberate search to this end. He took out a patent in 1707 for a particular way of casting iron pots. It was quite unconnected with the use of coal as a fuel in smelting. Later, after taking over a furnace and forge at Coalbrookdale, in Shropshire, he experimented successfully with the production of cast pots and similar utensils using iron smelted with coked coal; and unsuccessfully in efforts to produce commercial pig-iron by the same means. For long after his death in 1717, charcoal continued to be the main fuel in the iron industry, and coal was only very gradually coming into use by the end of our period. As in other industries, effective and widespread innovation waited until economic circumstances were propitious or needs more pressing. Sometimes the vital invention had a specific end in view; sometimes it owed far more to the particular curiosity, adventurousness, technical interest, or enterprise of one man.

Direct or indirect in its motivation, the increasing trend towards industrial innovation was more marked than it had

been in the preceding century of rapidly expanding population and therefore of easy labour supply. Patents are a poor
guide to invention because many crucial discoveries were
never thus registered (nobody patented convertible husbandry); and many gains in productivity came not from
single, once-and-for-all innovations but from an accumulation of minor changes, also outside the formal records. Still,
the records survive and are not to be wholly despised. This is
what they show, by decades:

TABLE 17
English patents sealed, 1610–1759

1610–19	15	1680–9	53
1620–9	33	1690–9	102
1630–9	75	1700–9	22
1640–9	4	1710–19	38
1650–9	—	1720–9	89
1660–9	31	1730–9	56
1670–9	50	1740–9	82
		1750–9	92

Source: B. R. Mitchell and P. Deane, *Abstract of British Historical Statistics*
(Cambridge, 1962).

Early patent specifications are exceedingly vague and in
many cases there is no real proof of any original invention
underlying the grant. Patents were (and still are) potential
money-spinners, because of the monopoly rights they confer.
Those of late Tudor and early Stuart times are notorious
because of their linkage with Crown grants to 'projectors'
and Court favourites, as devices for raising money. So the
high figures for the 1620s and 30s are better indicators,
albeit indirect, of the corruption and financial difficulties of
the Stuarts than of inventive activity. The slump in numbers
in 1640–59 may or may not testify to a slump in real inventive
activity; it is just as likely to be an administrative product of
the Crown's interregnum, as the revival in the 1660s was of
its restoration. The grants of the 1690s bear witness to a burst
of speculative enthusiasm which saw a substantial diversion
of funds away from trade and shipping (in difficulties during
the war) to a flood of dubious joint-stock companies many of
them floated on a sea of questionable patents (see below, pages

169–71). Nevertheless many of the post-Restoration patents testify to a genuine increase in inventive ideas; and to an interest in their application to industrial and commercial activity, sometimes specifically with the intent of lowering costs and increasing productivity. Compared with the upsurge after the mid-eighteenth century (there were 647 in the 1790s) the totals are small, but they are not pointers to a stagnant economy.

As the cost-price squeeze began to take effect, even the textile industry—so long dependent for its advance upon imitation, adaptation, mutation, and a plentiful supply of cheap labour—began to take cognizance of its changing economic position and to look to its main manufacturing processes. There is some evidence here and there, of minor, unspectacular advances: in about 1680, for example, a Wiltshire clothier said that spinning had so improved over the preceding 40 years that 1 lb of wool made twice as much cloth as before the Civil War. Some of its innovations were more radical; and—like Lombe's silk-throwing mill, already mentioned—came in from overseas. The Dutch small-wares loom or 'engine loom' (despite its name it was not originally power-driven) substantially increased productivity in the weaving of ribbons, tapes, and the like. It had caused trouble when introduced into London by immigrants in the early seventeenth century because it was seen as a threat to employment. In the 1660s, however, it was being adopted in the expanding textile town of Manchester, a focal point of enterprise and change in textiles; in 1750 the town had 1500 such looms, and experiments were being made with waterpower. What was to prove one of the most important technical innovations of the Industrial Revolution, power-spinning, also had its origins in this period, again in the Midlands and North-West. In 1673 and in 1723 two patents, vague in wording and unfruitful in practice, had been granted for devices designed to improve the output of spun textile yarns. A patent granted in 1738, to Lewis Paul, acquires significance in retrospect because it embodied the technique of spinning used in the machinery of Richard Arkwright's celebrated cotton spinning mills of a later era. The machine

which Paul and his partner, John Wyatt, brought into being
was intended to spin wool: so far as it is known, however, it
never did, and in its brief and obscure life in the 1740s spun
only cotton. The celebrated 'flying shuttle', patented in 1733
by John Kay, a maker of reeds for looms and a Lancastrian
by birth, met with a mixed reception, sometimes being
attacked as in the Essex bay-making industry, sometimes
being pirated, as in the woollen-weaving area of Lancashire.
But its spread in any textile area, woollen or cotton, remained
slow in our period.

In brief, English industry in the century from 1650 to 1750
can exhibit a variety of innovations, some of a radical nature
in that they represented injections of capital equipment which
had the effect of raising productivity. Some involved a new
use of power-driven machinery or opened up new possibilities
therein, for example, in silk-throwing or cotton-spinning;
some saw a replacement of one important input in the production process by another, for example, coal for charcoal,
steam and atmospheric pressure for horse- or man-power.
Such changes are antithetical to the pre-industrialized economy and *by definition* (see above, pages 1–3) must herald its
close. Contemporaries, of course, did not see it like that. It is
only by taking an economist's-eye view of the past that we do.
The historian, however, may reasonably draw conclusions
from the very appearance of these symptoms on a widening
front and in a number of different branches of industry. He
may see them as a sign that men were increasingly coming to
regard such innovations as likely methods of solving economic
problems. He may note, too, that they were to be found in
the particular context of a burgeoning interest in science and
technology and its application to economic problems; and of
a slackening enthusiasm for the delights of religious conflict
and the fascinations of irrationality. He must heed other
possible influences, such as the immigration of aliens—
especially the Huguenots, before and after the revocation of
the Edict of Nantes in 1685—who brought to this country
important increments of industrial knowledge as well as
capital, credit, and enterprise; and, quite differently, the
possible influence of State action, arising, intentionally or un-

intentionally, directly or indirectly, from the demands of war, the incidence of taxation, the building of a tariff wall, and the construction of various acts of economic policy (see below, Chapter 10). He must take cognizance of these things, but he will be brave to the point of bravado if he supposes that they can all be assigned quantifiable weights in an explanation, capable of prediction, which will tell him precisely why these changes were taking place in England at this time.

Although contemporaries could not see all that these signals portended, some at least showed themselves aware of what was happening. Here is John Cary, merchant of Bristol, writing in 1695:

The refiners of sugars lately sold for sixpence per pound what yielded twenty years since twelve pence; the distillers sell their spirits for one third part of what they formerly did; glass bottles, silk stockings, and other manufactures (too many to be enumerated) are sold for half the prices they were a few years since, without falling [i.e. lowering] the labour of the poor.

How, he went on to ask, was it done? He answered:

. . . it proceeds from the ingenuity of the manufacturer, and the improvements he makes in his ways of working: thus the refiner of sugars goes through that operation in a month, which our forefathers required four months to effect; thus the distillers draw more spirits, and in less time . . . than those formerly did who taught them the art. The glass maker hath found a quicker way of making it out of things which cost him little or nothing. Silk stockings are wove instead of knit. Tobacco is cut by engines instead of knives. Books are printed instead of written. Deal boards are sawn with a mill instead of men's labour. Lead is smelted by wind furnaces instead of blowing with bellows; all of which save the labour of many hands, so the wages of those employed need not be lessened. [2]

Here is a classic statement about productivity-increasing investments, lowered prices, and higher real wages. It did not all happen quite so easily and so quickly as Cary supposed; many new schemes proved to be visionary or fraudulent or simply ineffective. Progress was patchy. But it was real and Cary's successors saw it was. Otherwise Josiah Tucker could hardly have written in these terms in his *Instructions to Travellers* of 1757:

Few countries are equal, perhaps none excel, the English in the number of contrivances of their machines to abridge labour.

And, having provided examples, he drew the conclusions that:

The price of goods is thereby prodigiously lowered from what it might otherwise have been; and a much greater number of hands is employed. [3]

It was not just a display of economic patriotism, but a comment mirrored in reality, a reality which was, however, only just beginning to show itself in the indicators of economic quantities which we have to use.

(ii)

The difficulties of continuous measurement over the period 1650–1750, already observed in overseas trade, are even more evident in industry. Although some new sources, especially the returns of excise duties, help to remedy the paucity of information about the volume of production or of home sales, most of these unfortunately do not start until the second decade of the eighteenth century. Although the continuous trade statistics from 1697 provide bases for some tolerable inferences about the course of industrial output, the combination of few trade or production figures for the period 1650–1700 and a *relative* abundance thereafter has had some misleading consequences. Scholars engaged in sketching the prelude to industrialization have very naturally started their studies around 1700 for the good reason that the beginning of the eighteenth century looks like the beginning of useful statistics. Now it is clear that some of the major series for exports of domestic manufactures, imports of raw materials, and excisable production of certain wares show signs of being virtually stagnant from roughly 1710 to roughly 1740. A decade or so later and everything seemingly begins to hum and buzz. As it is these noises which are the real subject matter of the studies which start around 1700, the early eighteenth century and, sometimes by unspoken inference, the later seventeenth century, have come to be presented as an age of industrial immobility, a tranquil era in which nothing much happened, immediately preceding a period in which a great deal happened. This is almost certainly wrong. Very probably, if all the relevant statistics existed, they would show that the latter decades of the seventeenth century were marked by brisk industrial advance; and that this was followed by slower growth in the early eighteenth century, in turn followed by a spurt of renewed activity after about 1745. It is also probable that throughout the whole 1650–1750 period they would show an abnormally rapid process of internal change gathering momentum, that is, of old production lines decaying and new ones taking their place. Because we do not have the pre-1700 data, and because the new flowers only burst into spectacular bloom after 1750, we may too readily be led into supposing that little was happening beneath the surface. To counteract this possibility we have, as usual, to try to combine the quantitative and the non-quantitative.

In most periods of history it is not too difficult to catch the typical sounds of economic distress. The noise of complaint makes itself heard in the records; the silence of contentment does not. In 1669 a House of Lord's committee heard woeful tales about the cloth export to the effect that it was barely a fifth of what it had been forty years earlier; in 1707 there was a general complaint that the woollen manufacture was 'not carried on with the same advantage to this kingdom, as it was formerly'.⁴ The Norwich woollen workers were complaining in 1718, those in Wiltshire in 1737. Some such comments testify to the painful reality of short-term depressions, to slumps in trade induced by harvest failures which cut incomes, or to wars which interrupted exports. To some extent they can be countered by similar literary evidence, which tells an opposite tale. For example, the report on the nation's trade drawn up in 1697 by the newly created Commissioners of Trade and Plantations announced that the woollen manufacture had 'very much increased since . . . 1670' and cheerfully observed that weavers were 'improved in making several useful sorts with great variety'.[5] When we try to detect the economic reality of the textile industry's experience by measurement we cannot here be concerned with short-term fluctuations; it is the longer trends which we must heed. The nearest substitutes for output data are the 'hallage' figures (see above, page 75); textile exports; and the imports of textile raw materials. What do they all suggest?

For a number of technical reasons only limited reliance can be put on the 'hallage' data; they covered woollens and some new draperies, but with the notable exception of those from Norfolk. After 1710 the data became less and less representative as resistance to the compulsory use of the market increased (although it was not formally abolished until 1815). The broad picture revealed by the data is of a rise, punctuated by short-term fluctuations, from a low point around 1690 to a high point in 1707. Taking ten-year averages, the rise for the 60 years from 1645–54 to 1705–14 was 96 per cent. The export figures allow a longer period to be taken, although with these some problems arise from the changing valuations over time. Here are two versions:

TABLE 18

Estimates of woollen textile exports, circa 1640–1750

(£000s)

Period	(a)	(b)
circa 1640*	1621	
1663/9†	2100	
1697–1704‡		2427
1699–1701†	3045	
1720–9‡		3116
1722–4†	2986	
1745–54‡		3823
1752–4†	3930	

Sources: * J. D. Gould, 'Cloth Exports, 1600–40', loc. cit.

† R. Davis, as in Tables 13, 14, and 15. The 1663/9 figure of £2,100,000 is an estimate, obtained by assuming that the ratio of exports from the outports to exports from London in 1663/9 was slightly smaller than it was in 1699–1701, when the detailed breakdown in available.

‡ Deane and Cole, op. cit., pp. 59, 322. These figures are consistent with those used in Fig. 7 and as explained above (p. 135) have been adjusted to allow for a change in the Customs valuations of woollens in 1709. The figures in column (a) therefore form one roughly consistent series, and those in column (b) another, but the two should not be conflated.

Whichever version one chooses, the increase in value is there. According to column (a) it was about 87 per cent over the 1660s figure by the mid-eighteenth century, and with a possibly rather faster rate of growth in the later seventeenth century than in the early eighteenth. Neither the 'hallage' data nor the export figures suggest anything more than a fairly gentle rate of increase overall; certainly nothing like that achieved between 1450 and 1550. Within the aggregates lay variations in the export performance of different sorts of woollen or worsted fabrics. They reflect, for example, the complaints which betoken the slow decline of the Suffolk-Essex border area and of difficulties in Devon. The evidence of change becomes clearer after about the 1720s. Worsted stuffs from Norwich and Yorkshire, flannel from Lancashire, and stockings of Nottinghamshire took over from such old export staples as kerseys, and even from the serges and perpetuanas which had recently been so successful.

The Devonshire serge industry provides a striking example of rise and fall in this period. When Celia Fiennes visited Exeter in 1698 she wrote admiringly in her journal that the industry 'turns the most money in a week of anything in England'[6] (a characteristic piece of contemporary 'quantification'). She had caught the atmosphere of a boom town. Surviving figures show that Exeter's coastwise trade in serges, shipped mainly to London, had multiplied from a few hundred lbs in the 1660s and '70s to well over 1 million lbs in the 1680s and in 1700. Exeter's own export trade, mainly to Holland, had also expanded rapidly so that around the turn of the century it was probably responsible for nearly 50 per cent of the country's total exports of this type of fabric, which in turn accounted for about 20 per cent by value of all woollen exports. But the competition of Norwich, where wages were lower, and Yorkshire, already switching from its decaying kersey trade to the new worsted stuffs, soon began to leave its marks of distress. By the 1740s a correspondent could write of the 'lamentable condition of the woollen trade especially in these parts [between Taunton and Exeter], a thing so universally known that I think it almost needless to crowd a letter with any of my observations upon it'.[7]

The Lancashire linen industry began the process of transformation into its much more famous successor, the Lancashire cotton industry, in this period. It had already made the
acquaintance of cotton by developing the manufacture of
fustian, a fabric with a cotton weft and a linen warp. Cotton
was making further headway in the industry by its use in the
weaving of striped and checked fabrics of mixed cotton and
linen. English-made fustians, cotton-linens, and linens were
almost certainly sold mainly in the home market, for they
could hardly have been able to compete with the better-
quality and cheaper products of their rivals from old-
established linen and cotton centres in continental Europe.
But the whole industry was then given a tremendous jolt by
the very rapid surge of imported Indian calicoes, muslins,
and sundry other exotically-named cotton fabrics which
started to flood into England—and indeed into north-western
Europe generally—in the second half of the seventeenth century. They came as a consequence of the commercial doings
of the East India Companies. Table 19 charts the course of
the flood.

TABLE 19

Imports of textiles from Asia by the East India Co., 1664–1749

Average annual imports in 000 pieces

1664–9	162·5	1704–9	171·2
1674–9	554·6	1714–19	503·0
1684–9	748·8	1724–9	840·1
1694–9	301·5	1734–9	809·7
		1744–9	629·6

Source: Calculated from annual figures kindly made available to me by Dr.
K. N. Chaudhuri from the accounts of the East India Company in the India
Office Library. The great majority of the imports were of pure cottons, though
some were silks or cotton and silk mixtures.

Although the 1720s show the highest annual averages, the
biggest impact was felt in the 1680s when the peak total of
1·7 million pieces arrived in 1684.

This inflow produced a near-revolution in textile fashions.
It also posed the biggest economic threat which the existing
European textile industries had ever experienced. The result
was a lobbying activity which secured protection in various

countries. In England it produced an act in 1701 forbidding the import, save for re-export, of certain types, mainly printed calicoes; and in 1721 a further Act prohibiting the home consumption of all pure cotton prints, though this was modified in 1736 to permit the use of printed fustians. Partly as a consequence of these enactments, it encouraged the re-export trade. And it induced the customary reaction of stimulating attempts to imitate these much-desired fabrics. No very great success was achieved with pure cottons in our period. But a fillip was given to the textile-printing industry, using either plain Indian calicoes before 1720 or home-produced linens or cotton-linens thereafter; to the manufacture of fustians and other cotton-linen mixtures; and to the creation of a new body of experience in cotton textile technology, which was to have its bigger and more famous consequences in the second half of the eighteenth century.

The native silk industry also got a stimulus from events originating outside the English economy. It received the benefit of improved methods brought by immigrant Huguenots from France; it was provided with protection against imported French silks by periodic prohibitions of French imports and then of a high tariff; and it received, as already mentioned, the technical stimulus of the Italian type of silk-throwing mill.

TABLE 20
Imports of textile raw materials, 1663/9–1752–4

	(£000s) 1663/9 (London only)	1699–1701	1752–4
Raw wool	29	200	74
Textile yarns (mainly linen yarn)	83	232	250
Raw and thrown silk	263	346	671
	million lbs		
Retained imports of raw cotton	(1·6)	1·4	3·5

Sources: R. Davis, as in Tables 13, 14, and 15; retained cotton imports: 1663/9 estimates calculated from British Library Add. MSS., 36, 785 assuming that the percentage retained was the same as in 1699–1701; other figures from A. P. Wadsworth and J. de L. Mann, *The Cotton Trade and Industrial Lancashire, 1600–1780* (Manchester, 1931), App. G.

But, as in linen production, it was the home-market which took most of the output of this newly expanding industry.

Some summarized reflection of the course of change in textiles can be seen in Table 20 which presents figures for the imports of textile raw materials.

It was outside textiles, and especially outside the woollen industry, however, that many more notable advances were to be found. Some of the most striking came in the industries engaged in processing agricultural products, either imported or home-produced. The rapid growth in sugar and tobacco imports, and in the output of home-produced beer and, especially, spirits has already been noted in other contexts (above, pages 118–20); it provides some indication of the corresponding rise of the industries based upon them. Sugar refineries and works for preparation and processing tobacco spread in London, Liverpool, and Bristol. Bigger breweries multiplied, particularly in London where also were concentrated the growing number of distillers responsible for that tenfold rise in the output of spirits between the 1680s and 1750s. Though the excise statistics show little or no advance during the first half of the eighteenth century in such manufactures as starch and soap, the paper industry surged forward between approximately 1670 and 1720. During this half-century—when, like silk and linen, it benefited from Huguenot immigrants and protection against French imports —the number of mills probably multiplied about fourfold to reach about 200 by the time that the excise statistics become available. Although they record only a slow rate of advance between 1713 and the mid-century, over the whole period from 1650 to 1750 imports declined and home production rose about sevenfold as well as improving in quality. Another industry supplying more of the wants of a society gradually accumulating wealth was pottery, and not only those branches of the industry making expensive porcelain in London for the rich. In north Staffordshire and particularly the area in and around Burslem, the industry advanced especially rapidly between 1680 and 1750. It dispatched a wide range of products, many of them of the sort to meet a popular demand, to various parts of the country, using both overland transport and the navigable rivers Weaver and Trent; and drew its raw materials from local clay and coal deposits. Here was the early growth of an area which Josiah Wedgwood was later to make famous. But its advance is hard to measure. So too is that of a quite different industry—shipbuilding. Although London was the scene of much shipbuilding to meet the needs of the East India Company for big ships of 500 tons and upwards and, like Chatham and Portsmouth, of the Navy's demands for even bigger vessels, it was probably in provincial ports that much advance took place in this period. Most ships were still small, that is, less than 150–200 tons, and built in small yards all round the coast, with such places as Whitby and Newcastle coming to specialize in colliers and the bigger ships used in the timber and iron trade with the Baltic area.

For mining and metal manufactures some scraps of measurement are possible, though the later seventeenth century, as usual, presents problems. The consumption of lead almost certainly increased for it was used in a wide range of industries which must have expanded during the period. Building, its biggest single customer, gobbled up lead in the building and rebuilding of London, as well as in the new provincial towns and in all those solid country houses; the printing industry used it in type-founding; it went into pewter and lead shot, into paint, pottery, and glass, not to speak of coffins. Estimates of production suggest an increase of about 10 per cent between 1705 and 1755, though rising to 110 per cent if the guesses are taken forward to 1770, revealing thereby a very rapid increase in 1755–70 and/or a wide margin of error. Cornish tin production went up by 63 per cent between 1695–1704 and 1745–54; and copper output in the same county by 38 per cent between 1725–34 and 1745–54.

The iron industry presents clear evidence both of expansion and of increasing productivity, yet also of inability to meet home demand. The estimated 86 blast furnaces at work in England and Wales in the 1650s had fallen to 49 in the 1740s, but meanwhile estimated output had risen from about 23–24,000 tons to around 30–33,000 in 1750, almost all of which was still produced with charcoal. This increase was due substantially to bigger and better furnaces and to the near-elimination of the inefficient working of the low-grade ores of the Wealden area. By the mid-century the industry was largely concentrated in the Midlands, the North-West, and south Wales. It proved impossible, however, to produce enough to meet the bar-iron needs of the rapidly expanding wrought-iron industry. So imports of bar-iron rose rapidly. From the 3,000 tons of the 1630s they grew to 16-18,000 in the 1680s and had reached nearly 30,000 tons in the 1750s. Most of it came from Sweden; some of it was high-grade iron necessary for steel making, but it came in largely because the home industry remained a high-cost producer compared with that of Sweden (and Russia). It did so not so much because of a shortage of charcoal as because of the higher cost in England of the main elements in the price of charcoal delivered to the furnace or forge, that is, labour and transport. The industry was far from wilting under a 'national fuel shortage', though it certainly did encounter localized difficulties in securing adequate supplies of reasonably priced charcoal; as well as such quite different problems as summer shortages of water to operate the water-wheels at the furnaces and forges, a problem which began to be solved at some works in the Midlands by the installation of Newcomen-type engines to pump water back over the dam.

The metal-using end of the industry was meanwhile continuing its expansion in the west Midlands and contributing to the rapid growth of such towns as Walsall, Wednesbury,

TABLE 21
Exports of metal goods, 1663/9-1752-4
(£000s)

		Percentage increase
1663/9 (London only)	44	
(England and Wales) estimate	57	
1699-1701 (England and Wales)	114	100
1752-4 (England and Wales)	587	415

Source: R. Davis, as in Tables 13, 14, and 15. The England and Wales estimate for 1663/9 assumes the same ratio between London and national exports as in 1699-1701.

and Birmingham. From there and from the copper-, tin-, brass-, and lead-using industries came the exports of metal goods which show a substantial increase over the period. The rate of advance shown in Table 21 is impressive, but it must be remembered that even by 1752–4 the total export value of these metal wares was only 15 per cent of that of woollen textiles.

The fuel for the smithies of this incipient 'Black Country' was coal from the coalfields of the west Midlands. Total output undoubtedly increased over the period but by how much it is impossible to say. London's sea-borne imports, virtually all from the Northumberland and Durham fields, rose from an average of 372,000 tons per annum in 1680/1–1686/7 to 701,000 in 1748–52, an increase of 88 per cent which is much less than in the preceding century. But there can be little doubt that total production rose far more than this as the other coalfields, in the Midlands, in Lancashire, Yorkshire, and south Wales, began to be exploited more intensively. Sporadic figures, for example of coastwise trade, cannot be taken as indicative of total trends without embarking upon guess-work more hazardous than useful. This has not, of course, deterred some people from making such guesses; and they include the alternative estimates that total production rose from about $2\frac{1}{4}$ million tons *circa* 1660 to over 6 million in the 1770s or from nearly 3 million in the 1680s to over 10 million in the 1780s. We cannot measure the course of change, but a reasonable inference is that as population and industry grew in areas contiguous to coalfields, for example around Nottingham, Sheffield, and Birmingham, more coal must have been extracted and moved locally by land or navigable river. It has left little or no quantitative traces in the records; but the very activity, already mentioned, in improving the navigability of rivers bears witness to its movement. Certainly, the use was overwhelmingly internal. Although exports—negligible in the mid-seventeenth century—rose to an average value of £51,000 in 1697–1704 and £155,000 in 1752–4, these amounts are still relatively trivial. As coal was increasingly moved about in the internal economy so, because of its high ratio of bulk and weight to value, was it providing an ever more powerful stimulus to improved transport. And it was creating a base for Northern and Midland wealth; contemporary descriptions of Newcastle present that town almost as one of the new wonders of the age.

(iii)

These patterns of industrial change brought with them some corresponding shifts in organization and finance. Again, few were striking or spectacular; but the trend was evident enough, a gradual, piecemeal move towards a greater capital intensity in mining and manufacture.

Because the insertion of new and relatively expensive pieces of capital was most evident in such activities as coal-mining or iron-smelting it is there that one recognizes the symptoms of an industrial capitalism more commonly associated with a later era. The greater depths reached in mining increased alike the risks to human life and the capital needed in the undertaking. By the early eighteenth century some coal mines in the North-East had reached a depth of 400 feet. As a contemporary observed in 1713 'where the seam lies deep you are always attended with vast quantities of water which must be drawn by horses and at a prodigious expense from £500 to £1500 yearly.' Going on to spell out the dangers of fire damp, he admitted that this frequently '. . . does blow up numbers of workmen and consequently where this hazard is run men will have a proportionate addition of price for the working'. [8] The reasons for considering the use of Newcomen-type engines were obvious enough. Such installations and an increasing scale of operations likewise increased the capital intensity of the whole enterprise. In contrast to the large collieries in that area, employing men, women, and children in an elaborate division of labour, many Midland and other shallower mines were worked on a much smaller scale. This contrast in size of operation was also evident in the iron industry. At one end were such men as Ambrose Crowley, whose substantial metal-working factory at Winlaton was an exceptional undertaking for the age and whose fortune, made out of contracting for the navy, moved him and his family smartly up the social scale. So likewise did the Foley family prosper on their control of a substantial part of the Midlands iron industry. This enterprise, organized within three interlocking partnerships of family and friends, financed and ran an iron empire embracing furnaces, forges, slitting mills, and warehouses, stretching from the Forest of Dean to Yorkshire. At the other end of the scale were the small masters, employing one or two men, who were numerous in the cutlery industry of the Sheffield region; and who were to be found interspersed with—and sometimes almost indistinguishable from—the domestic outworkers of the small metalwares industry of the west Midlands.

This range in types of enterprise appears right across the industrial scene. A large number of small units rather than a small number of large units: this was still the characteristic structure of almost all industries in the land despite, of course, a few exceptions. Amongst those exceptions some of the biggest were such State enterprises as the naval dockyards which grew very rapidly during this period. Around the end of the seventeenth century Chatham and Portsmouth yards each employed well over 1,000 men in big centralized works unlike almost anything that private enterprise could offer at the time. Small craftsmen still abounded. Their independence was limited by the power of the market, of dealers who bought their wares, of suppliers who sold them raw materials, and of all who supplied credit. But 'the butcher, the baker, and the candlestick maker' of the nursery rhyme were still individual realities, part neither of a putting-out system nor of a large centralized organization.

One sort of enterprise in industrial organization proved premature. The joint-stock company experienced in this period a boom, a slump, and in 1720, legal restrictions. Between 1660 and 1719 some 54 major joint-stock companies were given charters (as well as numerous lesser, unincorporated companies) as compared with only 19 in the preceding half-century. Of those 54 companies, 23 were for mining or manufacturing, 11 for overseas trade, and the remaining 20 distributed over the fields of banking and finance, water supply, insurance, and fishing. There is a temptation to see this as evidence of a real boom in economic activity. The reality was less attractive. It was the first big performance in England by that familiar and dangerous comedian of the capitalist stage: the company promoter. One decade, the 1690s, saw the flotation of 32 out of the 54 companies, and 23 of those were in the five years 1691–5. It was precisely at this time that there also arrived the host of lesser companies which never received charters. It is estimated that in 1695 some 93 joint-stock companies, incorporated and unincorporated, existed in England, as well as another 47 in Scotland. A vigorous and highly speculative market in stocks and shares flowered in the City; thunders of disapproval rumbled against the 'pernicious art of stock-jobbing'; and the boom burst in 1697–8. By 1717 there were about 21 companies left in England. Only one of them could be described (question-ably) as concerned with manufacturing and three with mining. The repetition of a speculative boom in the South Sea Company episode of 1720 (see below, page 194) brought the Bubble Act which inhibited the flotation of further such companies.

From this whole sequence of events between 1660 and 1719 two conclusions may be drawn. First, there was no real need in industry for the apparatus of the joint-stock company. Normally, the fixed capital needs of most industry simply did not require this pattern of organization. What was valuable for long-distance foreign trade or for the finance of such undertakings as water supply or insurance, where the return on capital was slow or risks needed to be spread, was still irrelevant to most manufacturing. It had some relevance to mining but even there, as in the iron industry, the unincor-porated partnership with its strong personal linkages, a social as well as a business nexus, proved adequate and effective, and continued to do so well into the nineteenth century. Second, it demonstrated that there was no shortage of capital funds, no lack of enterprise in seeking ways to use them. The 1691–5 boom was overwhelmingly in domestic projects whilst overseas trade was disrupted by war. A contemporary, John Houghton, put the sequence clearly in 1694:

. . . a great many stocks have arisen since this war with France; for trade being obstructed at sea, few that have money were willing it should lie idle, and a great many that wanted employments studied how to dispose of their money, that they might be able to command whensoever they had occasion, which they found they could more easily do in joint-stocks, than in laying out the same in lands, houses or commodities, these being more easily shifted from hand to hand.[9]

This was not an economy without an investable surplus nor without a willingness, indeed eagerness, to look for investment outlets.

Notwithstanding these developments, the structure of the putting-out system remained strong despite the slackening in population and the rise in real wages. Its shrinkage in the older, southern areas of woollen textile manufacture left problems of poverty and unemployment. Unless alternative jobs developed the gains in real wages did not readily materialize here. Short-term slumps became long-term decay. Elsewhere, the extension of putting-out was creating work and speeding up that same type of rural industrialization which was now waning in the South. In Lancashire the older and smaller linen industry, still full of many independent weavers in the early seventeenth century, began to feel the effects of a more rigorously commercial economy. Puttingout arrangements fastened themselves upon this branch of manufacture as they did on the fustian and cotton industries from the beginning. In the Midlands, the spread of the putting-out system amongst the framework-knitters of the hosiery industry went ahead rapidly. The total number of frames in the three counties of Nottinghamshire, Derbyshire, and Leicestershire is said to have risen from 140 in 1664 to 3,500 in 1727. In all these regions, as amongst the worsted makers of Yorkshire, and the metal-workers of Worcestershire and Staffordshire, putting-out spread, sometimes still part of the agricultural scene, sometimes spawning a near-proletariat of predominantly industrial workers. At the same time it was gradually becoming more integrated with the new centralized plants: calico-printing shops, water-powered silk-throwing mills, glass-works, blast furnaces and forges, and mines, some of them using the new atmospheric engines as well as water power. The conditions for the further changes which we call the Industrial Revolution were being created.

The State and its Impact

<hr>

(i)

The 'rise of the nation state' has become one of the less-disputed clichés in the political history of early modern Europe. Its economic counterpart 'mercantilism' has had the opposite fate, having given rise to debates about its existence, nature, or value as a conceptual tool. That this should have happened is not a little due to its origins in the mind of the first great systematizer of economic ideas, Adam Smith. Most of Book IV of his *Wealth of Nations* of 1776 is concerned with what he saw as the principles and practice of something which he called the 'mercantile system'. He regarded it, in part at least, as a creation of merchants and manufacturers shaping the course of State economic action to their own ends, to the advantage of producers and the detriment of consumers. Thus born as the brain-child of an economist, the concept in its life has been abused by historians, mishandled by economists, transmuted into *Merkantilismus*, and variously paraded, for praise or blame, by anyone seeking historical illustrations for the latest nostrum in political economy. Guides to the debate exist. It may now therefore be sensible to move on to consider the topic of this chapter without further reference to mercantilism as such.

In our period State action in economic and social matters can be seen as having four main ends in view: the maintenance of social stability and order; the encouragement and regulation of the internal economy; the encouragement and regulation of overseas trade and shipping; and the raising of revenue. Within each category a complex of purposes operated. Legislation about overseas commerce, for example, often aimed directly at raising national wealth and power in relation to other states but it also sought, from time to time, to encourage domestic employment and thus to conduce to internal stability and order, or to improve the flow of revenue to the Crown. Specific instances of State action could sometimes conflict with one another. The State's not infrequent attempts, for example, to restrain internal labour mobility in the supposed interest of public order almost certainly conflicted with its efforts to create jobs by stimulating industry. Such conflicts and contradictions are still with us today just as are controversies about economic policies. The modern debates differ from those of the sixteenth and seventeenth centuries in that they are informed by a body of distinct economic theories which provide the bases for various policy recommendations (only too often mutually incompatible). Those of the earlier period were far less informed by such theories because it was only in the course of the eighteenth century that the latter came to exist as recognizable, analytical entities. Instead, the actions of the State, as well as the policy recommendations which it received, drew upon a complex of prevailing assumptions about the nature of economic and social life and the proper role of the State within it. These, in turn, jostled with the lobbying of pressure groups, the clamour of courtiers, the growing power of a parliament jealous of its rights, and the persistent urgency of a State treasury forever short of cash, to determine the ultimate shape of practical policy. It would therefore seem suitable to try to illustrate the nature of economic and social policy over the four main categories outlined above by considering some specific areas of action within certain fields of interest. An appropriate starting point is the attitude of the State towards agriculture; specifically, its varying policies on the question of enclosure and depopulation, the trade in grain, and the price of foodstuffs

(ii)

According to Francis Bacon, Henry VII 'bowed the ancient policy of this State from consideration of plenty to consideration of power'.[1] A half-truth, because the State's concern to try to ensure an adequate supply of foodstuffs ('plenty') remained real, and became more so as population growth pressed upon food supply, but it will serve to indicate a continuous thread of distinction between two of the many aims of State action. Despite Bacon's comment, it is broadly true to say that before the downturn of population and prices in the mid-seventeenth century, Tudor and early Stuart governments generally tried either to stem the course of agricultural change or at least to soften the involuntary hardships which the poor experienced; to control prices in the interest of 'plenty'; to maintain the output of cereals; and to discourage what were seen as excessive shifts, in land-use, towards sheep-rearing. This is not to say that they received accurate information on these subjects or that they were right in their judgments, nor, least of all, that they were successful.

The problem, real or imaginary, of depopulating enclosure (see above, pages 35–6) stimulated a roughly consistent and continuous anti-enclosure policy, the chronological limits of which run from the first statute against depopulation in 1489 until the last bill to regulate enclosure was rejected by Parliament in 1656. Meanwhile, there were sundry commissions of enquiry—in 1517–18, 1548, 1607, and 1635, to give only some of their dates—as well as Acts bearing upon the issue, various proclamations, and a series of cases heard in the prerogative courts. Successive governments entertained some real fears: that the countryside might lose useful population, useful for the defence of the realm or for paying taxes; that conversion to pasture from tillage, by lessening employment, might cause disaffection and public disorder; that there might be a shortage of grain which would necessitate imports and thus increase our dependence on others, thereby militating against a vaguely held ideal of self-sufficiency. The complexity of motivation behind such policy is incomparably conveyed in the words of the day. Here is part of the preamble to the Act of 1489 against depopulation:

. . . great inconveniences daily doth increase by desolation and putting down and wilful waste of houses and towns within this his realm, and laying to pasture lands which customarily have been used in tilth, whereby idleness—ground and beginning of all mischiefs—daily doth increase, for where in some towns two hundred persons were occupied and lived by their lawful labours, now be there occupied two or three herdmen and the residue fallen in idleness, the husbandry, which is one of the greatest commodities of this realm, is greatly decayed, churches destroyed, the service of God withdrawn, the bodies there buried not prayed for, the patron and curates wronged, the defence of this land against enemies outward feebled and impaired: to the great displeasure of God, to the subversion of the policy and good rule of this land . . .[2]

The splendid language no doubt conceals some unintentional inaccuracy and a little deliberate exaggeration. But the passage encapsulates some of the essence of Tudor policy in this field as well as pointing to the common social assumptions of the 'political nation'.

    This policy was, as in related matters, a blend of political, economic, and social regulation. That regulation was maintained by an authoritarian, though not absolute, monarchy ruling with the periodic aid of Parliament and with the prescriptive power of the Church; and its controlling purpose operated upon an underdeveloped and underemployed economy on the margin of national self-sufficiency in foodstuffs. This combination was similarly manifest in the attempts to control the doings of victualling middlemen. Acts of 1552 and 1563 required the licensing of corn dealers. We can be sure that many operated without licence; and a rapid increase during the second half of the sixteenth century in the numbers of allegations by informers about engrossing grain is a testimony at once to more dealing and to higher grain prices. The government, notably under the administrative zeal of William Cecil, Lord Burghley, and again during the years of Charles I and Archbishop Laud, tried to exercise an elaborate control of markets. Such outbursts of energy can be seen as episodes in a longer tradition of control of the export of grain. During the period, grain exports were periodically forbidden, allowed, permitted

under licence, allowed when the price was not above a specified figure, or otherwise regulated. Given this continuity of
attitude, shifts of immediate policy corresponded broadly to
shifts in prices. After the relatively stagnant prices of the
1560s, for example, the Justices of the Peace—to whom so
much of the local exercise of the central government's
economic and social policy was entrusted—were told in 1571
to determine whether grain prices were sufficiently 'reasonable and moderate' to permit export. In the 1580s and '90s,
however, with the return of sharply rising prices, they were
confronted with the 'Book of Orders' from the Privy Council
requiring them, *inter alia*, to stop exports. At such times, as
again in 1622–3 or 1630–1, they had to deal with situations
in which profits (sometimes their own), public order, and
humanity had to be nicely balanced.

After the 1650s the change in the trend of policy is clear
enough. Lower grain prices, the growing approval of enclosure for arable farming, and the fall in the rate of population
increase all meant less anxiety about food supply and more
about farmer's profits and landowners' rents. So in a society
in which political power, at least in home affairs, was coming
to rest more strongly in Parliament, it is not wholly surprising
to find that body, dominated by landowners as it was, voting
agrarian encouragement and protection in the shape of the
Corn Laws. The laws about grain dealing were relaxed and
in 1670 the export of grain was allowed, whatever its price.
Three years later, at a time when complaints about falling
rents were particularly rife, came the institution of bounties
on grain exports. In 1689 duties on exports were removed.
The complement to encouragement for home production
was protection against imports. Parliament voted it in 1660
and again in 1670 in the shape of sliding scales of import
duties on foreign grain—low when prices were high, high
when prices were low.

Despite all these radical changes in the direction of policy
there was still a real continuity in its nature. Although the
tendency was clearly to favour the producer, the consumer
was not simply abandoned to the free play of market forces.
Nor was the new line unbroken; the bounty lapsed between

1681 and 1689; and grain exports were forbidden in years of bad harvests, for example, 1698, 1709, and 1741. In 1773, when population pressure on food supplies reasserted itself, the statutory price limit for exports was revived. Meanwhile, when harvests were bad, authority could be heard thundering against the ancient sins of forestalling, engrossing and regrating (that is, buying up victuals with a view to retailing at a profit); and Justices of the Peace were busy with the licensing of corn dealers and attempting to uphold that medieval symbol of consumer protection, the Assize of Bread. When, for example, we read of Kentish bakers in 1693 and 1710 being indicted for not baking bread according to the Assize, or of a butcher in 1701 presented at Quarter Sessions for 'buying of fat bullocks and selling them to other butchers',[3] we should at least hesitate before accepting the notion, popularized by some historians, that the English economy had already succumbed to the 'bourgeois' principles of 'laissez faire'.

(iii)

A similar pattern of rise and decline, embodying both continuity in nature but adaptation to changing economic conditions, can be seen in the State's efforts to encourage and regulate industry, to control the supply and movement of labour, and to relieve the poor.

Because woollen textiles dominated the English manufacturing scene, the policy of industrial regulation can there be seen at its clearest. Attempts to lay down the proper length, width, weight, etc. of cloths had two main justifications: to maintain standards; and, very important for the State, to provide specifications on the basis of which Customs duties were charged on export or taxes levied on output. To this end the office of the Aulnager had been instituted in 1315; he and his officials were supposed to inspect cloths to see that they corresponded to the specifications, and also to collect an output tax, the aulnage duty. With the expansion of the industry in the fifteenth and sixteenth centuries, it became very evident that the job was being done with little efficiency and some fraud. But the need to deal with frequent complaints about what an investigating committee in 1622 called 'false and deceitful making, dyeing and dressing of our cloth and stuff which disgraceth and discrediteth it in foreign parts'[4] provoked a series of regulative enactments, between 1464 and 1640, designed to maintain standards. Not surprisingly, they often followed major depressions, for example those of 1552, 1622, and 1640. The enforced use of the London cloth market at Blackwell Hall, statutory since 1397, was part of the policy. But, despite more recommendations on similar lines by royal proclamations, councils, and committees between 1638 and 1669, the enthusiasm for regulation was waning in the face of the rapid diversification of English textiles. A last legislative attempt at a general regulation of the cloth industry failed to become law in 1678. The aulnage, corrupt, unloved, farmed out to a royal favourite by James I, finally expired in 1724, useless as a controlling device and negligible as a source of revenue.

Only from about the end of the seventeenth century does the decay in the policy of regulation become evident. Until then the continuing belief in its necessity was powerful and pervasive, despite the failings in practice to which the sheer frequency of repeated policy pronouncements pays tribute. The decay, again, had less to do with any burgeoning concepts of economic liberalism than with the increasing practical difficulties of applying an ancient policy to a changed structure of output—and, moreover, in circumstances in which the urge to reduce costs or to adapt production to new market trends was now far more pressing than the desire to adhere to traditional specifications. While the long history of the aulnage had identified control with corruption and an unpopular tax on woollens, other industries—gunpowder, linen, iron-smelting, paper-making, small metalwares, bricks, tobacco processing, sugar-refining, to name but some—had grown up without an apparatus of control. As the industrial structure became more diverse, so did the pressure to dispense with control become stronger. Not that action was always so positive as the word 'pressure' implies. Much of the decay was a product of inertia, as legislature and executive alike became increasingly involved in the protection and encouragement of overseas trade and, especially between 1689 and 1713, in the immensely more urgent needs of revenue collection for war.

Meanwhile, another policy had waxed and waned. The Tudors made several attempts to regulate, control, and generally impose order upon the whole complex muddle of work (or lack of it). The high points of this policy were the Weavers Act of 1555, the Statute of Artificers of 1563, and the Poor Law enactments of 1536, 1572, and 1576, together with the consolidating statutes of 1597 and 1601. Looked at with a long focus, in terms of embodied ideas, this body of legislation exhibits many remarkable continuities with earlier attitudes and practices. The requirement of a fixed term of apprenticeship and the assessment of maximum wages by the Justices of the Peace: both of these provisions in the Statute of Artificers had a respectable medieval ancestry. The limitation of the number of looms to be owned by persons outside corporate towns and the injunction that weavers should not have fulling mills nor fullers have looms: these and other requirements of the Weavers Act point to the familiar tradition of ordered demarcation between crafts and craftsmen, seen as essentially urban. The restriction on labour mobility; the attempt to ensure stable and regular labour supply by means of the long contract; the requirement for compulsory work in agriculture for all except those in specified occupations, categories, or social strata: such clauses in the Statute of Artificers again belong to the ideal of an ordered, stratified, controlled society. Harvest work, too, was to be compulsory on order from the Justices of the Peace for any 'artificers and persons as be meet to labour'. And the preamble typifies the contemporary economic hopes of the governing political nation in its attitude to labour. The Act was, inter alia, to 'banish idleness, advance husbandry, and yield unto the hired person both in time of scarcity and in time of plenty a convenient proportion of wages'.[5]

Yet if these various enactments are looked at more closely they often appear as reactions to specific economic and social problems. The Weavers Act has to be seen in the context of the ending of the long upswing in cloth exports. The Statute of Artificers, so far from being a clearly thought-out product of Elizabethan economic statesmanship, was a hotchpotch of compromise between the efforts of the Queen's councillors and numerous amendments originating in the House of Commons. Its timing has to be seen in the context of a temporarily curtailed labour supply after the heavy mortality of the late 1550s. The Act of 1604 which in effect required the assessment of minimum wages in the cloth industry was a direct outcome of the complaints of impoverished weavers and spinners. Rising prices, economic changes, and fluctuating but periodically rapid population changes were powerful stimulants to acts of State.

Most noticeably does this seem to be so in the efforts to deal with the problem of the poor. The secularization of poor relief, and the creation of a new system to replace haphazard alms-giving, stands out as a major achievement of Tudor social policy. Much of it nearly came in with the Act of 1536. Drawing incompletely upon a scheme for centrally administered and comprehensive poor relief, this Act distinguished between the voluntary and involuntary unemployed, prohibited begging, provided for the apprenticing of pauper children, and for the distribution of money to the aged and incapable. It was not, however, until the Act of 1572 that the vital concomitant of compulsory assessment, the poor rate (collected on a parish basis), was adopted as national policy. In 1576 came the requirement that each county should establish a 'house of correction' (often called a 'Bridewell' after the name of the London exemplar). Here the voluntary unemployed, male and female, were to be put to work in what were considered to be suitably disagreeable circumstances; and towns were required to maintain stocks of materials on which the involuntary unemployed should be put to work. Despite many other experiments in trying to deal with these problems, some on a national scale, some in particular towns, it was the strands of policy enshrined in these Acts which were finally put together, with minor variations, into the consolidating Acts of 1597 and 1601.

Although population growth and rising prices certainly

exacerbated the problems with which this evolving policy
had to contend, the first steps towards its inception were
taken in 1535–6 when prices and population had only recently started their upward move, but precisely when another
great act of secularization was under way: the dissolution of
the monasteries, the former fount of almsgiving. In brief,
although the increasing pressure of economic and social
difficulties made the completion of an effective policy ever
more urgent, its origins lay in an effort by the State to take
over and deal with a problem long persistent in the pre-
industrialized economy. Moreover, though administrative
arrangements were thus changed, the emergent Elizabethan
poor law showed no more awareness than its predecessors of
the underemployment, the casual labour, the inadequate
economic investment which lay at the base of these social
difficulties. It tried to create work for some, to enforce work
for others; but in the very nature of its efforts, it revealed a
continuity of economic and social attitudes. Like so much of
this domestic policy it was essentially restrictive; it sought
stability and social order. In no way did it seek a solution via
what we would call economic growth.

If the final century of our period seems to contain, once
again, a decaying phase of this Tudor policy, it is less because
of a change of heart than because the changing economic
context sometimes evoked indifference to enforcement. All
sorts of circumstances conduced to that end. Some areas in
which industrial development took place were specifically
exempted, wholly or in part, from the Weavers Act or the
Statute of Artificers. Jobs unknown to those who had drawn
up the Tudor legislation had come into being. Just as the
older regulations specific to textile manufacture either
decayed or were not amended to fit changing circumstances,
so this more general Tudor regulative apparatus experienced
a similar fate. Wages, for example, continued to be assessed
by the Justices of the Peace in Quarter Sessions, fairly regu-
larly until about the end of our period. But increasingly the
assessments were ignored or were inoperative. New industrial
developments in new areas meant that higher wages were
paid to attract labour, supply no longer being abundant,

just as change brought unemployment and lower wages in other areas. Wages in many new trades went unassessed while those in dying, if not defunct, occupations in a particular area continued to be assessed. Attempts to enforce the full seven-year apprenticeship demanded by the Statute of Artificers were enfeebled, even in the early seventeenth century, by the consideration that it might be better to have employment created by those who had not served a proper apprenticeship than no employment at all.

The upward trend in real wages brought, as already mentioned (above, pages 103–4), complaints by employers of 'idleness', that is, voluntary underemployment (*not* unemployment). The increasing diversity of the economy resulted in greater labour mobility, even though over shorter distances, as more towns and other focal points of industry and trade developed. The response to what were seen as the social problems thereby created, so far from revealing indifference to Tudor policy, produced attempts to strengthen it. Whatever the events of the Interregnum may have done to weaken the control of the central government over such matters, there seems to be evidence that locally, at the level of the Justices of the Peace and the parochial overseers of the poor, Tudor-type social control and poor relief continued to be operated. In a further effort to tackle that perennial problem, the 'loose and straggling' poor, in reprehensible motion for whatever reason, the Settlement Act of 1662 empowered Justices of the Peace, in certain circumstances, to remove recent settlers in a parish back to the parish where they were last legally settled. Variously amended, and especially in 1697 by the introduction of certificates permitting limited settlement, the Act remained contentiously in being throughout, and long after, our period. The idea was not new; sixteenth-century regulations had tried to make the too-mobile poor return whence they came. Once poor rates were compulsory and rising, however, it was more or less inevitable that further efforts would be made to keep out those unwanted persons who might add to the rate burden; and, once cheap labour had become less abundant, to dissuade those already in employment from moving elsewhere.

The old policy of trying to 'set the poor on work' was likewise continued by the development of workhouses. London and Bristol led the way but other towns followed, empowered by private Act to set up workhouses; and in 1723 a general measure was passed to facilitate their progress.

How much was achieved by these interlocking policies of poor relief, labour control, and social policing is quite another matter. Between 1480 and 1660 there was a substantial increase in private charitable benefactions; at least there was in their total monetary value though probably not in real value per head of the population. The sundry alms-houses and charitable trusts created thereby may have done as much to relieve suffering as the moneys collected and disbursed to the poor under statutory provisions. It is unlikely that the State's efforts to encourage employment made any significant difference to the course of the country's economic development. Perhaps the most important quality of these acts of State lay in their continuing embodiment, throughout the whole period, of the attitude of mind of the political nation. 'Plenty' had not only to be balanced against 'power' but seen to be; social control was imperative but had to be balanced by social obligations; the submerged third, quarter, half— whatever the varying proportion may have been—who were the poor, that other entity, had to be regulated, succoured, defined for varying treatments, controlled, prevented from causing trouble—but not eliminated. Without them the economy would have collapsed.

(iv)

In their attempts to encourage and regulate trade and shipping, English governments deployed certain well-tried weapons. Some have already been examined, notably the making of commercial treaties or similar bargains, and the chartering of trading companies (see above, pages 58-60, 148-50). The rise and fall of the latter, between 1553 and 1720, as the joint products of State and private interests have already been considered in some detail and there is no need to repeat that here. Treaty-making and the like continued throughout the whole period. It varied from Henry VII's Intercursus Magnus of 1496, by which commerce was restored between England and the Netherlands, after an interruption largely political in origin, to the Methuen treaty of 1703 between England and Portugal, by which the latter agreed to accept English woollens as a quid pro quo for England accepting Portuguese wines at two-thirds of the duty imposed on French wines. Many more examples could be cited. They all had in common the linkage of political power to eonomic privileges or concessions for particular groups. As the process of international trade came more and more to be seen as part of an international conflict, so was the country's total overseas trade seen as an aggregation of a number of separate, self-financing 'trades', to be judged as good or bad according to whether they produced a favourable or adverse balance and thus led to a net inflow or outflow of bullion. At least, that is what was claimed as the criterion of judgement. In practice, as was revealed by the controversy over the Anglo-French commercial treaty of 1713, a combination of pressure groups and political allegiances often mattered more than economic arguments of this sort. Of course, because bullion, specie, or 'treasure' (as contemporaries called it) was the hard currency of the time, needed for the coinage which financed everyday transactions as well as for the conduct of certain branches of trade, notably that with Asia, it is not surprising that the government should have been interested in helping to secure it. It was partly to these ends that regular commercial statistics started to be collected in 1696. Neither statistics nor a belief in particular balances of trade helped very much in reality, as the indicator that really mattered, the national balance of payments, remained unrevealed.

A rather different line of government policy was that aimed at the encouragement of native shipping and the control of colonial commerce. Medieval efforts to favour English ships at the expense of foreign were fitful, if only because they were unlikely to have had much success. Altogether more purposeful were the various enactments generally known as the Navigation Acts passed between 1651 and 1733, the most important of which were those of 1660, 1663, 1673, and 1696.

The major provisions of these Acts were: most imports from Europe had to come into England either in an English ship or in a ship of the country in which the goods were produced; all colonial trade was reserved to English or colonial ships; certain enumerated colonial products could be exported from the colonies only to England; with certain exceptions, European goods were not to be imported directly into the colonies but only indirectly via England and in English ships; a staff of officials was set up in the colonies to enforce the laws controlling colonial trade. The two most prominent features of this policy were that it was uncompromisingly aimed at Dutch supremacy in the carrying trade; and that it sought to keep foreigners out of the colonial trade and to preserve it for the benefit of the mother country. In so far as this latter feature was part of a wider colonial economic policy, other enactments (with little effect) tried to discourage manufacturing in the colonies by prohibiting the export therefrom of woollens (1699) and beaver hats (1732). With some modifications, Ireland was brought within the ambit of the Navigation Act as a colony; with the Act of Union of 1707, Scotland was brought in as part of Britain.

In the evolution of this policy long-held ideas of discrimination against the foreigner can be seen at work. Heavier customs duties on alien than on English merchants exporting cloth or wool, for example, date back to 1303. In its attempts to reserve all colonial trade for Englishmen, the English State was doing nothing different from what Spain or Portugal had done before. The timing of the policy, however, owes much to the gradual build-up of the English merchant navy, thus creating a stronger situation for the launching of these economic weapons in the international combat; and to the pressures of increasingly powerful interest groups emerging along with the growth of the Atlantic economy. As the fires of Anglo-Dutch and then Anglo-French economic rivalry burst into flame, helping to ignite wider political and dynastic issues into open warfare, so did the State bring colonial commerce within the ambit of its control. The timing of the first, and strongly anti-Dutch, Navigation Act of 1651 owed not a little to the ending of the period in which English shipping had enjoyed the fruits of neutrality (see above, pages 67–8); and to the presence on the committees and councils of trade set up under the Commonwealth of many influential 'new men', active in colonial trade and enterprise. The establishment in 1696 of the 'Lords Commissioners of Trade and Plantations' (the Board of Trade as it later became) was related, in its general timing, to the problems created by French attacks úpon colonial trade; but in its immediate timing, to a deliberate act by the royal government to defeat a proposal from the Commons to set up a similar body under Commons' control. If the motives for specific action were thus as complex as we should properly suppose them to be, there was nevertheless a continuity of attitude well summed up in the observation that policy on trade, enterprise, and the colonies should contrive:

all possible encouragements and advantages for the adventurer, planter and English merchants, in order also to the shutting out all strangers from that trade, by making them not necessary to it, and by drawing it wholly . . . into our ports here. [6]

The author of these remarks of 1657 was Thomas Povey. He symbolizes a continuity of attitudes, for not only was he a member of various government committees on trade and the colonies both before and after the Restoration, but his nephew William Blathwayt was almost continuously concerned with colonial trade and administration from 1675 to 1707, achieving a position of notable influence and authority, and expounding views which his uncle would surely have endorsed.

Another weapon with which the State helped to wage the battle of international trade was the power to manipulate the level of customs duties, to impose tariffs or even trade embargoes. Some prohibitions were specific, such as those imposed in the interests of the cloth industry: the prohibition on the import of foreign woollen cloth dated back to 1337; in the early seventeenth century the export of English wool, woollen yarn, and fuller's earth was statutorily banned. Trade with France offers a rich field for examples of the use of the embargo, the treaty and the tariff wall. Going by stops

and starts between the 1640s and the failure of the commercial treaty of 1713, Anglo-French trade became a classic
example of legal strangulation by prohibitions or very high
duties for most of the rest of the eighteenth century. The use
of differential customs duties, to discourage some imports and
encourage some exports, did not however appear as a prominent weapon in the state armoury until the seventeenth
century. In the fifteenth and sixteenth centuries both exports
and imports paid duty, although from the mid-fifteenth
century export duties on wool became significantly higher
than those on cloth. A tentative move in a protectionist
direction came in 1610, more positive ones in 1643 and 1660,
and many more after 1689. The maintenance, indeed the
raising, of import duties in conjunction with the ending of
export duties on woollen cloth in 1700 and the general aboli-
tion of most export duties in Walpole's Customs reform of
1722, signified the State's willingness to encourage home
industry or, at least, to heed the clamour of the producers'
lobbies. This was not a simple burst of enthusiasm for industrial protection. It was a complex product of the needs of
wartime finance which led to higher import duties and
helped thereby to build a protective wall, and of the already
proceeding industrial diversification. This combination then
created interest groups which demanded a continuance of
protection; and the changed nature of government, with the
evolution of a party system in an increasingly powerful House
of Commons, facilitated the effective granting of protection.
But the whole policy, as it emerged, cannot be understood
without regard to that most important of all the State's
economic functions in this period, the raising of revenue.

(v)

The financial doings of the central government affect the
economic and social life of a community according to the
nature and quantity of expenditure, and the ways in which
the revenue to meet that expenditure is raised. During the
whole of the period with which this book is concerned almost
all expenditure had two objects only: the maintenance of the

Court and provision for defence and public order in peace-time; and, overwhelmingly important, war. War spending brought not only sharp increases in the need for revenue generally but also for a particular sort of revenue, that is, cash, immediate income. In the course of the period, the methods of revenue-raising underwent drastic changes; and most of those changes are directly attributable to war time needs. Moreover, it was precisely the urgency of wartime finance that led to actions which, though not in themselves part of the revolution in the methods of public finance, had substantial repercussions on wider aspects of economic and social life whilst bringing in cash to the government. Two obvious examples: the sales of former monastic lands, esti-mated to have yielded about £800,000 between 1539 and 1547; and the debasement of the coinage, thought to have profited the Crown to the extent of some £1,200,000 between 1542 and 1551. Given that expenditure on war was thus the crucial determinant, it was the solutions found to the prob-lems of raising revenue that effected change. The only signi-ficant change that happened on the expenditure side was. that warfare became more expensive, both in capital costs (more and bigger warships and guns) and in cash demands (more soldiers, sailors, and dockyard workers to pay and victual).

The government's revenue came from three main sources: royal lands; taxation; and borrowing. The revolution wrought in English public finance saw the elimination of the first as a significant source of government income; the imposition of total parliamentary control over the second; and the transformation of the third from *ad hoc* Crown bor-rowing at high rates of interest to a well-secured national debt at a low rate of interest.

The rise and fall of the Crown's hopes for financial in-dependence of Parliament are approximately delimited by Edward IV's telling the Commons in 1467 that 'I purpose to live upon mine own, and not to charge my subjects but in great and urgent causes'[7] and Charles I's reluctant recall of the Long Parliament in 1640. Yorkist accumulation of royal lands was continued by the first of the Tudors, and in 1502–5 about 30 per cent of Henry VII's total income came from that source. Henry VIII's two main pastimes, war and sex, proved, directly or indirectly, so costly and the monastic lands so tempting that a big increase in landed wealth was made after 1536. But, as already mentioned in a different context, income was not enough; capital had to be sold to meet 'great and urgent causes' of war, and monastic properties were put on the market to raise cash. Royal lands were again sold under Elizabeth to help finance the war with Spain; and yet again by both of the early Stuarts. Despite the restoration of royal lands in 1660 after further sales by the Commonwealth, this source of income had already become a virtually insignificant proportion of the total revenue by 1640. This particular pursuit of State finance had thus helped to redistribute wealth by dispersing Crown and Church lands to the benefit of the nobility and gentry.

Until the 1640s there were only two prime objects of taxation: overseas trade and landed property. The yield of the customs duties was normally granted by Parliament to the king for life. Because the Customs were then regarded chiefly as sources of revenue rather than as instruments of commercial policy, they were generally fixed at a low level; and their yield thus depended upon the volume of trade and the efficiency of collection. Although the proportion of total revenue which they contributed obviously varied greatly, it was normally substantial and reasonably certain. So it was in the royal interest to favour trade by keeping it flowing; and to have effective Customs administration. To the latter end, the duties were periodically revised, as in 1558, by the issue of new 'books of rates' to take account of changes in the commodity-structure of trade and in the level of prices; and until 1672 the collection of the duties was from time to time, wholly or in part, farmed out to businessmen (or royal favourites). Grants of parliamentary taxation were normally made to meet 'extraordinary' costs, that is, war, and control of them was, of course, a powerful parliamentary weapon in the developing conflict with royal power. But under the Tudors it became evident that tax-grants were coming to be made by Parliament in peace as well as in war; and Charles

I had to discover just how great was his degree of financial dependence upon Parliament. In relation to the concerns of this book, however, the two most important facts about Tudor and early Stuart land taxes were that they became so fossilized in assessment that their yield declined not only in real but even in monetary terms; and that they (and indeed later taxes of this sort) never effectively taxed total income but only landed wealth. Consequently, the government, by failing to tap effectively some of the most rapidly growing incomes in the economy, was forced, by economic as well as constitutional constraints, to seek a variety of fiscal expedients. Moreover, because both land taxes and customs duties were relatively light, and thus made little impact on prices or purses, any such expedients which were truly effective, as was 'ship money' in the 1630s, or which raised prices, as did the new customs duties or 'impositions' of 1608 and 1610, rapidly became exceedingly unpopular. But State power demanded revenue. So it had to turn to a new sort of tax— the excise—and to borrowing.

The excise was introduced by Parliament in 1643, again to help meet the financial needs of war, this time of civil war. Like so much in the English economy of the day, it was an import from continental Europe; and its unpopularity was instant, for it touched the purses of all and, as a regressive tax affecting the prices of ordinary consumables, bore especially upon wage-earners and the poorer strata of the community. It thus brought into the tax net groups previously almost unaffected. This parliamentary tax was retained at the Restoration to compensate for the ending of 'feudal' revenues, such as those arising from the Court of Wards. Although then diminished in its application, its rates were increased in 1671; its application extended again in 1711 to a much wider range of products; and in 1694 another sort of excise, the salt duty, was added. At all these dates—1671, 1694, 1711—the country was at war.

English kings had borrowed money on the security of the wool trade in the fourteenth century, but at the beginning of our period the scale of borrowing was much smaller than it had been previously. It continued sporadically at home, the loanable funds of such City bodies as the Merchant Adventurers being appropriately persuaded into Crown hands. Borrowing on the international money market at Antwerp, however, increased considerably between 1540 and 1570. After the decline of Antwerp, the English governments turned once more to the growing wealth of the City of London; and both James I and Charles I borrowed substantially from individual magnates, from the City Corporation, and especially from the various syndicates of Customs farmers who collected the customs duties after 1604. Charles' failure to maintain his credit with such lenders left his financial position impossible by 1640. The governments of the Interregnum were no more successful in developing efficient techniques of borrowing; nor were those of the Restoration, despite the heightened parliamentary control of taxation and despite the efforts of Sir George Downing to induce the public to lend money. A mountain of inadequately secured-short-term debts still left unpaid sailors, rioting dockyard workers, and clamorous creditors; created fortunes for a handful of financiers; and, in 1672, brought on the Stop of the Exchequer.

When the wars came yet again, in quick succession, in 1689–96 and 1701–13 they proved to be longer, bigger, and vastly more expensive. The growing wealth of the economy could pay for them; and it had got a fillip from the trading boom of the peace period, 1674–88. The overriding problem of public finance was how to channel that wealth to provide the immediate liquidity, the cash, which the State needed for the conduct of the wars. Customs duties were raised and the excise extended. One important new tax arrived to stay. The land tax of 1693 replaced both the inefficient and unpopular hearth tax (1660–89) and the assessments, effective under the Commonwealth, and sporadically continued after the Restoration. It became, in effect, a national rate on landed property varying from two to four shillings in the pound, and lasted as the main direct tax of the eighteenth century. But taxes were not enough.

Lending to the State had long been a lucrative, if dangerous, business. Private financiers, individually or in syndicates, continued to do well out of the State's needs. Indeed, the whole later Stuart period was a particularly happy hunting ground for the skilful operator who could find cash for the government, make remittances to the troops abroad, or emerge from naval victualling or contracting with his debts repaid—usually at rates of interest covertly higher than overtly allowed. Many of the business fortunes of the time—like those of Sir John Banks, Sir Charles Duncombe, Sir Gilbert Heathcote, or Sir Henry Furnese—were built up more from such financial or contracting activities than from orthodox overseas commerce. Borrowing schemes abounded. The establishment of the New East India Company of 1698 did not even pretend to be merely a matter of trade, for the very title of the Act incorporating the company began with the words 'An Act for raising a sum not exceeding two millions upon a fund for payment of annuities . . .' One such scheme had been accepted in 1694 and incorporated, in very traditional wording, as 'The Governor and Company of the Bank of England'. Its basis was a loan of £1,200,000 at 8 per cent; the whole sum was subscribed within twelve days. It succeeded; began to make further cash advances to the government; and the interest charges and management costs were charged as an annuity against the yield of the Customs and excise. Here was one element in what was to become the national debt. The securing of loans against anticipated tax yields was not new; creating permanent charges and giving them parliamentary, and not merely royal, guarantee was. Already in 1692 a Commons' committee had been appointed to consider 'proposals for raising a sum of money towards carrying on the war against France upon a fund of perpetual interest'. Money was raised by lotteries and the sale of life annuities. But still the mass of short-term debt grew; in 1696 the discount on some government debt was at 30–40 per cent, similar to the worst days of naval credit during the second Anglo-Dutch war, which Pepys had so bewailed in his diary. The solution was found in the creation of long-term funded debt; and in the development of the Exchequer bill, receivable in payment of taxes and, after 1707, cashable on sight at the Bank of England. Many of the facilities for these moves were made possible by Acts of 1697 and 1717. The creation of the South Sea Company in 1711 was essentially another lending and funding operation; the company took over a still existent mass of short-term debt, much of it owing to contractors who had supplied the navy. The subsequent sensational orgy of fraud, bribery, political corruption, and financial speculation in 1720, known as the South Sea Bubble, followed a further attempted conversion operation in 1719. It made little difference to the development of funding what had come to be called, and recognized as, 'the national debt'. All sorts of charges were added to it: more loans on lotteries and annuities, moneys due to the Bank of England (increasingly concerned with the management of the debt), and to the South Sea and East India companies. But all the time the rate of interest was pushed down as funding proceeded, aided by the work of Robert Walpole, under parliamentary fiat. On this basis, the State was able to finance without notable difficulty the war of 1739–48. In 1750 the national debt stood at £78 million; and in 1751 a number of funds and annuities were grouped together at 3 per cent to become known as the '3 per cent consolidated annuities' or 'Consols'. A new British institution had been founded.

These radical changes in public finance did not happen without opposition. 'Dutch finance' gave way to 'moneyed interest' as terms of abuse by landowning Tories against the Whig supporters of the Bank of England and 'the City'. The crude political labels were to be worn for years to come; the reality was, of course, infinitely more complex. Much has been written on the execution and administration of this revolution in public finance; remarkably little on its effects upon economy and society. A few points can be made.

At the end of our period the State was annually extracting from its citizens a very much larger amount per head of the population than formerly, even in real terms. Much of the change was concentrated into the period after 1660. The immediate stimulus had come from the financial demands of war. But the results were evident in peace: between the 1660s and the 1730s the government's peacetime revenue multiplied nearly fourfold, from approximately £1·5 million annually to £5·8 million. This was partly because of the maintenance, even in peace, of a larger and costlier navy and army but still more because of substantial interest payments to the holders of government stock. In the peace-years 1729–38 almost as much went in this debt service (an average of £2·1 million annually or 40 per cent of total net expenditure) as to the army, navy, and ordnance combined (£2·3 million or 42 per cent). There was, in short, a considerable transfer of income from tax-payers to interest-receivers. Large, safe, and new outlets for investable funds helped to sustain an urban or less-landed gentry, a comfortably-off middle class, the social clientèle of Bath and Tunbridge Wells. The transfer did not pass unnoticed by contemporary payers of the land tax or of Customs and excise duties, but it did not break the social and political stability of the times. Moreover, despite the great increase in the State's tax demands, the ordinary early eighteenth-century Englishman was still left with a probably deserved reputation for enjoying a higher standard of living than his European counterpart: surely an indirect witness to a massive accumulation of wealth, however unequal its distribution. The effect of the increased taxation upon prices is far from clear; but it is evident that the new methods of raising revenue gave increased scope for the use of Customs' tariffs as politico-economic weapons rather than simply as fiscal devices. Even when excise demands are set off against the Customs, the result was almost certainly a strengthening of the protective wall around English industry. The economy whose entrepreneurs were the first to launch into industrial revolution did not do so on a basis of free trade and economic liberalism, but of protection created, in part at least, by the needs of war finance.

Conclusion: the Divergence of England

'From the late fifteenth century until well into the beginning of the eighteenth century,' it has been authoritatively stated 'the standard of living in Europe progressively declined.'[1] As has already been indicated, there is indeed evidence to suggest that many of the poorer sections of the English population may have shared in this worsening European situation, especially in the sixteenth and early seventeenth centuries. But if it holds true as fully for England as elsewhere, and it continued 'well into the beginning of the eighteenth century', it raises an interesting problem when considered in relation to the unique onset of the Industrial Revolution in England only a few decades later. How did the Industrial Revolution launch itself in an economy which, on this reading, had been experiencing a progressively declining ability to buy goods and services over the past two and a half centuries? Whichever way it is posed, we return to the question earlier raised but not answered (above, page 2). How and why did England become so differentiated from the rest of pre-industrialized Europe by about 1750 that its economy could take off into the first industrial revolution?

Implicit in the very posing of such a question is the assumption that was made explicit on the first page of this book: that is, that a past defined as pre-industrialized is here being examined from the vantage point of an industrialized present. Such a stance is in certain ways a-historical in that it is at least partially analogous to the celebrated Whig interpretation of history, to the production of 'a story which is the ratification if not the glorification of the present'.[2] In so far as one tries to marry that disputatious pair, history and economics, the dilemma seems inescapable. This is not the occasion to seek to resolve it. But some stress upon its existence may serve to emphasize that we walk on shifting and treacherous sands when we try to separate out certain themes, forces, or factors, from the totality of the past and say of them that this or that was the crucial determinant in the coming of industrialization. Anyone who supposes that he can readily reveal how it all began is deceiving himself.

The generalization quoted at the beginning of this chapter cannot in reality be fully applicable to England. It seems likely, instead, that after about 1650 there was gradually building up in England a more substantial and more widely distributed reserve of disposable income than anywhere else in Europe. If so, this offers some support for arguments which have stressed the width and depth of home market demand as particularly important in the coming of the first industrial revolution. This is not to dismiss other potential causes. If true, however, it must necessarily lessen the importance of those common to other economies which might have earlier burst into industrialized flame but did not. There is, for example, no particular evidence that England was uniquely in possession of important technical or scientific knowledge peculiarly pertinent to what happened in the later eighteenth century. In manufacturing industry, mining, shipping, and commerce there existed a body of technical knowledge which was broadly common to England, France, Holland, and some other areas in Europe around 1700. England had been, and to some extent still was, trailing in technical expertise, catching up on continental practices, whether in silk throwing or public finance. (A 'late-start' hypothesis for the English Industrial Revolution might be worth investigating.) Nor is commercial expansion in itself enough to provide an explanation. Portugal, Spain, Holland, and France had each undergone such experiences; each had overseas settlements, more or less colonial in type. All were beaten to the post. Admittedly, England's North American colonies probably offered the most striking net increase in demand after 1650, thereby opening up an exclusive market for English industrial output precisely when intra-European trade was depressed and competition intensifying. Even so, total exports probably took only a minor proportion of total industrial output. So although the rapid expansion in transatlantic activity may have given a useful marginal stimulus to industrialization at home, it is unlikely to have provided much more than that. In any event, calculations about the proportionate contribution of overseas trade or home demand or technology or any other single, seemingly separable factor cannot be very convincing because of the complex, and often unstated, assumptions on which they must build and the historical questions which they perforce leave unanswered. For example, without prior English export expansion would her merchants have been able to acquire the Spanish silver necessary to participate successfully in Asiatic trade? And without that participation which, after 1660, brought in such a flood of Indian cottons, would the native English textile industry have been appropriately challenged and stimulated to make the technical revolution that it subsequently did? And without the growth of English naval power would continued access to America and India have been secured?

If, however, the English economy was diverging from some common European experience in showing rising standards of living in the later stages of our period, we may reasonably ask why this was so, although remaining cautious meanwhile about attributing some unique causative value to this divergence.

The basis of judgements about the standard of living during the period is, of course, the comparison between wages and prices, mainly cereal prices. Consequently, the determinants of change in the standard would include changes in agricultural productivity, in the proportion of wage-workers in the community, in the level of employment offered to those workers, and in their productivity and earnings. As explained in earlier chapters, there is reason to think that agricultural productivity rose significantly in England especially after the mid-seventeenth century. At the same time as this was happening the whole English economy was also undergoing a substantial geographical expansion north of that line between the Severn and the Wash which had delimited the southern concentration of most late fifteenth- and sixteenth-century wealth and economic activity. That geographical expansion—some of it associated with the opening up of the transatlantic market, some with the growing trade between England and Scotland, some with coal-based growth in the west Midlands or in the Newcastle area—drew its labour force from an only moderately rising population and from migration to the lively new towns. Thus was scope created for increases in levels of employment, in earnings and productivity, in industry as well as agriculture. The changes were limited and patchy but they were sufficient to give a significant lift to the level of demand in the home market. They rested on improvements in agricultural productivity; and on the moving frontier of the internal economy.

One general point of divergence needs to be stressed. In any changing economy, the larger the share of the population which is becoming wholly urban or otherwise not contributing to agriculture, the higher does productivity have to be in the agricultural sector; alternatively the more does the economy have to depend on its ability to export goods and services in exchange for imported food. Just as Spain and Italy provide examples of economies which in the seventeenth century conspicuously failed to maintain their urban splendours by these means, so England and Holland succeeded. But England was probably unique in the century after 1650 in significantly increasing its urban and non-agrarian population, in diversifying its manufacturing industry, in extending its exports of goods and services, and yet at the same time in becoming a net exporter of foodstuffs. To have been able to achieve this implies an improvement in agricultural productivity sufficient to represent a real divergence from the rest of Europe.

Were comparable developments taking place in continental Europe? England's great seventeenth-century rival, Holland, lost its grip on European commerce; and its internal

resources were an inadquate base for pioneering industrialization. What of England's most obvious eighteenth-century
competitor, France? This is no place to rehearse all the relevant evidence. Suffice to note that it seems to point to a
longer continuance in France of depressed internal demand,
of lowered standards of living for the mass of the people. Much
of this seems to have rested, as would be expected in the
pre-industrialized economy, on an inadequate agricultural
base, a failure to raise productivity in the agrarian sector.
The opportunities for expanding internal demand were not
helped by a tax structure more onerous and regressive than
that in England. The achievement of internal economic and
administrative unity remained incomplete despite the labours
of Colbert; and this relative lack of coherence stood in marked
contrast to the political unity and increased economic integration of England. The absence of internal customs barriers
in England, and the expansion of inland and coastwise trade
had gone far towards the creation of a national market. In
France the opposite was true. So the expansion of French
overseas commerce, whatever the wealth it generated in such
towns as Bordeaux, failed to provide the same stimulus to the
internal economy as did its English counterpart.

Some of this is well known; some of it is guess-work; some
seems so obvious that it is probably wrong. None of it says or
is intended to say that the period examined in this book was
followed by the Industrial Revolution in England but not in
France simply because of certain differences in agricultural
productivity and the internal market. All it does is to suggest
that these may have been among the more important divergences opening up between England and continental Europe.
It is tempting to suppose that the social structure and *mores*
of England were somehow more conducive to economic
change than were their French equivalents. Maybe they
were. But we must not suppose this to be so simply because
the eighteenth century ended with an economic revolution
in the one country and a political revolution in the other.
This is a temptation peculiarly to be resisted. For we have,
as yet, no means of ascribing causality, necessary or sufficient.
We need to know more; particularly do we need comparative

studies of economy and society in the varied political entities which made up Europe and of which England was a part, then as now. If this book helps to stimulate such studies, thus to further our understanding, it will have done something.

Notes

CHAPTER I

[1] From the *Political Register*, 1768, quoted in S. Maccoby, *English Radicalism, 1762–85* (1955), p. 84, n. 4. The sixteenth-century categorization will be found in both Sir Thomas Smith's *De Republica Anglorum* (1583) and William Harrison's *The Description of England* (1577).

[2] *De Republica Anglorum*, ed. L. Alston (Cambridge, 1906), pp. 38–40.

[3] *The Autobiography and Correspondence of Sir Simonds d'Ewes*, ed. J. O. Halliwell (1845), I, pp. 308–9

CHAPTER 2

[1] *Discourse of Western Planting* in *The Original Writings and Correspondence of the two Richard Hakluyts*, ed. E. G. R. Taylor, (Hakluyt Society, 1935), II, p. 234.

[2] John Stow, *Annals of England* (1592), p. 1076.

[3] See F. J. Fisher, 'Influenza and Inflation in Tudor England', *Econ. Hist. Rev.*, 2nd Ser. XVIII (1965).

[4] *The Paston Letters* (Everyman edn.), II, p. 116.

[5] *Tudor Economic Documents* [henceforth *T.E.D.*], ed. R. H. Tawney and E. Power (1924), I, p. 359, II, p. 237.

[6] Quoted in E. H. Phelps Brown and Sheila V. Hopkins, 'Wage Rates and Prices: evidence for population pressure in the sixteenth century', *Economica*, No. 1957, pp. 294–5.

[7] Eric Kerridge, *The Farmers of Old England* (1973), pp. 160, 162–3.

[8] Christopher Hill, *Reformation to Industrial Revolution* (The Pelican Economic History of Britain, Vol. II, 1969), pp. 69, 83.

CHAPTER 3

[1] *A Discourse of the Common Weal of this Realm of England*, ed. E. Lamond (Cambridge, 1929), p. 59.

[2] Quoted in M. W. Beresford, *The Lost Villages of England* (1954), p. 183.

[3] *Two Italian Accounts of Tudor England* (translated and published by C. V. Malfatti, Barcelona, 1953), p. 41.

[4] Respectively: Eric Kerridge, *The Agricultural Revolution* (London, 1967) and Joan Thirsk (ed.) in *The Agrarian History of England and Wales*, IV (Cambridge, 1967).

[5] *T.E.D.*, I, p. 74.

6 David G. Hey, *An English Rural Community: Myddle under the Tudors and Stuarts* (Leicester, 1974), p. 33.

7 Quoted in Kerridge, *Agricultural Revolution*, pp. 184–5.

8 *Robert Loder's Farm Accounts, 1610–20*, ed. G. E. Fussell (Camden Series, 1936), p. 157.

CHAPTER 4

1 Quoted in E. A. J. Johnson, *American Economic Thought in the Seventeenth Century* (London, 1932), p. 38.

2 ibid, p. 52.

3 *T.E.D.*, II, pp. 49–50.

4 *English Economic History: Select Documents*, ed. A. E. Bland, R. A. Brown, and R. H. Tawney (1914), p. 444.

5 Quoted in Harland Taylor, 'Trade, Neutrality and the "English Road"', 1630–48, *Econ. Hist. Rev.*, 2nd Ser. XXV (1972).

CHAPTER 5

1 Both this and Camden's comment are quoted in E. Lipson, *The Economic History of England* (4th edn. 1947), II, p. 10.

2 *T.E.D.*, III, p. 322.

3 2 & 3 Philip and Mary, c. 11, quoted in *T.E.D.*, I, p. 185.

4 R. Reyce, *Breviary of Suffolk*, quoted in G. Unwin, *Studies in Economic History* (1927), p. 280.

5 *T.E.D.*, I, p. 192.

6 Historical Manuscripts Commission, *Calendar of the Sackville MSS.* II, *The Cranfield Papers, 1597–1612*, ed. F. J. Fisher (1966), p. 146.

7 From a letter written by the Governor of the Russia Company to the company's chief agent in Russia, quoted in T. S. Willan, *The Early History of the Russia Company, 1553–1603* (Manchester, 1956), pp. 246–7.

8 William Harrison, *The Description of England*, ed. G. Edelen (1587, Ithaca, New York, 1968), p. 67.

CHAPTER 6

1 Quoted in P. E. Razzell, 'Population Change in Eighteenth-Century England: A Reinterpretation', *Econ. Hist. Rev.*, 2nd Ser. XVIII (1965).

2 Quoted in Alan Macfarlane, *The Family Life of Ralph Josselin* (Cambridge, 1970), pp. 73–4.

3 Thomas Manly, *Usurie at Six Per Cent* (1669), p. 19.

4 Arthur Young, *The Farmer's Tour through the East of England* (1771), IV, p. 361.

5 John Houghton, *A Collection of Letters for the Improvement of Husbandry and Trade* (1681–3), ed. R. Bradley (1728), IV, p. 383.

6 Quoted in Norman Cohn, *The Pursuit of the Millenium* (1957, paperback edn. 1970), p. 301.

7 Charles Davenant, *Discourse . . . on the Plantation Trade* in *Works*, ed. C. Whitworth (1771), II, p. 45.

CHAPTER 7

[1] B. H. Slicher Van Bath, *The Agrarian History of Western Europe, A.D. 500–1850*, translated from the Dutch by Olive Ordish (1963), p. 206.

[2] 15 Car. 2, c. 7.

[3] John Evelyn, *Diary*, 12 April 1656, ed. E. S. de Beer (6 vols., Oxford, 1955).

[4] D. Defoe, *A Tour through England and Wales* (Everyman edn., 1928), II, p. 89.

[5] For examples of such comments, see E. Furniss, *The Position of the Laborer in a System of Nationalism* (New York, 1920), pp. 180–4.

[6] *Seventeenth Century Economic Documents*, ed. Joan Thirsk and J. P. Cooper (Oxford, 1972), p. 177.

[7] Davenant, *Second Report . . . to the Commissioners . . . for Stating the Public Accounts*, in *Works*, V, p. 424.

[8] British Library: Add. MSS. 34, 164, f. 86.

[9] J. Child, *A Discourse about Trade* (1690).

[10] Quoted in G. E. Mingay, 'The Agricultural Depression, 1730–50', *Econ. Hist. Rev.*, 2nd Ser. VIII (1956).

[11] Quoted in Edward Hughes, *North Country Life in the Eighteenth Century* (Oxford, 1952), p. 1.

[12] *The Letters of Henry St. John to the Earl of Orrery, 1709–11*, ed. H. T. Dickinson, *Camden Miscellany*, XXVI (1975).

CHAPTER 8

[1] D. Defoe, *A Plan of English Commerce* (Oxford, 1927), p. 244.

[2] *Discourse . . . on the Plantation Trade*, in *Works*, II, pp. 37–8.

[3] These figures are derived from J. R. Ward, *The Finance of Canal Building in Eighteenth Century England* (Oxford, 1974), p. 164.

CHAPTER 9

[1] Quoted in *History of Technology*, ed. Charles Singer and others, IV (Oxford, 1958), pp. 173–4.

[2] John Cary, *An Essay on the State of England* (1695), quoted in *Seventeenth Century Economic Documents*, pp. 322–3.

[3] Quoted in A. P. Wadsworth and J. de L. Mann, *The Cotton Trade and Industrial Lancashire, 1600–1780* (Manchester, 1931), pp. 411–2.

[4] H.M.C., *Calendar of MSS. of the House of Lords*, VII (new series), 1706–8 (1921), p. 249.

[5] *Calendar of MSS of the House of Lords*, X (new series), 1712–14, ed. M. F. Bond (1965), p. 159.

[6] *The Journeys of Celia Fiennes*, ed. C. Morris (London, 1947), p. 245.

[7] Quoted in W. G. Hoskins, *Industry, Trade and People in Exeter, 1688–1800* (Manchester, 1935), p. 76.

[8] Quoted in Hughes, op. cit., p. 156.

[9] John Houghton, *Husbandry and Trade Improved* (1692–1703), ed. R. Bradley (1727), I, p. 251.

CHAPTER 10

1 *The History of the Reign of King Henry the Seventh*, quoted in E. Heckscher, *Mercantilism* (2nd edn., 1955), II, p. 16.

2 4 Hen. VII. c. 19, quoted in *T.E.D.*, I, pp. 4–5.

3 Kent Archives Office: Quarter Sessions papers.

4 Quoted in B. E. Supple, *Commercial Crisis and Change in England, 1600–42* (Cambridge, 1959), p. 59.

5 5 Eliz. I c. 4., quoted in *T.E.D.*, I, pp. 339, 344.

6 British Library: Add. MSS., 11, 411, ff. 11–12.

7 *Rotuli Parliamentorum*, V, p. 572, quoted in B. P. Wolffe, *The Crown Lands, 1461–1536* (1970), p. 102.

CHAPTER 11

1 F. P. Braudel and F. Spooner, in *Cambridge Economic History of Europe*, IV, p. 429.

2 H. Butterfield, *The Whig Interpretation of History* (1931, Pelican edn. 1973), p. 9.

Select Bibliography

To read more deeply in this subject is to plunge into the world of articles in learned journals, of specialized monographs, and volumes of detailed essays. In recent years a number of collections of reprinted articles have appeared. Here are some of them together with the abbreviations used in this bibliography.

Carus-Wilson (ed.) = *Essays in Economic History*, ed. E. M. Carus-Wilson, Vol. I (1954), Vols. II and III (1962). Very useful and wide ranging collection of important reprinted articles. Those on 1450–1750 are mainly in Vols. I and II.

The following four collections of reprints are all in the Methuen *Debates in Economic History* series. Some are of fundamental importance to an understanding of the period. They all contain useful bibliographies.

Coleman (ed.) = *Revisions in Mercantilism*, ed. D. C. Coleman (1969)

Jones (ed.) = *Agriculture and Economic Growth in England, 1650–1815*, ed. E. L. Jones (1967)

Minchinton (ed.) = *The Growth of English Overseas Trade in the Seventeenth and Eighteenth Centuries*, ed. W. E. Minchinton (1969)

Ramsey (ed.) = *The Price Revolution in Sixteenth Century England*, ed. P. Ramsey (1971).

Two other useful collections of reprints in the O.U.P./Economic History Society series are:

Flinn & Smout (eds.) = *Essays in Social History*, ed. M. W. Flinn and T. C. Smout (1974)

Floud (ed.) = *Essays in Quantitative Economic History*, ed. R. Floud (1974).

The following abbreviations have been used for frequently quoted learned journals:

Agric. Hist. Rev. = *Agricultural History Review*
Econ. Hist. Rev. = *Economic History Review*
P. & P. = *Past and Present*
Trans. R. Hist. Soc. = *Transactions of the Royal Historical Society;*

and certain frequently quoted collaborative works are abbreviated thus:

C.E.H.E.   = *Cambridge Economic History of Europe*

Clark & Slack (eds.)   = *Crisis and Order in English Towns, 1500–1700*, ed. P. Clark and P. Slack (1972)

Fisher (ed.)   = *Essays in the Economic and Social History of Tudor and Stuart England*, ed. F. J. Fisher (1961)

Thirsk (ed.)   = *The Agrarian History of England and Wales*, Vol. IV, 1500–1640, ed. J. Thirsk (1967)

GENERAL

A very useful introduction to some of the basic features of the England of the time is presented in *A New Historical Geography of England*, ed. H. C. Darby (1973). Amongst general studies of the economy the following may be consulted with advantage: *C.E.H.E.*, especially Vol. II; A. R. Bridbury, *Economic Growth: England in the Later Middle Ages*—interesting and controversial; C. H. Wilson, *England's Apprenticeship, 1603–1763* (1965); L. A. Clarkson, *The Pre-Industrial Economy in England, 1500–1750* (1971), which has a very useful and extensive bibliography; and T. S. Ashton, *An Economic History of England: the Eighteenth Century* (1955). For those who like explanation in bold categories, Christopher Hill, *From Reformation to Revolution* (1969) offers class-conflict and exploitation of the working man by the rising bourgeoisie, and D. C. North and R. P. Thomas, *The Rise of the Western World* (1973) offers rational, optimizing economic man in pursuit of efficient organization. Economic growth during the last half-century of our period is analysed in P. Deane and W. A. Cole, *British Economic Growth, 1688–1959* (2nd ed. 1967), though, naturally enough, the analysis is largely in relation to what was to follow rather than what preceded. It is important to see the English economy in its European context and an admirable aid in so doing is R. Davis, *The Rise of the Atlantic Economies* (1973); see also *The Fontana Economic History of Europe*, ed. C. M. Cipolla, Vol. II: *The Sixteenth and Seventeenth Centuries* (1974); and some pertinent chapters in the relevant volumes of *C.E.H.E.* and the *New Cambridge Modern History*. B. R. Mitchell and P. Deane, *Abstract of British Historical Statistics* (1962) contains some useful series for some parts of the period.

CONTEMPORARY WRITINGS

Only by some acquaintance with what contemporaries wrote can one begin to understand an historic period. William Harrison's *Description of England* (1587) and Daniel Defoe's *Tour through England and Wales* (1724–6) provide readable introductions to contemporary views. They can be supplemented by collections of documents, for example, *Tudor Economic Documents*, ed. R. H. Tawney and E. Power (1924) and *Seventeenth Century Economic Documents*, ed. J. Thirsk and J. P. Cooper (1972). The contemporary tracts in *Early English Tracts on Commerce*, ed. J. R. McCulloch

(1856, reprinted 1952), well illustrate prevailing views on economic matters.

POPULATION

A lively interest in historical demography is one of the big new themes in the study of our economic and social past, and the forthcoming book by R. S. Schofield and E. A. Wrigley, *Population Trends in Early Modern England* will be of particular relevance to this period. Meanwhile, Dr. Wrigley's *Population and History* (1969) provides a useful introduction to the subject, and *An Introduction to English Historical Demography*, ed. E. A. Wrigley (1966) deals with a number of questions specific to this pre-census age. Later seventeenth-century interest in analysing the population may be examined at first-hand in Gregory King's *Natural and Political Observations*, reprinted in *Two Tracts by Gregory King*, ed. G. E. Barnett (1936); and important articles on his work, as well as on other aspect of the subject, will be found in *Population in History*, ed. D. V. Glass and D. E. C. Eversley (1965). Some useful recent articles are: J. M. W. Bean, 'Plague, Population and Economic Decline in England in the Later Middle Ages', *Econ. Hist. Rev.*, 2nd. Ser. XV (1963); I. Blanchard, 'Population Change, Enclosure and the Early Tudor Economy', *Econ. Hist. Rev.*, 2nd Ser. XXIII (1970); J. Cornwall, 'English Population in the Early Sixteenth Century', *Econ. Hist. Rev.*, 2nd Ser. XXIII (1970); F. J. Fisher, 'Influenza and Inflation in Tudor England', *Econ. Hist. Rev.*, 2nd Ser. XVIII (1965); A. B. Appleby, 'Disease or Famine? Mortality in Cumberland and Westmoreland 1580–1640', *Econ. Hist. Rev.*, 2nd Ser. XXVI (1973). For a survey of continental European population movements, see *C.E.H.E.* IV.

AGRICULTURE

The two main modern general works on agriculture are Thirsk (ed.) and E. Kerridge, *The Agricultural Revolution* (1967). The former is thorough and wide-ranging; the latter is interesting, controversial and, in certain respects, perverse. On the whole question of fifteenth- and sixteenth-century enclosure for sheep farming see M. W. Beresford, *The Lost Villages of England* (1954). For the later part of the period see especially Jones (ed.); also A. H. John, 'The Course of Agricultural Change 1660–1760' in *Studies in the Industrial Revolution*, ed. L. S. Pressnell (1960); G. Mingay, 'The Size of Farms in the Eighteenth Century', *Econ. Hist. Rev.*, 2nd Ser. XIV (1962) and 'The Agricultural Depression, 1730–50', *Econ. Hist. Rev.*, 2nd Ser. VIII (1955); and an important recent study of a famous estate, R. A. C. Parker, *Coke of Norfolk: A Financial and Agricultural Study, 1707–1842* (1975). Price indices for agricultural products will be found in Thirsk (ed.); and in two articles by W. G. Hoskins which emphasize the importance of harvests for economic and social life, 'Harvest Fluctuations and English Economic Life, 1480–1619' and 'Harvest Fluctuations and English Economic Life, 1620–1759' in *Agric. Hist. Rev.*, XII (1964) and XVI (1968). For change

in rents see the article by E. Kerridge reprinted in Carus-Wilson (ed.) II.
W. E. Minchinton (ed.), *Essays in Agrarian History* Vol. I (1968) reprints a
number of useful articles including some of the above.

SOCIETY, SOCIAL CHANGE, AND LOCAL STUDIES

Two stimulating books on the relationship between society and the
demographic structure are P. Laslett, *The World we have Lost* (1965) and
J. D. Chambers, *Population, Economy and Society in Pre-Industrial England*
(1972). A less fashionable type of book but well worth reading is A.
Wagner, *English Genealogy* (1960). Some general questions of social
mobility are discussed in two articles, by Lawrence Stone and by Alan
Everitt in *P. & P.* 33 (1966). Much of the debate about social change in
the sixteenth and seventeenth centuries has sprung, indirectly, from
R. H. Tawney's *The Agrarian Problem of the Sixteenth Century* (1912) and
specifically from his famous 1941 article, 'The Rise of the Gentry, 1558–
1640', reprinted in Carus-Wilson (ed.) I. For further light on this debate,
see L. Stone, *The Crisis of the Aristocracy, 1558–1641* (1965); M. Campbell,
The English Yeoman under Elizabeth and the Early Stuarts (1942); the chapters
by G. Batho, A. Everitt, and J. Youings in Thirsk (ed.); and E. Kerridge, *Agrarian Problems in the Sixteenth Century and After* (1969)—an
important corrective to Tawney on some matters, though rather
obsessed by the need to prove him wrong. Stone's *Crisis* has not com-
manded unalloyed acceptance: see the controversy 'Stone and Anti-
Stone', *Econ. Hist. Rev.*, 2nd Ser. XXV (1972). See also his *Family and
Fortune* (1973) for a fascinating account of five aristocratic family fortunes. For other ways of looking at the distribution of wealth see the
articles by R. S. Schofield and by J. P. Cooper reprinted in Floud (ed.).
On the later part of the period see H. J. Habakkuk, 'English Landownership 1680–1740', *Econ. Hist. Rev.*, X (1940) and 'Landowners and
the Civil War', *Econ. Hist Rev.*, 2nd Ser. XVIII (1965); C. Clay, 'Marriage, Inheritance, and the Rise of Large Estates in England 1660–1815',
Econ. Hist. Rev, 2nd Ser. XXI (1968); and G. E. Mingay, *English Landed
Society in the Eighteenth Century* (1963).

Local and regional studies are often the best path to an understanding
of change in social and economic life. Some examples: W. G. Hoskins,
Essays in Leicestershire History (1950) and *Provincial England* (1963); J. T.
Cliffe, *The Yorkshire Gentry from the Reformation to the Civil War* (1969);
A. Simpson, *The Wealth of the Gentry, 1540–1640: East Anglian Studies*
(1961); M. E. Finch, *Five Northamptonshire Families* (1956); and E.
Hughes, *North Country Life in the Eighteenth Century* (1952). Two very good
recent local studies are D. Hey, *An English Rural Community: Myddle under
the Tudors and Stuarts* (1974) and M. Spufford, *Contrasting Communities:
English Villages in the Sixteenth and Seventeenth Centuries* (1974).

There is a growing body of scholarly analysis on the economic and
social features of urban life. See, for example, Sylvia Thrupp, *The
Merchant Class of Medieval London* (1948, paperback 1962); Dorothy

George, *London Life in the Eighteenth Century* (3rd edn. 1951) and the interesting collection in Clark and Slack (eds.), touching diverse aspects of urban life; C. W. Chalklin, *The Provincial Towns of Georgian England* (1974); and, for a mix of town and country, the *Festschrift* to W. G. Hoskins, *Rural Change and Urban Growth, 1500–1800*, ed. C. W. Chalklin and M. A. Havinden (1974). Some relevant articles on London include two important ones by F. J. Fisher reprinted in Carus-Wilson (ed.), I and II; E. A. Wrigley, 'A Simple Model of London's Importance in a Changing English Society and Economy, 1650–1750', *P. & P.* 37 (1967); and D. V. Glass, 'Socio-economic Status and Occupations in the City of London at the End of the Seventeenth Century', in *Studies in London History Presented to P. E. Jones*, ed. A. E. J. Hollaender and W. Kellaway (1969). Useful analyses of work in provincial towns and villages are A. J. and R. H. Tawney, 'An Occupational Census of the Seventeenth Century', *Econ. Hist. Rev.*, V (1934), J. F. Pound, 'The Social and Trade Structure of Norwich 1525–75', *P. & P.* 34 (1966), and J. Patton, 'Village and Town: An Occupational Study', *Agric. Hist. Rev.*, XX (1972).

Biographies of businessmen moving up the social scale, or failing to, are another way of looking at social change. Some examples include L. Stone, *An Elizabethan: Sir Horatio Palavicino* (1956), Menna Prestwich, *Cranfield: Politics and Profit under the Early Stuarts* (1966), A. F. Upton, *Sir Arthur Ingram, circa 1565–1642* (1961), and D. C. Coleman, *Sir John Banks* (1963). A useful study of a lesser, and more representative, businessman is *The Autobiography of William Stout*, ed. J. D. Marshall (1967). See also R. Lang, 'Social Origins and Social Aspirations of Jacobean London Merchants', *Econ. Hist. Rev.*, 2nd Ser. XXVII (1974). On the distribution of business wealth, see R. Grassby, 'The Personal Wealth of the Business Community in Seventeenth Century England', *Econ. Hist. Rev.*, 2nd Ser. XXIII (1970).

Historical man, neither living by bread alone nor being merely an economic animal, demands study in a wider social context. See Alan Macfarlane's interesting exercise in historical anthropology, *The Family Life of Ralph Josselin* (1970) and Keith Thomas's masterly *Religion and the Decline of Magic* (1971), a book with an importance for our knowledge of sixteenth- and seventeenth-century society wider than its title implies. For a brief introduction to the troubles of the mid-seventeenth century, see *The English Revolution, 1600–60*, ed. E. Ives (1968); for more detailed examination of some of the social ideas aired at the time, see C. Hill, *The World Turned Upside Down* (1972) and B. S. Capp, *The Fifth Monarchy Men* (1972). An expert enquiry into the historical roots of some of the socio-religious ideas will be found in N. Cohn, *The Pursuit of the Millenium* (3rd edn. 1970). On the relations, real or alleged, between religion and economic activity, see R. H. Tawney, *Religion and the Rise of Capitalism* (1926, paperback 1938), C. Hill, *Society and Puritanism in Pre-Revolutionary England* (1964) and K. Samuelsson, *Religion and Economic Action* (1957).

Attitudes to work are examined in E. S. Furniss, *The Position of the Laborer in a System of Nationalism* (1920), in the article by D. C. Coleman reprinted in Carus-Wilson (ed.) II, and in the articles by E. P. Thompson and by A. W. Coats reprinted in Flinn and Smout (eds.).

PRICES AND CURRENCY

The detailed study of prices and currency can be very arcane. R. B. Outhwaite, *Inflation in Tudor and Stuart England* (1969), one of the books in the Macmillan/Economic History Society *Studies in Economic and Social History* series, provides an excellent brief introduction. It should be supplemented by Ramsey (ed.) in which are reprinted some important articles and, in particular the price- and wage-index constructed by E. H. Phelps Brown and S. V. Hopkins (also reprinted in Carus-Wilson (ed.) II). See also their further article, 'Wage Rates and Prices: Evidence for Population Pressure in the Sixteenth Century', *Economica*, November 1957. For the European context of price changes, see F. P. Braudel and F. C. Spooner in *C.E.H.E.* IV. On the Tudor currency see C. E. Challis in Ramsey (ed.), his 'The Debasement of the Coinage 1542–51', *Econ. Hist. Rev.*, 2nd Ser. XX (1967), and J. D. Gould, *The Great Debasement* (1970). J. K. Horsefield, *British Monetary Experiments, 1650–1710* (1960) deals with some monetary problems of a later period. Two valuable articles on quite different aspects of needing and using money are B. E. Supple, 'Currency and Commerce in the Early Seventeenth Century', *Econ. Hist. Rev.*, 2nd Ser. X (1957) and J. Sperling, 'The International Payments Mechanism in the Seventeenth and Eighteenth Centuries', *Econ. Hist. Rev.*, 2nd Ser. XIV (1962).

INDUSTRY

A general introduction to industry and industrial change in the period is provided in D. C. Coleman, *Industry in Tudor and Stuart England* (1975) —another of the books in the Macmillan/Economic History Society *Studies in Economic and Social History* series—which also provides an annotated bibliography. Amongst the more important general articles or monographs which should be consulted are: on rural industry, the chapter by J. Thirsk in Fisher (ed.) and E. L. Jones, 'Agricultural Origins of Industry', *P. & P.* 40 (1968); on the guilds, S. Kramer, *The English Craft Gilds* (1927), G. Unwin. *The Gilds and Companies of London* (1908), and a pair of interesting chapters—by D. M. Palliser and C. Phythian-Adams—in Clark and Slack (eds.).

The textile industries have generated a substantial historical literature. A selection must suffice here. P. J. Bowden, *The Wool Trade in Tudor and Stuart England* (1962) deals with the vital raw material of the woollen industry. For some particular branches of it see H. Heaton, *The York-shire Woollen and Worsted Industries* (1920), G. D. Ramsay, *The Wiltshire Woollen Industry in the Sixteenth and Seventeenth Centuries* (1943), J. de L. Mann, *The Cloth Industry in the West of England from 1640 to 1880* (1971). Other sorts of textiles are considered in A. P. Wadsworth and J. de L.

Mann, *The Cotton Trade and Industrial Lancashire, 1600–1780* (1931) and N. Lowe, *The Lancashire Textile Industry in the Sixteenth Century* (1972), as well as in two chapters in *Textile History and Economic History*, ed. N. B. Harte and K. Ponting (1973), specifically those by N. Harte (linen) and J. Thirsk (stocking knitting). On this latter subject see also the valuable article by S. D. Chapman, 'The Genesis of the British Hosiery Industry, 1600–1750', *Textile History* III (1972). An important article on international specialization in cloth making in C. Wilson, 'Cloth Production and International Competition in the Seventeenth Century', *Econ. Hist. Rev.*, 2nd Ser. XIII (1960); and D. W. Jones, 'The "Hallage" Receipts of the London Cloth Markets 1562–c. 1720', *Econ. Hist. Rev.*, 2nd Ser. XXV (1972) is a valiant attempt to provide some statistical evidence of changes in output.

Other industries are gradually catching up textiles as generators of learned works. M. W. Flinn, 'The Growth of the English Iron Industry 1660–1760', *Econ. Hist. Rev.*, 2nd Ser. XI (1958) and G. Hammersley, 'The Charcoal Iron Industry and its Fuel, 1540–1750', *Econ. Hist. Rev.*, 2nd Ser. XXVI (1973) are two important articles which change many of the earlier views on the progress of this industry in England; and A. Raistrick, *Dynasty of Iron Founders: the Darbys and Coalbrookdale* (1953) introduces an important figure in the iron revolution. For reasons indicated in my *Industry in Tudor and Stuart England*, J. U. Nef, *The Rise of the British Coal Industry* (2 vols. 1932) should be absorbed with caution. J. Hatcher, *English Tin Production and Trade before 1550* (1973), D. C. Coleman, *The British Paper Industry, 1495–1860* (1958), P. Mathias, *The Brewing Industry in England, 1700–1830* (1959), and L. Weatherill, *The Pottery Trade and North Staffordshire, 1660–1700* (1971) are simply a few of many monographs on diverse industrial activities. As in other areas of economic and social change, local studies are illuminating. J. D. Chambers, *The Vale of Trent, 1670–1800*, Supplement No. 3 to the *Econ. Hist. Rev.* (1957) is valuable for industry, agriculture, and population change in this important Midland region; C. W. Chalklin, *Seventeenth Century Kent* (1965) covers a wide range of activities; W. H. B. Court, *The Rise of the Midland Industries* (1938) and M. B. Rowlands, *Masters and Men in the west Midlands Metalware Trades before the Industrial Revolution* (1975), together provide an excellent survey of early industrial change in the west Midlands.

The growing seventeenth-century interest in science and technology and their application to industrial activity has stimulated lively debate. For some information see A. R. Hall in *C.E.H.E.* IV and *A History of Technology*, ed. C. Singer and others, *Vol. III, 1500–1750* (1957). For an introduction to the debate, see H. F. Kearney, 'Puritanism, Capitalism, and the Scientific Revolution, *P. & P.* 28 (1964) and the subsequent discussion in *P. & P.* 1965–6. For interesting preludes to later developments, see A. E. Musson and E. Robinson, *Science and Technology in the Industrial Revolution* (1969).

SELECT BIBLIOGRAPHY 213

TRADE AND SHIPPING

The commercial history of the period, like the industrial history, has a general introduction in the *Studies in Economic and Social History* series: R. Davis, *English Overseas Trade, 1500–1700* (1973), complete with a useful bibliography. Much of the general analysis of commerce after 1500 is contained in four crucial articles, two by F. J. Fisher reprinted in Carus-Wilson (ed.) I and in Minchinton (ed.), and two by R. Davis reprinted in Carus-Wilson (ed.) II and in Minchinton (ed.). See also Davis's 'England and the Mediterranean 1570–1670' in Fisher (ed.). For the earlier part of the period: E. M. Carus-Wilson, *Medieval Merchant Venturers* (1954), her chapter in *C.E.H.E.* II, and *English Overseas Trade in the Fifteenth Century*, ed. E. E. Power and M. M. Postan (1933). Some useful studies of particular aspects of Tudor commerce include A. Ruddock, 'London Capitalists and the Decline of Southampton in the Early Tudor Period', and L. Stone, 'Elizabethan Overseas Trade' both in *Econ. Hist. Rev.*, 2nd Ser. II (1949), and T. S. Willan, *Studies in Elizabethan Foreign Trade* (1959). B. E. Supple, *Commercial Crisis and Change in England, 1600–42* (1959) is a very valuable study of early Stuart trade on which also see W. B. Stephens, 'Cloth Exports of the Provincial Ports 1600–40', *Econ. Hist. Rev.*, 2nd Ser. XXII (1969), J. D. Gould, 'Cloth Exports 1600–40', *Econ. Hist. Rev.*, 2nd Ser. XXIV (1971), and H. Taylor, 'Trade, Neutrality and the "English road" 1630–48', *Econ. Hist. Rev.*, 2nd Ser. XXV (1972). General statistics of overseas commence are to be found in E. M. Carus-Wilson and O. Coleman, *England's Export Trade, 1275–1547* (1963) and E. B. Schumpeter, *English Overseas Trade Statistics, 1697–1808* (1960). On shipping the standard work is R. Davis, *The Rise of the English Shipping Industry in the Seventeenth and Eighteenth Centuries* (1962); and, for the earlier part of the period, see two articles by G. V. Scammell, 'English Merchant Shipping at the End of the Middle Ages', *Econ. Hist. Rev.*, 2nd Ser. XIII (1961), and 'Shipowning in the Economy and Politics of Early Modern England', *Historical Journal* XV (1972).

Some studies of particular branches of trade are crucial to an understanding of the period. See, especially, K. N. Chaudhuri, *The English East India Company, 1600–40* (1965) and his 'Treasure and Trade Balances: The East India Company's export trade 1660–1720', *Econ. Hist. Rev.*, 2nd Ser. XXI (1968), and watch out for his forthcoming work, *The English East India Company in the Trade of Asia, 1660–1760*. R. Davis, *Aleppo and Devonshire Square* (1967) examines the Levant trade in the late seventeenth and early eighteenth centuries through the records of a particular family. K. G. Davies, *The Royal African Company* (1957) is important for an understanding of English participation in the slave trade; and his *The North Atlantic World in the Seventeenth Century* (1974) offers a valuable introduction to English, Dutch, and French commercial expansion in America and Africa. On the Baltic trade, see R. W. K. Hinton, *The Eastland Company and the Commonwealth in the Seventeenth Century* (1959) and H. Zins, *England and the Baltic in the Elizabethan*

Era (1972). These are merely a few of a large number of specialized works of which details can be found in bibliographies. Some also deal with the organization and finance of trade but see also on this W. R. Scott, *The Constitution and Finance of English, Scottish and Irish Joint Stock Companies, 1558–1720* (3 vols, 1910–12) which, despite its age, length and formidable title, remains a remarkable work on many aspects of the economic history of the period including business fluctuations. On this latter topic see also T. S. Ashton, *Economic Fluctuations in England 1700–1800* (1959).

The following are useful on internal trade and communications: T. S. Willan, *The English Coasting Trade, 1600–1750* (1938) and *River Navigation in England, 1600–1750* (1936), J. R. Ward, *The Finance of Canal Building in Eighteenth Century England* (1974), W. Albert, *The Turnpike Road System in England, 1663–1840* (1972), and R. B. Westerfield, *Middlemen in English Business, 1600–1760* (1915).

THE STATE

General problems of economic thought and of economic policy (sometimes confused with each other) have often been subsumed under the general title of 'mercantilism'. A number of pertinent articles on this theme are gathered together in Coleman (ed.), together with an introduction, which tries to clarify the debate, and a guide to further reading. On commercial policy, see L. Stone, 'State Control in Sixteenth Century England', *Econ. Hist. Rev.* XVII (1947), Supple, *Commercial Crisis and Change*, M. Ashley, *Financial and Commercial Policy under the Cromwellian Protectorate* (1934), L. Harper, *The English Navigation Laws* (1939), and R. Davis, 'The Rise of Protection in England 1688–1780', *Econ. Hist. Rev.*, 2nd Ser. XIX (1966). C. Wilson, *Profit and Power* studies the nature of Anglo-Dutch commercial rivalry and conflict in the seventeenth century.

The State in pursuit of money can be examined in some old but not very accurate books by F. C. Dietz: *English Government Finance, 1485–1588* and *English Public Finance, 1558–1641* (1921 and 1932 respectively, 2nd edns. 1964). Less general but more accurate studies of some specific matters or periods are: B. P. Wolffe, *The Crown Lands, 1461–1536* (1970), Joyce Youings, *The Dissolution of the Monasteries* (1971), R. B. Outhwaite, 'The Trials of Foreign Borrowing: the English Crown and the Antwerp Money Market in the Sixteenth Century', *Econ. Hist. Rev.*, 2nd Ser. XIX (1966), R. Ashton, *The Crown and the Money Market, 1603–40* (1960), C. D. Chandaman, *The English Public Revenue, 1660–88* (1975), J. H. Clapham, *The Bank of England*, vol. I, 1694–1797 (1944), P. G. M. Dickson, *The Financial Revolution in England, 1688–1756* (1967), and J. Carswell, *The South Sea Bubble* (1960).

The State's efforts to regulate in agriculture and industry, to control labour, or to deal with the problems of poverty and vagrancy have given birth to many writings. Here are a few: G. R. Elton, 'An Early Tudor

Poor Law', *Econ. Hist. Rev.*, 2nd Ser. VI (1953); S. T. Bindoff, 'The Making of the Statute of Artificers' in *Elizabethan Government and Society*, ed. S. T. Bindoff and others (1961); R. K. Kelsall, *Wage Regulation under the Statute of Artificers* (1938); M. G. Davies, *The Enforcement of English Apprenticeship, 1563–1642* (1956); J. F. Pound, *Poverty and Vagrancy in Tudor England* (1971); P. Slack, 'Vagrants and Vagrancy in England 1598–1664', *Econ. Hist. Rev.*, 2nd Ser. XXVII (1974); A. L. Beier, 'Poor Relief in Warwickshire 1630–60', *P. & P.* 35 (1966); M. W. Beresford, 'The Common Informer, the Penal Statutes and Economic Regulation', *Econ. Hist. Rev.*, 2nd Ser. X (1957); J. P. Cooper, 'Economic Regulation and the Cloth Industry in Seventeenth Century England', *Trans. R. Hist. Soc.* XX (1970).

ADDENDUM (1978)

The following items include a few of the many books and articles on this period which appeared after this bibliography was originally prepared.

GENERAL

W. G. Hoskins, *The Age of Plunder: The England of Henry VIII, 1500–1547* (1976), an idiosyncratic and Cobbett-like foray, provides a contrast to B. A. Holderness, *Pre-Industrial England: Economy and Society from 1500 to 1750* (1976), a detached and useful general survey, stronger on social than on economic matters. An interesting brief discussion on the course of economic change will be found in A. J. Little, *Deceleration in the Eighteenth Century British Economy* (1976). D. C. Coleman and A. H. John (eds.), *Trade, Government and Economy in Pre-industrial England* (1976) contains a number of relevant articles, some of which are mentioned under particular headings below.

CONTEMPORARY

A remarkable seventeenth-century diary touching upon many topics is *The Diary of Ralph Josselin, 1616–1683* (ed. Alan Macfarlane, 1976); and a valuable supplement to, but *not* a substitute for, reading Defoe is Peter Earle, *The World of Defoe* (1976).

POPULATION

J. Hatcher, *Plague, Population and the English Economy, 1348–1530* (1977), another addition to the *Studies in Economic and Social History* series, is helpful for the beginning of our period; L. A. Clarkson, *Death, Disease and Famine in Pre-industrial England* (1975) offers an introductory survey of just those grisly topics; and Lawrence Stone's *The Family, Sex and Marriage in England 1500–1800* (1977) provides a lengthy examination of (and some sweeping conclusions upon) an earlier stage of the life circle.

AGRICULTURE

A useful general analysis of an important subject is J. A. Yelling,

Common Field and Enclosure in England 1450–1850 (1977); and the contribution by A. H. John 'English Agricultural Improvement and Grain Exports, 1660–1765' to Coleman and John (eds.) is pertinent not only to agriculture but also to the wider question of economic performance in the early eighteenth century.

SOCIETY, SOCIAL CHANGE AND LOCAL STUDIES

The discussion about landownership is furthered by J. V. Beckett, 'English Landownership in the Later Seventeenth and Eighteenth Centuries: the Debate and the Problems', *Econ. Hist. Rev.* 2nd Ser. XXX, (1977); and the gentry surveyed in G. E. Mingay, *The Gentry: the Rise and Fall of a Ruling Class* (1976). The economic and social background of protest is variously considered in J. Walter and K. Wrightson, 'Dearth and the Social Order in Early Modern England', *P. & P.* 71 (1976) and in Peter Earle, *Monmouth's Rebels* (1977). Towns are well represented in recent publications: see, in particular, Peter Clark and Paul Slack, *English Towns in Transition, 1500–1700* (1976); the article by F. J. Fisher 'London as an "Engine of Economic Growth"' reprinted in P. Clark (ed.), *The Early Modern Town* (1976); and two articles in Coleman and John (eds.), viz. Penelope Corfield, 'Urban Development in England and Wales in the Sixteenth and Seventeenth Centuries' and M. Falkus, 'Lighting in the Dark Ages of English Economic History: Towns and Streets before the Industrial Revolution'. Peter Clark also figures amongst the contributers to local history in this period with his wide-ranging study, *English Provincial Society from the Reformation to the Revolution. Religion, Politics and Society in Kent, 1500–1640* (1977).

PRICES AND CURRENCY

The prime contribution in this area is C. Challis, *The Tudor Coinage* (1978).

INDUSTRY

Joan Thirsk, *Economic Policy and Projects: the Development of a Consumer Society in Early Modern England* (1978) falls under both this heading and 'The State' as it is much concerned with state support of various industrial projects.

TRADE AND SHIPPING

Internal trade has been further examined in two valuable publications: T. S. Willan, *The Inland Trade* (1976) and, another useful survey of both our knowledge and our ignorance, in the *Studies in Economic and Social History* series, J. A. Chartres, *Internal Trade in England 1500–1700* (1977).

THE STATE

A number of examples of state action in this period are considered in Coleman and John (eds.): see, for example, N. B. Harte, 'State Control of Dress and Social Change in Pre-industrial England' and D. C. Coleman, 'Politics and Economics in the Age of Anne: the Case of the Anglo-French Trade Treaty of 1713'.

Index